PRENTICE-HALL
FOUNDATIONS OF MODERN SOCIOLOGY SERIES
Alex Inkeles, Editor

INDUSTRIAL SOCIOLOGY
Ivar Berg

INTRODUCTION TO SOCIAL RESEARCH, Second Edition
Ann Bonar Blalock/Hubert M. Blalock, Jr.

RACE AND ETHNIC RELATIONS
Hubert M. Blalock, Jr.

DEVIANCE AND CONTROL
Albert K. Cohen

MODERN ORGANIZATIONS
Amitai Etzioni

SOCIAL PROBLEMS
Amitai Etzioni

LAW AND SOCIETY: An Introduction
Lawrence M. Friedman

THE FAMILY, Second Edition
William J. Goode

SOCIETY AND POPULATION, Second Edition
David M. Heer

WHAT IS SOCIOLOGY? An Introduction to the Discipline and Profession
Alex Inkeles

THE SOCIOLOGY OF SMALL GROUPS
Theodore M. Mills

SOCIAL CHANGE, Second Edition
Wilbert E. Moore

THE SOCIOLOGY OF RELIGION
Thomas F. O'Dea

THE EVOLUTION OF SOCIETIES
Talcott Parsons

RURAL SOCIETIES
Irwin T. Sanders

THE AMERICAN SCHOOL: A Sociological Analysis
Patricia C. Sexton

THE SOCIOLOGY OF ECONOMIC LIFE, Second Edition
Neil J. Smelser

FOUNDATIONS OF MODERN SOCIOLOGY
Metta Spencer/Alex Inkeles

SOCIAL STRATIFICATION
Melvin M. Tumin

second edition
THE FAMILY

second edition
THE FAMILY

WILLIAM J. GOODE
Stanford University

Prentice-Hall, Inc., Englewood Cliffs, New Jersey 07632

Library of Congress Cataloging in Publication Data

GOODE, WILLIAM JOSIAH.
    The family.

    Bibliography: p.
    Includes index.
    1. Family. 2. Marriage. 3. Social
change. I. Title.
HQ728.G56 1982   306.8   81-19970
ISBN   0-13-301762-1   AACR2
ISBN   0-13-301754-0 (pbk.)

Printed in the United States of America

10 9 8 7 6 5 4 3 2 1

Prentice-Hall International, Inc., *London*

Prentice-Hall of Australia Pty. Limited, *Sydney*

Prentice-Hall of Canada, Ltd., *Toronto*

Prentice-Hall of India Private Limited, *New Delhi*

Prentice-Hall of Japan, Inc., *Tokyo*

Prentice-Hall of Southeast Asia Pte. Ltd., *Singapore*

Whitehall Books Limited, *Wellington, New Zealand*

CONTENTS

PREFACE TO THE SECOND EDITION

George Bernard Shaw once commented that first editions are rare but tenth editions are rarer still; however, he referred to the unlikelihood of so great a market success. There is a deeper reason for the rarity of successive editions. To recapture the intensity and excitement of the earlier creation is difficult. More important, most of us, looking over what we once wrote, are likely to concede painfully that we now have precious little to add to it; or with unbecoming modesty we may simply be unable to see many errors in it. If at best we can only "bring the figures up to date," we may feel little motivation to fashion a genuine new edition.

But whether or not the author musters the will to accomplish a new version of his or her thinking about a field, the discipline moves on anyway, leaving behind the errors the first edition contained, and sometimes its strengths as well. In this arena of life, as in others, the world moves on, changed, whether or not it makes any progress. An author must at least consider those changes.

Many political and philosophical attacks have been mounted against sociology during the past decade. The field of the family has not been spared, but in one way it has refuted at least one accusation made against the discipline as a whole: This subfield *has* made progress. Not only do we now possess more accurate information about the family than Marx, Durkheim, or Wever ever knew—we also know more than did the family scholars of the 1950s and 1960s. What we know more of is not simply a few additional descriptions (a Civil War divorce rate for Talladega County, the "secret money" of the Chinese wife); we also understand better many *relationships* (class and race differences in divorce rates, and in their consequences for children; the conditions for the maintenance of large, extended family households).

This small volume cannot summarize all that work, although we shall incorporate it where it is relevant. Here, I should like to do no more than note some sources and areas of progress in the field.

The most spectacular development has occurred in our historical knowledge of the family. In the first edition I deplored the absence of adequate histories of the family, though of course I utilized historical materials where possible. For example, I pointed out that long before industrialization the family systems of the West were neolocal (newly married couples set up a new home, and were not usually incorporated into large, extended households), and had been different in several ways from other family systems for perhaps a thousand years. My contemporaneous analytical work, *World Revolution and Family Patterns,* was also a "history," focusing on alterations in family and social structure over the past century in China, Japan, India, sub-Saharan Africa, Arabic Islam, and the West.

But though my use of historical materials at that time was fortunate, since many of my formulations have been confirmed by better historical data, those earlier analyses cannot do justice to the immense amount of material now available. Since that time, hundreds of articles and monographs have probed the obscurities of this social institution whose daily life mostly disappears from the archives. To be sure, not all of these historical studies are of the same high quality. Indeed, because these are relatively new areas for historians, I believe that they do not yet apply as rigorous standards to these works as in areas where many scholars have an entrenched or vested interest, such as the French Revolution or the Elizabethan Age. Nevertheless, the quality has been generally high, and large enough in quantity that several attempts at historical synthesis have already been made, notably those by Peter Laslett and Lawrence Stone.

A second major addition to the literature, research on women, partly overlaps with the foregoing body of research, for a substantial segment has been focused on historical questions. This new material is a step forward, because both history and comparative sociology had neglected women in various ways. Since my much earlier work had also noted the disadvantages suffered by women, the importance of this new research is not that it documents the obvious, but that it broadens our understanding of what women have actually done in both the family and the larger society. Some few examples may be noted: the reports by women anthropologists on the complexity of the woman's role in North African and Mediterranean "male vanity" cultures; the relations between the relative power of women and the modes of making a living; the increasing evidence that masculine and feminine roles have only a loose connection with the inborn capacities of the two sexes; the pervasiveness and interconnectedness of the social forces that hold women in their allotted place in family and society; and the extent to which the actions as well as the perceptions of women had been omitted from analyses of the family.

The revival of *evolutionism* as a mode of speculation has added a considerable literature to older guesses about the prehistory of the family. Just when did the family evolve? What was the sequence of family forms as human species arose? Such essays have also been stimulated by the work of "sociobiology" as well, since this new orientation has tried to interpret family behavior as determined by biological predispositions that evolved along with the family. Cautiously evaluated, however, these sequences do not seem to be any more plausible than those of decades past, for reasons given in this volume. Very likely we shall never know with any certainty the evolutionary sequences of family patterns. On the other hand, as in the past, this subject matter will always be a stimulating topic on which to exercise one's imagination.

A small but theoretically significant set of inquiries has tried, in many countries, to chart the importance of *kin relations* outside the immediate or conjugal family. Although I had noted long ago that there is no such thing as a "nuclear family system," in which the only significant family relations occur within the social unit of husband, wife, and children, and I had pointed out some of the conditions under which interaction with extended kin flourished or declined, more recent research permits us to make a more systematic statement of those conditions.

Related to that development is a broader question, which has not been answered but which has been posed by our stronger data base about families in many societies. Our newer census and survey data force us to accept the wide variety of social units we would like to call "families," within the same society. Thus, we cannot think of the completed nuclear family (husband, wife, and children) as "the" family and all others as "deviants." Then the question arises, what are the social conditions that determine the distribution of these various kinds of families in the society? Some part of the problem can be avoided or answered by thinking of some of these forms as *phases* of a "family life cycle," so that the distribution of all families is simply a composite of those various phases in succession: the childless couple, the couple with one or more children, a divorced parent with children, an older person living with adult children, and so on. However, that is not a full answer, and it may not be a theoretically fruitful answer. For that matter, we may decide that these various categories are so different from one another that putting them all together does not suggest many fruitful ideas or hypotheses.

In the first edition, I noted that it was meant to "exemplify, rather than argue, the fruitfulness of sociological theory when applied to family relations." I believed then, as I believe now (and in harmony with Robert K. Merton's classic statement), that many kinds of intellectual activity are called "theory," but the theoretical core of any field is a structure or architectonic of empirical relationships. Some of these, but not most, can be derived deductively from a set of axioms, postulates, and definitions. In an early stage of theory making, we are likely to apply a general relationship to several different social settings or historical periods (such as variations in the parental control of courtship patterns under different conditions of parental power or the social rank of the family line). More recently, and perhaps challenged by the larger number of works on theory construction in general sociology, more family analysts have begun to engage in *formal theory construction*. That is, they have brought together a wide range of research literature bearing on a specific topic, such as class and courtship, and have tried to approximate as closely as possible the models of axiomatization and formalization long followed in the field. Many of these explorations then attempt to develop new propositions as well.

What is significant for the progress of the field is not how closely a given inquiry has been able to reduce a given set of propositions to a few axioms, postulates, and definitions, and thereupon reproduce the original findings or new ones. It is rather that a larger number of family analysts are actively seeking to develop a systematic, theoretical approach that links many empirical findings with both general sociology and with broader principles of family sociology, rather than being content with simply one more descriptive finding about some segment of families in twentieth-century urban United States.[1] It should also be pointed out that this kind of endeavor, focused as it is on the actual analysis of real behavior, usually glosses over (as being relatively unimportant) whether the empirical relationships are to be classified as "functionalist," "symbolic interactionist," or part of "conflict theory."

As can be seen from the foregoing areas of development, the field of the family has also been marked recently by a large growth in studies devoted to social change: Industrialization and the family, economy and history, changes in sex patterns and the place of women, and extended kin relations, in both the present and centuries past. This development is related to larger theoretical concerns, in part because sociology itself has once more begun to focus on social change and thereby on the larger questions of power, stratification, the development of modern states, and revolution. In industrial societies, changes in family relations have seemed so marked that hundreds of commentators have raised the question as to whether it is simply disappearing as a social institution, its various tasks being taken over by other agencies or discarded altogether. Since it is so difficult to ascertain precisely why a given family pattern does change, numerous speculations

---

1.   My colleagues and I also attempted to help somewhat in this endeavor by furnishing a substantial amount of building material, in the form of thousands of empirical propositions about the family, in *Social Systems and Family Patterns,* by William J. Goode, Elizabeth Hopkins, and Helen M. McClure (Indianapolis: Bobbs-Merrill, 1971).

have been offered as to the meaning and the origin of these alterations in family behavior.

It is not possible to evaluate all these guesses, and the complexity of modern society suggests we should be cautious about supposing we have finally hit upon a single cause of anything. With reference to the most general thesis, that somehow industrialization causes all these changes, I should like to repeat what I have said in various contexts before. First, both industrialization and urbanization represent a kind of grab bag, containing dozens of very different kinds of forces or processes. They do not have much explanatory power, unless we can specify exactly *which* subfactor is causal, as well as the *linkage* by which it has its effect. Second, many family changes occurred long before industrialization, and doubtless have occurred over many thousands of years, under the impact of entirely different forces. Third, many family patterns that we used to think were "modern" (the neolocal family) are very ancient, and could not have been caused by industrialization. Fourth, it is clear that some family patterns may resist the forces of industrialization far more than others. For example, I suggested some years ago that the intensity of the mother-son relationship in India would be far more resistant than the cooperation of brothers in joint family households. Finally, of course, we should remember that family processes do not seem to be entirely determined by political and economic structures; they are *interdependent*, and have some independent power of their own. Their consequences may facilitate *or* hinder the operation of political and economic institutions. In any event, unless the needs of individuals are partly satisfied by families, it is unlikely that larger economic processes will work efficiently either, whatever the economic system.

In short, to invoke the magic word, *industrialization*, will not suddenly cause all family processes to fall into a set of orderly regularities. Family and friendship are not important only because they are ancient residues or survivals from simpler, happier times. What happens within these arenas is not determined solely by the industrial system. If we wish to use the imagery of causation, we must also be willing to do the hard work necessary to pinpoint precisely how anything causes anything.

By pointing to the complex relations between family systems and the larger social structure, I am arguing implicitly that the family can no longer be treated as a simple set of dependent variables to be explained by cryptic remarks about "economic forces." First of all, the aim of a social theorist is to state and demonstrate determinate relationships between sets of central variables, no matter which may turn out to be "dependent." It is discovering the relationship that is important, not whether one or another variable is the primary cause. Second, even if economic, political, or other traditional variables are prepotent, we must nevertheless specify in precise detail through which processes they have their effects upon family patterns. For example, if we wish to assert that industrialization has some specific effect, we have to show that it has by stating just how it changes the resources for social control that are at the disposal of husband, wife, children, or kin. Finally, a systematic attempt to explain *any* important institution is likely to force the researcher to explore the larger social structure. Thus, I am urging the wise student of society to give serious thought to the importance of the family system.

Let me make a last comment, repeating a philosophical position that I expressed in my original Preface, with respect to to the general problem of values. It is useful to remember that science cannot tell us how we ought to behave. It can only tell us how people actually behave and feel. It is therefore almost unnecessary to state that my analyses of particular family patterns do not imply approval of them, though occasionally I have expressed some evaluation of them, as distinct from the analysis itself. However, I wish to imply more than that. We need not look only at family patterns as they actually exist, or societies as they actually exist. An important theoretical task is to explore the implications of possible utopias, for whole societies as well as for family systems. That is partly an expression of one's ideology, but it can also be a serious application of principles we already know to new solutions for contemporary problems.

That is not, however, a task of salon sociology. We should be well equipped with sound theory and facts before proposing such solutions. Whether or not we work out better family systems, at least some of our future social planning will be wiser if we base it on the best of sound sociological research; and sociological wisdom will increasingly have to take systematic account of family patterns.

Updating descriptive data and rethinking family processes requires time and labor, and I have had the help of many friends and fellow workers in this task. I cannot list here all the friends and colleagues who have aided me in these matters, but I express my thanks to them now. Barbara Grandin was of help at the beginning of this research, and Laura Bean was most effective in carrying it through to its completion. Along the way, others have contributed: Edward Gilliland and Mitchell LaPlante deserve my thanks too. The Hoover Institution at Stanford University gave research support to this set of inquiries, and I am grateful for that help.

second edition
THE FAMILY

CHAPTER 1
THE THEORETICAL
IMPORTANCE
OF THE FAMILY

Through the centuries, thoughtful people have observed that the family was disintegrating. In the past several decades, this idea has become more and more common. Many analysts have reported that the family no longer performs tasks once entrusted to it—production, education, protection, for example. From these and other data we might conclude that the family is on its way out.

But almost everyone who lives out an average life span enters the married state. Most eventually have children, who will later do the same. Of the increasing number who divorce, many will hopefully or skeptically marry again. In the Western nations, a higher percentage of people marry than a century ago. Indeed, the total number of years spent within marriage by the average person is higher now than at any previous time in the history of the world. In all known societies, almost everyone lives enmeshed in a network of family rights and obligations. People are taught to accept these rules through a long period of childhood socialization. That is, people come to feel that these family patterns are both right and desirable.

At the present time, human beings appear to get as much joy and sorrow from the family as they always have, and seem as bent as ever on taking part in family life. In most of the world, the traditional family may be shaken, but the institution will probably enjoy a longer life than any nation now in existence. The family does not seem to be a powerful institution, like the military, the church, or the state, but it seems to be the most resistant to conquest, or to the efforts people make to reshape it. Any specific family may appear to be fragile or unstable, but the family system as a whole is tough and resilient.

1

THE FAMILY: VARIOUS VIEWS

The intense emotional meaning of family relations for almost everyone has been observed throughout history. Philosophers and social analysts have noted that any society is a structure made up of families linked together. Both travelers and anthropologists often describe the peculiarities of a given society by outlining its family relations.

The earliest moral and ethical writings of many cultures assert the significance of the family. Within those commentaries, the view is often expressed that a society loses its strength if people do not fulfill family obligations. Confucius thought that happiness and prosperity would prevail if everyone would behave "correctly" as a family member. This meant primarily that no one should fail in his filial obligations. That is, the proper relationship between ruler and subjects was like that between a father and his children. The cultural importance of the family is also emphasized in the Old Testament. The books of Exodus, Deuteronomy, Ecclesiastes, Psalms, and Proverbs, for example, proclaim the importance of obeying family rules. The earliest codified literature in India, the Rig-Veda, which dates from about the last half of the second millennium B.C., and the Law of Manu, which dates from about the beginning of the Christian era, devote much attention to the family. Poetry, plays, novels, and short stories typically seize upon family relationships as the primary focus of human passion, and their ideas and themes often grow from family conflict. Even the great epic poems of war have subthemes focusing on problems in family relations.[1]

From time to time, social analysts and philosophers have presented plans for societies that *might* be created (these are called utopias) in which new family roles (rights and obligations of individual members) are offered as solutions to traditional social problems. Plato's *Republic* is one such attempt. Plato was probably the first to urge the creation of a society in which all members, men and women alike, would have an equal opportunity to develop their talents to the utmost, and to achieve a position in society solely through merit. Since family patterns in all societies prevent selection based entirely on individual worth, in Plato's utopia the tie between parents and children would play no part, because knowledge of that link would be erased. Approved conception would take place at the same time each year at certain hymeneal festivals; children born out of season would be eliminated (along with those born defective). All children would be taken from their parents at birth and reared by specially designated people.

Experimental or utopian communities like Oneida, the Shakers, the Mormons, and modern communes have typically insisted that changes in family relations were necessary to achieve their goals. Every fundamental political upheaval since the French Revolution of 1789 has offered a program that included profound changes in family relations. Since World War

---

1.   See in this connection Nicholas Tavuchis and William J. Goode (eds.) *The Family through Literature* (New York: Oxford University Press, 1973).

II, most countries of the world have written new constitutions. In perhaps all of them, but especially in all the less developed nations, these new laws have been far more advanced than public opinion in those countries. They have aimed at creating new family patterns more in conformity with the leaders' views of equality and justice, and often antagonistic to traditional family systems. This wide range of commentary, analysis, and political action, over a period of twenty-five hundred years, suggests that throughout history we have been at least implicitly aware of the importance of family patterns as a central element in human societies.

THE CENTRAL POSITION OF THE FAMILY
IN SOCIETY

In most tribal societies, kinship patterns form the major part of the whole social structure. By contrast, the family is only a small part of the social structure of modern industrial societies. It is nevertheless a key element in them, specifically linking individuals with other social institutions, such as the church, the state, or the economy. Indeed modern society, with its complex advanced technology and its highly trained bureaucracy, would collapse without the contributions of this seemingly primitive social agency. The class system, too, including its restrictions on education and opportunity, its high or low social mobility rates, and its initial social placement by birth, is founded on the family.

Most important, it is within the family that the child is first socialized to serve the needs of the society, and not only its own needs. A society will not survive unless its needs are met, such as the production and distribution of commodities, protection of the young and old or the sick and the pregnant, conformity to the law, and so on. Only if individuals are motivated to serve these needs will the society continue to operate, and the foundation for that motivation is laid by the family. Family members also participate in informal social control processes. Socialization at early ages makes most of us wish to conform, but throughout each day, both as children and as adults, we are often tempted to deviate. The formal agencies of social control (such as the police) are not enough to do more than force the extreme deviant to conform. What is needed is a set of social pressures that provide feedback to the individual whenever he or she does well or poorly and thus support internal controls as well as the controls of the formal agencies. Effectively or not, the family usually takes on this task.

The family, then, is made up of individuals, but it is also a social unit, and part of a larger social network. Families are not isolated, self-enclosed social systems; and the other institutions of society, such as the military, the church, or the school system, continually rediscover that they are not dealing with individuals, but with members of families. Even in the most industrialized and urban of societies, where it is sometimes supposed that people lead rootless and anonymous lives, most people are in continual interaction with other family members. Men and women who achieve high social position usually find that even as adults they still respond to their parents' criticisms, are still angered or hurt by a sibling's scorn. Corporations that offer substantial opportunities to rising executives often find that their proposals are turned down because of objections from family members.

So it is through the family that the society is able to elicit from the individual his or her contributions. The family, in turn, can continue to exist only if it is supported by the larger society. If these two, the smaller and the larger social system, furnish each other the conditions necessary for their survival, they must be interrelated in many important ways. Thus, the two main themes in this book will be the relations among family members, and the relations between the family and the society.

PRECONCEPTIONS ABOUT THE FAMILY

The task of understanding the family presents many difficulties, and one of the greatest barriers is found in ourselves. We are likely to have strong emotions about the family. Because of our own deep involvement in family relationships, objective analysis is not easy. When we read about other types of family behavior, in other classes or societies, we are likely to feel that they are odd or improper. We are tempted to argue that this or that type of family behavior is wrong or right, rather than to analyze it. Second, although we have observed many people in some of their family behavior, usually we have had very limited experience with what goes on behind the walls of other homes. This means that our sample of observations is very narrow. It also means that for almost any generalization we create or read about, we can often find some specific experience that refutes it, or fits it. Since we feel we "already know," we may not feel motivated to look for further data against which to test generalizations.

However, many supposedly well-known beliefs about the family are not well grounded in fact. Others are only partly true and must be studied more precisely if they are to be understood. One such belief is that "children hold the family together." Despite repeated attempts to affirm it, this generalization does not seem to be very strong. A more correct view seems to be that there is a modest association between divorce and not having children, but it is mostly caused by the fact that people who do not become well adjusted, and who may for some reasons be prone to divorce, are also less likely to have children.

Another way of checking whether the findings of family sociology are obvious is to present some research findings, and ask whether it was worth the bother of discovering them since "everybody knew them all along." Consider the following set of facts. Suppose a researcher had demonstrated those facts. Was it worthwhile to carry out the study, or were the facts already known?

1. Because modern industrial society breaks down traditional family systems, one result is that the age of marriage in Western nations (which was low among farmers) has risen greatly over many generations.

2. Because of the importance of the extended family in China and India, the

average size of the household has always been large, with many generations living under one roof.

3. In polygynous societies, most men have several wives, and the fertility rate is higher than in monogamous societies.

Although these statements sound plausible to many people, and impressive arguments have been presented to support them, in fact they are all false. For hundreds of years, the age at marriage among farmers in Western nations has been relatively high (25–27 years), and though it rises and falls somewhat over time, there seems to be no important trend in any particular direction. With reference to multifamily households, every survey of Chinese and Indian households has shown that even generations ago they were relatively modest in size (from four to six persons, varying by region and time period). Only under special historical circumstances will large, extended households be common. As to polygyny, the fact is that except under special circumstances, almost all men in all societies must be content with only one wife, and the fertility rate of polygynous marriages (one man married to several wives) is lower than that for monogamous marriages. Thus we see that with reference to the incorrect findings just cited, common beliefs did require testing, and they were wrong.

On the other hand, of course, many popular beliefs about how families work *are* correct. We cannot assume their correctness, however. Instead, we have to examine our observations, and make studies on our own to see how well these data fit in order to improve our understanding of the dynamics of family processes in our own or in other societies. If we emphasize the problems of obtaining facts, we should not lose sight of the central truth of any science: vast quantities of figures may be entirely meaningless, unless the search is guided by fruitful hypotheses or broad conceptions of social behavior. What we seek is organized facts, a structure of propositions, in which theory and fact illuminate one another. If we do not seek actual observation, we are engaged in blind speculation. If we seek facts without theoretical guidance, our search is random and often yields findings that have no bearing on anything. Understanding the family, then, requires the same sort of careful investigation as any other scientific endeavor.

WHY THE FAMILY IS THEORETICALLY SIGNIFICANT

Because the family is so much taken for granted, we do not often stop to consider the many traits that make it theoretically interesting. A brief consideration of certain peculiarities of the family will suggest why it is worthwhile exploring this social unit.

The family is the only social institution other than religion that is formally developed in all societies: a specific social agency is in charge of a great variety of social behaviors and activities. Some have argued that legal systems did not exist in preliterate or technologically less developed tribes or societies because there was no formally organized legislative body or judiciary. Of course, it is possible to abstract from concrete behavior the legal *aspects* of action, or the economic aspects, or the political dynamics, even when there are no explicitly labeled agencies formally in control of these areas in the society. However, kinship statuses and their responsibilities are the object of both formal and informal attention in societies at a high or a low technological level.

Family duties are the direct role responsibility of everyone in the society, with rare exceptions. Almost everyone is both born into a family and founds one of his or her own. Each individual is kin to many others. Many people, by contrast, may escape the religious duties others take for granted, or military or political burdens. Moreover, many family role responsibilities cannot usually be delegated to others, while in a work situation specialized obligations can be delegated.

Taking part in family activities has the further interesting quality that though it is not backed by the formal punishments supporting many other obligations, almost everyone takes part nonetheless. We must, for example, engage in economic or productive acts, or face starvation. We must enter the army, pay taxes, and appear before courts, or face money penalties and force. Such punishments do not usually confront the individual who does not wish to marry, or refuses to talk with his father or brother. Nevertheless, so pervasive are the social pressures, and so intertwined with indirect or direct rewards and punishments, that almost everyone conforms, or claims to conform, to family demands.

Although the family is usually thought of as an *expressive* or emotional social unit, it serves as an *instrumental* agency for the larger social structures, and all other institutions and agencies depend upon its contributions. For example, the role behavior learned within the family becomes the model or prototype for behavior required in other segments of the society. Inside the family, the content of the *socialization* process is the cultural tradition of the larger society. Families are also themselves *economic* units with respect to production and allocation. With reference to *social control,* each person's total range of behavior, and how his or her time and energies are budgeted, is more easily visible to family members than to outsiders. They can evaluate how the individual is allocating his or her time and money, and how well he or she is carrying out various duties. Consequently, the family acts as a source of pressure on the individual to adjust—to work harder and play less, or go to church less and study more. In all these ways, the family is partly an instrument or agent of the larger society. If it fails to perform adequately, the goals of the larger society may not be effectively achieved.

Perhaps more interesting theoretically is the fact that the various *tasks of the family are all separable* from one another, but in fact are not separated in almost all known family systems. We shall discuss these functions or tasks in various contexts in this book, so no great elaboration is needed at this point. Here are some of the contributions of the family to the larger society: reproduction of young, physical maintenance of family members, social placement of the child, socialization, and social control.

Let us consider how these activities could be separated. For example, the mother could send her child to be fed in a neighborhood mess hall, and of course some harassed mothers do send their children to buy lunch in a local snack bar. Those who give birth to a child need not socialize the child. They might send the child to specialists, and indeed specialists do take more responsibility for this task as the child grows older. Parents might, as some eugenicists have suggested, be selected for their breeding qualities, but these might not include any great talent for training the young. Status placement might be accomplished by random drawing of lots, by IQ tests or periodic examinations in physical and intellectual skills, or by popularity polls. This assignment of children to various social positions could be done without regard to an individual's parents, those who socialized or fed the child, or others who might supervise the child's daily behavior.

Separations of this kind have been suggested from time to time, and a few hesitant attempts have been made here and there in the world to put them into operation. However, three conclusions relevant to this kind of division can be drawn: (1) In all known societies, the *ideal* (with certain qualifications to be noted) is that the family be entrusted with all these functions. (2) When one or more family tasks are entrusted to another agency by a revolutionary or utopian society, the change can be made only with the support of much ideological fervor, and usually political pressure as well. (3) These experiments are also characterized by a gradual return to the more traditional type of family. In both the Israeli *kibbutzim* and the Russian experiments in relieving parents of child care, the ideal of completely communal living was once urged. Husband and wife were to have only a personal and emotional tie with one another: divorce would be easy. The children were to see their parents at regular intervals but look to their nursery attendants and mother surrogates for affection and direction during work hours. Each individual was to contribute his or her best skills to the cooperative unit without regard to family ties or sex status (there would be few or no "female" or "male" tasks). That ideal was attempted in a modest way, but behavior gradually dropped away from the ideal. The only other country in which the pattern has been attempted on a large scale is China. Already Chinese communes have retreated from their high ambitions, following the path of the *kibbutz* and the Russian *kolkhoz*.

Various factors contribute to these deviations from attempts to create a new type of family, and the two most important sets of pressures cannot easily be separated from each other. First is the problem, also noted by Plato, that individuals who develop their own attitudes and behaviors in the usual Western (European and European-based) family system do not easily adjust to the communal "family" even when they believe it is the right way. The second is the likelihood that when the family is radically changed, the various relations between it and the larger society are changed. New strains are created, demanding new kinds of adjustments on the part of the individuals in the society. Perhaps the planners must develop somewhat different agencies, or a different blueprint, to transform the family.

These comments have nothing to do with "capitalism" in its current political and economic argument with "communism." They merely describe the historical fact that though various experiments in separating the major functions of the family from one another have been conducted, none of these evolved from a previously existing family system. In addition, the several modern important attempts at such a separation, including the smaller communes that were created in the United States during the 1960s and 1970s, mostly exhibit a common pattern, a movement *away* from the utopian blueprint of separating the various family activities and giving each of them to a different social unit.

It is possible that some of these activities (meals) can be more easily separated than others; or that some family systems (for example, matrilineal systems) might lend themselves to such a separation more easily than others. On the other hand, we have to begin with the data that are now available. Even cautiously interpreted, they suggest that the family is a rather stable institution. On the other hand, we have not yet analyzed what this particular institution is. In the next section we discuss this question.

DEFINING THE FAMILY: A MATTER OF MORE OR LESS

Since thousands of publications have presented research findings on the family, one might suppose that there must be agreement on what this social unit is. In fact, sociologists and anthropologists have argued for decades about how to define it. Indeed, creating a clear, formal definition of any object of study is sometimes more difficult than making a study of that object. If we use a *concrete* definition, and assert that "a family is a social unit made up of father, mother, and children," then only about 35 percent of all U.S. households can be classed as a family. Much of the research on the family would have to exclude a majority of residential units. In addition, in some societies, one wife may be married to several husbands, or one husband to several wives. The definition would exclude such units. In a few societies there have been "families" in which the "husband" was a woman; and in some, certain "husbands" were not expected to live with their "wives." In the United States, millions of households contain at least one child, but only one parent. In a few communes, every adult male is married to all other adult females. That is, there are many kinds of social units that seem to be *like* a family, but do not fit almost any concrete definition that we might formulate.

We can escape such criticisms in part by claiming that most adults eventually go through such a *phase* of family life; that is, almost all men and women in the United States marry at some time during their lives, and most of them eventually have children. Nevertheless, analysis of the family would be much thinner if we focused only on that one kind of household. In ordinary language usage, people are most likely to agree that a social unit made up of father, mother, and child or children is a genuine family. They will begin to disagree more and more, as one or more of those persons or social roles is missing. Few people would agree that, at the other extremes, a household with only a single person in it is a family. Far more would think of a household as a family if it comprised a widow and her several children. Most people would agree that a husband-wife household is a family if they have children, even if their children are now living somewhere else. However, many would not be willing to class a childless couple as a family, especially if that couple planned never to have children. Very few people would be willing to accept a homosexual couple as a family.

What can we learn from such ordinary language usage? First, that *family* is not a single thing, to be captured by a neat verbal formula. Second, many social units can be thought of as "more or less" families, as they are more or less similar to the traditional type of family. Third, much of this graded similarity can be traced to the different kinds of role relations to be found in that traditional unit. Doubtless the following list is not comprehensive, but it includes most of those relationships: (1) At least two adult persons of opposite sex reside together. (2) They engage in some kind of division of labor; that is, they do not both perform exactly the same tasks. (3) They engage in many types of economic and social exchanges; that is, they do things for one another. (4) They share many things in common, such as food, sex, residence, and both goods and social activitites. (5) The adults have parental relations with their children, as their children have filial relations with them; the parents have some authority over their children, and both share with one another, while also assuming some obligation for protection, cooperation, and nurturance. (6) There are sibling relations among the children themselves, with, once more, a range of obligations to share, protect, and help one another. When all these conditions exist, few people would deny that the unit is a family. As we consider households in which more are missing, a larger number of people would express some doubt as to whether it really is a family. Thus, if two adults live together, but do nothing for each other, few people would agree that it is a family. If they do not even live together, fewer still would call the couple a family.

Individuals create all sorts of relations with each other, but others are more or less likely to view them as a family to the extent that their continuing social relations exhibit some or all of the role patterns noted above. Most important for our understanding of the family is that in all known societies, and under a wide range of social conditions, some kinds of familistic living arrangements seem to emerge, with some or all of these traits. These arrangements can emerge in prisons (with homosexual couples as units), under the disorganized conditions of revolution, conquest, or epidemic; or even when political attempts are made to reduce the importance of the family, and instead to press people to live in a more communal fashion. That is, people create and re-create some forms of familistic social patterns even when some of those traditional elements are missing.

This raises the inevitable question: Why does this happen: Why do people continue to form familistic relations, even when they are not convinced that it is the ideal social arrangement? Why is *this* and not some *other* social pattern so widespread? Of course, this is not an argument for the *universality* of the conjugal family. Many other kinds of relations between individuals are created. Nevertheless, some approximation of these familistic relationships do continue to occur in the face of many alternative temptations and opportunities as well as counterpressures. Unless we are willing to assert that people are irrational, we must conclude that these relationships must offer some *advantages*. What are they?

ADVANTAGES OF THE "FAMILISTIC PACKAGE"

We suppose that the most fundamental set of advantages is found in the division of labor and the resulting possibility of social exchanges between husband and wife (or members of a homosexual couple), as well as between children and parents. This includes not only economic goods, but help, nurturance, protection, and affection. It is often forgotten that the modern domestic household is very much an *economic* unit even if it is no longer a farming unit. People are actually producing goods and services for one another. They are buying objects in one place, and transporting them to the household. They are transforming food into meals. They are engaged in cleaning, mowing lawns, repairing, transporting, counseling,—a wide array of services that would have to be paid for in money if some member of the family did not do them.

Families of all types also enjoy some small economies of scale. When there are two or more members of the household, various kinds of activities can be done almost as easily for everyone as for a single person; it is almost as easy to prepare one meal for three or four people as it is to prepare a similar meal for one person. Thus, the cost of a meal is less per person within a family. Families can cooperate to achieve what an individual cannot, from building a mountain cabin to creating a certain style of life. Help from all members will make it much easier to achieve that goal than it would be for one person.

All the historic forms of the family that we know, including communal group marriages, are also attractive because they offer *continuity*. Thus, whatever the members produce together, they expect to be able to enjoy together later. Continuity has several implications. One is that members do not have to bear the costs of continually searching for new partners, or for new members who might be "better" at various family tasks. In addition, husband and wife, as well as children, enjoy a much longer line of social credit than they would have if they were making exchanges with people outside the family. This means that an individual can give more at one time to someone in the family, knowing that in the longer run this will not be a loss: the other person will remain long enough to reciprocate at some point, or perhaps still another member will offer help at a later time.

Next, the familistic mode of living offers several of the advantages of any informal group.[2] It exhibits, for example, a very short line of communication; everyone is close by, and members need not communicate through intermediaries. Thus they can respond quickly in case of need. A short line of communication makes cooperation much easier. Second, everyone has many idiosyncratic needs and wishes. In day to day interaction with outsiders, we need not adjust to these very much, and they may be a nuisance; others, in turn, are likely not to adjust to our own idiosyncracies. However, within the familistic mode of social interaction, people learn what each other's idiosyncratic needs are. Learning such needs can and does make life together somewhat more attractive because adjusting to them may not be a great burden, but does give pleasure to the other. These include such trivia as how strong the tea or coffee should be, how much talk there will be at meals, sleep and work schedules, levels of noise, and so on. Of course with that knowledge we can more easily make others miserable, too, if we wish to do so.

Domestic tasks typically do not require high expertise, and as a consequence most members of the family can learn to do them eventually. Because they do learn, members derive many benefits from one another, without having to go outside the family unit. Again, this makes a familistic mode of living more attractive than it would be otherwise. In addition, with reference to many such tasks, there are no outside experts anyway (throughout most of world history, there have been no experts in childrearing, taking care of small cuts or bruises, murmuring consoling words in response to some distress, and so on). That is, the tasks within a family setting are likely to be tasks at which insiders are at least as good as outsiders, and typically better.

No other social institutions offer this range of complementarities, sharing, and closely linked, interwoven advantages. The closest possible exception might be some ascribed, ritual friendships in a few societies, but even these do not offer the range of exchanges that are to be found in the familistic processes.

We have focused on advantages that the *members* of families obtain from living under this type of arrangement. However, when we survey the wide range of family patterns in hundreds of societies, we are struck by the fact that this social unit is strongly supported by *outsiders*—that is, members of the larger society.

It is supported by a structure of norms, values, laws, and a wide range of social pressures. More concretely, other members of the society believe such units are necessary, and they are concerned about how people discharge their obligations within the family. They punish members of the family who do not conform to ideal behavior, and praise those who do conform. These intrusions are not simply whimsical, or a matter of oppression. Other members of the society do in fact have a stake in how families

2. For further comparisons of bureaucracy and informal groups, see Eugene Litwak, "Technical Innovation and Theoretical Functions of Primary Groups and Bureaucratic Structures," *American Journal of Sociology,* 73 (1968), 468–481.

discharge their various tasks. More broadly, it is widely believed that the collective needs of the whole society are served by some of the activities individual families carry out. In short, it is characteristic of the varieties of the family that participants on an average enjoy more, and gain more comfort, pleasure, or advantage from being in a familistic arrangement than from living alone; and *other* members of the society view that arrangement as contributing in some measure to the survival of the society itself. Members of societies have usually supposed it important for most *other* individuals to form families, to rear children, to create the next generation, to support and help each other—whether or not individual members of specific families do in fact feel they gain real advantages from living in a familistic arrangement. For example, over many centuries, people opposed legal divorces, whether or not they themselves were happily married, and with little regard for the marital happiness of others.

This view of what makes up the "familistic social package" explains several kinds of widely observable social behavior. One is that people experiment with different kinds of arrangements, often guided by a new philosophy of how people ought to live. They do so because their own needs have not been adequately fulfilled in the traditional modes of family arrangements available to them in their own society. Since other people have a stake in the kinds of familistic arrangements people make, we can also expect that when some individuals or groups attempt to change or experiment with the established system, various members of the society will object, and may even persecute them for it. We can also see why it is that even in a high-divorce society such as our own, where millions of people have been dissatisfied or hurt by their marriages and their divorces, they nevertheless move back into a marital arrangement. That is, after examining various alternatives, the familistic social package still seems to offer a broader set of personal advantages, and the outside society supports that move. And, as noted earlier, even when there are strong political pressures to create new social units that give far less support for the individual family, as in China, Russia, and the Israeli *kibbutzim,* we can expect that people will continue to drift back toward some kind of familistic arrangement.

A SOCIOLOGICAL APPROACH TO FAMILY RESEARCH

The unusual traits the family exhibits as a type of social subsystem require that some attention be paid to the analytic approach to be used in studying it. First, neither ideal nor reality can be excluded from our attention. It would, for example, be naive to suppose that because some 40 percent of all U.S. couples now marrying will eventually divorce, they do not cherish the ideal of remaining married to one person. Contemporary estimates suggest that about half of all married men engage in extramarital intercourse at some time, but public opinion surveys report that a large majority of both men and women in the United States, even in these permissive times, approve of the ideal of faithfulness. On a more personal level, every reader of these lines has lied at some time, but nevertheless most believe in the ideal of telling the truth.

A sociologist ascertains the ideals of family systems partly because they are a rough guide to behavior. Knowing that people prefer to have their sons and daughters marry at least at the same class level, we can expect them to try to control their children's mate choices if they can do so. We can also specify some of the conditions under which they will have a greater or lesser success in reaching that goal. We also know that when a person violates the ideal, he or she is likely to conceal the violation if possible. If that is not possible, people will try to find some excuse for the violation, and are likely to be embarrassed if others find out about it.

The sociology of the family cannot confine itself only to contemporary urban (or suburban) American life. Conclusions of any substantial validity or scope must include data from other societies, whether these are past or present, industrial or nonindustrial, Asian or European. Data from the historical past, such as Periclean Athens or imperial Rome, are not often used because no sociologically adequate account of their family systems has as yet been written.[3] On the other hand, the last two decades have seen the appearance of many studies about family systems in various European cities of the last five centuries.

The study of customs and beliefs from the past yields a better understanding of the possible range of social behavior. Thereby, we are led to deny or at least to qualify a finding that might be correct if limited only to modern American life (such as the rise in divorce rates over several decades). The use of data from tribal societies of the past or present helps us in testing conclusions about family systems that are not found at all in Western society, such as matrilineal systems or polygyny. Or, an apparently simple relationship may take a different form in other societies. For example, in the United States most first marriages are based on a love relationship (whatever else they may be based on), and people are reluctant to admit that they have married someone with whom they were not in love. By contrast, though people fall in love in other societies, love may play a small or a large part in the marriage system. We shall analyze this difference in the chapter on mate choice.

It is possible to study almost any phenomenon from a wide range of viewpoints. We may study the economic aspects of family behavior, or we may confine ourselves to the biological factors in family patterns. A full analysis of any concrete object is impossible. Everything can be analyzed from many vantage points, each of them yielding a somewhat different but still limited picture. Everything is infinitely complex. Each science limits its perspective to the range of processes that it considers important. Each such approach has its own justification. Here we examine the family mainly from a sociological perspective.

---

3.   However, Keith Hopkins has published several specialized studies on various aspects of Roman families. See his *Conquerors and Slaves* (Cambridge, Eng.: Cambridge University Press, 1978).

The sociological approach focuses on the family as a social institution, the peculiar and unique quality of family interaction as *social*. For example, family systems exhibit the characteristics of legitimacy and authority, which are not biological categories at all. The values and the prescribed behavior to be found in a family, or the rights and duties of family statuses such as father or daughter, are not psychological categories. They are peculiar to the theoretical approach of sociology. Personality theory is not very useful in explaining the particular position of the family in Chinese and Japanese social structures, although it may help us understand how individuals respond emotionally to those rights and obligations. If we use a consistently sociological approach, we will miss some important information about concrete family interaction. The possible gain when we stay on one theoretical level may be the achievement of some increased systematization, and some greater rigor.

At a minimum, however, when an analyst moves from the sociological to the psychological level of theory, he or she ought at least to be conscious of it. If the investigation turns to the impact of biological or psychological factors on the family, they should be examined with reference to their *social* meaning. For example, interracial marriage appears to be of little biological significance, but it has much social impact on those who take part in such a marriage. A sociologist who studies the family is not likely to be an expert in the *psychodynamics* of mental disease, but is interested in the effect of mental disease on the social relations in a particular family or type of family, or in the adjustment different family types make to it.

Since all these sciences of human behavior contribute to our understanding of the family, we should use the information as it becomes available. In the next chapter, we consider the biological bases of the family, the extent to which we can use the findings from biology to explain family behavior patterns.

CHAPTER 2
THE BIOLOGICAL FOUNDATIONS OF FAMILY BEHAVIOR

Stimulated by a growing body of knowledge about animal behavior and by spectacular advances in genetics, some biologists (as well as nonbiologists) have begun to build a new synthesis of ideas under the label of *sociobiology*, and have challenged sociologists on their own ground. Their general thesis is that far more of human behavior is caused by biological forces than once was believed. This is an ancient set of claims, now renewed. Some of these claims rest on strong foundations. It would be unreasonable to suppose that a social institution so intertwined with biological events would have evolved without being shaped to some extent by biological forces. After all: people marry in part because of their sexual drives; reproduction is a biological process; social training, however persistent, cannot transform a human infant into an adult chimpanzee; biologically, the infant is helpless and requires adult care to survive.

The broader claims of sociobiologists are based on much new research on both human beings and other animals. First, many studies of the social (and thus family) life of animals in their natural habitat have revealed patterns of interaction very close to those of human beings (cooperation, play, mothers' care of infants, adult males' protection of the group, deference, leadership). Since their family life is presumably determined by biology rather than culture, perhaps more of our behavior is biologically inherited than was thought possible two decades ago. Second, just as the human infant seems to be neurologically "programmed" or "wired" for speech, so is it also apparently programmed for maximizing social interaction with whoever acts as parent. For example, infants not only suckle automatically, but also adjust their bodies to increase contact with adults. Third, studies of biochemical changes during physical growth, the effects of glandular secretions, and the effect of chemicals on both the mind and social behavior all suggest that under-lying physiological states of the human body shape some part of the per-sonality, sex role behavior, and social action. Thus, what was thought to be caused by culture or social experience may instead be caused by biological processes.

Scholars who assert the prepotence of biology have not all made the same claims, of course. However, many of those who have contributed to this body of hypotheses have argued that the following types of family behavior are mainly determined by biological factors:

1. The dominance of males over females, and of husbands over wives.
2. The division of labor between husbands and wives.
3. The feminine roles of caring for children, preparing food, and assuming responsibility for domestic chores.
4. Male initiative in sexual activities, polygyny, and male promiscuity; female coyness, resistance to sexual overtures, and attempts to ensure large male investments in domesticity before agreeing to mate.
5. Sacrificing oneself for a member of the kin group or tribe, even for those who are not one's sons or daughters.
6. Defense of one's territory, and war between societies.
7. Male jealousy.
8. Rules against incest.
9. The organization of males into dyads or larger groups—male bonding.
10. Willingness to murder other human beings (most killer animals do so rarely), or engage in war.

On a general level, of course, some evidence supports these assertions, even if they are unlikely to be correct as stated. Human family patterns are surely determined in part by the peculiar task imposed on them: The family is the only social institution charged with transforming a biological organism into a human being. On the other hand, this is a very special kind of animal, the result of millions of years of evolutionary development. Cultural systems and social patterns are not simply plastered, like a thin layer of civility, on top of a raging animal that has remained unchanged from its first appearance as an apelike hunter-gatherer. The human animal and its culture have been adapting to each other for at least three to five million years.

More precisely, it is likely that human biological patterns adjusted long ago to something unique in the history of the world: Environmental problems began to be solved mainly by social and cultural innovations (a sharper arrowhead), not by genetic changes that embedded solutions in an automatic biological response (the infant monkey's ability to hang onto its mother when she is moving through the trees). Any competing humanlike species that might have followed the path of biological adaptation would have been left far behind, since social and cultural inventions offer quicker answers to environmental challenges than genetic solutions (and quicker corrections if the answers are wrong).

Almost certainly that talent for sociocultural advance took the form of a larger and more complex brain, plus a set of biological processes that did not specify a rigid, narrow set of behavior patterns. Since the humanoid brain continued to increase in size long past the point where it might have been needed to compete with other animals, we have to suppose that this continued development was a response to the social and cultural environment of human society, not to the challenge of the *nonhuman* environment. Over time, the individuals with higher brain capacities survived better because they were better suited to the cultural and social patterns of human life. If this is so, it may well be that our new knowledge about biological factors will not yield the conclusion that they are prepotent, but will simply help us better to understand how biological, social, and cultural factors interact to create the many forms of family life that we can observe. Let us first consider the problem of finding the facts.

THE NATURE AND NURTURE DEBATE

The Problem of Proof

How much of family behavior can be explained by biological factors is part of the age-old question of nature versus nurture: Do human traits arise mainly from social influences, or from our biological heritage? It is not certain that we *can* answer the question if it is stated in that form, but each decade of research brings more knowledge about both biological and social factors.

We cannot easily answer the question because the problem of proof is difficult. It is difficult primarily because of one stubborn fact: In order to ascertain what kinds of family behavior might be determined by "purely" biological factors, we have to observe a wide range of family patterns that are of some importance (courtship, respect paid to elders, division of labor in the family). But by the time any human being is old enough to take part in such behaviors, he or she has already been shaped in many ways by social and cultural influences. In short, it is not possible to isolate in a pure form either social influences or biological factors. On the other hand, because the problem is of some importance in understanding family behavior, social analysts for many generations have made the attempt to solve it. Let us consider some of the kinds of evidence that have been adduced and why each is unsatisfactory, although none of these sets of data can be dismissed as wholly irrelevant. The main kinds of evidence are these:

1. Biological evolution of the human species, over the past three to five million years.
2. Observations of higher mammals, especially of our four great anthropoid cousins (gorillas, chimpanzees, orangutans, and gibbons) made under natural conditions in the wild.
3. Studies of human societies at a low technological level (people who use no metal tools).
4. Studies of human children reared in social isolation.
5. Endocrinal or hormonal studies, mostly on lower animals.

Let us consider each of these briefly.

Evolution.   As the archeological record becomes richer, we know more about our distant ancestors as they gradually evolved from apelike creatures to become human in appearance. We learn more about what they ate, how they hunted, and so on. It is tempting to correlate that development in some way with the gradual evolution of human *family* systems. Unfortunately, we know and shall know nothing important about this latter evolution prior to written history. The data are lost forever. Precisely the kinds of information we need—how men and women, parents and children, interacted together—left no traces. Even with respect to the purely biological evolution, our knowledge is entirely anatomical. We do not have any knowledge of the physiological evolution of human beings, of endocrinal or hormonal changes, or even the quality of human mental behavior as distinct from the sheer physical size of the brain. We do not know, for example, why Neanderthal people died out, but we know their brains were large.

The more fundamental lesson we learn from evolution is that the processes of selection determine both our cultural *and* our genetic heritage, and very likely on the same basis. But which of the new traits that arose in prehistory helped the individual to survive better and to pass on these characteristics (cultural *or* biological) to succeeding generations? That view cannot presuppose that any widespread human pattern is genetic, because so many such traits seem clearly cultural (such as religion). Since culture can change more rapidly than biology, and is more variable because it has to fit very different types of environments, a panorama of human changes over thousands of years would probably suggest the cultural as having had far more effect on family patterns.

Mammal Studies.   Sociobiologists have relied on field studies of animals in their natural setting. Some have also done quasi-experiments with animals and birds living under relative freedom. The apparent logic being followed is that if we can specify some kinds of family behavior that seem to be common to several types of apes, we can suppose that shared behavior is biological, rather than cultural. Unfortunately, the four anthropoid apes (gibbon, orangutan, chimpanzee, and gorilla) branched off separately from human evolution during the Miocene age or perhaps somewhat later, but in any event some twenty or more million years ago, according to some estimates. This makes their similarity with human patterns questionable in evolutionary terms; more important, it is precisely during this most recent period of evolution that human beings came to rely less on their biological heritage, and to cope with their environment through social learning.

Equally important, we now have reasonably good field studies of family behavior among the four anthropoids, and in fact their domestic patterns are dissimilar: gibbons are monogamous and both sexes are jealous, while gorilla family life is polygynous and jealousy is uncommon; the male orangutan seems to have relatively little to do with the female and her children on a day-to-day basis; and so on.

Societal Studies.   Parallel to the line of speculation about family patterns among apes is the notion that we could examine the family life of modern tribal societies, arranged by technological level, and then deduce or speculate about their family life in the distant past when those technologies were dominant. Thus, for example, we could suppose that the family life of Australian aborigines, who were still living at a Stone Age level in a gathering and hunting economy, would be like the family life of human beings in the Paleolithic period, say fifty to one hundred thousand years ago. Unfortunately, recent tribal societies at a Stone Age level are no "older" than modern industrial societies: both have the same number of years behind them. We have no way of guessing whether such families were similar to those of people who lived a hundred millennia ago. Knowledge about all such societies helps us to understand family behavior, but we have no way of linking that knowledge to the distant past.

Children Reared in Isolation. At first, the notion of rearing infants in isolation from all human relations, and then comparing their adult behavior with that of normally socialized adults, might seem to be a promising direction of inquiry: We would thereby ascertain which patterns of behavior are "purely" biological, uncontaminated by social learning. Indeed, that idea has been mentioned many times by philosophers over the past two thousand years. We might go further, and rear several children in isolation and then bring them together in adulthood to see what kinds of "families" they might form.

There are, of course, humanitarian objections to such a cruel experiment. Scientifically, however, it is also self-contaminating. A child reared in social isolation does not develop normally, and cannot function adequately *even as an animal.* We now know that this is true of monkeys as well: Their adult behavior is bizarre and distorted if they are reared without social contact with others of their species. Some analysts have supposed that the so-called wolf children, children who seem to have grown up in the wild, and even possibly reared by wild animals, would throw light on this matter. As far as can be ascertained, no such children have ever existed. On the other hand, from time to time, children who were reared in more or less social isolation have been discovered. When found, they do not appear to be "animals," but without the surface polish of social learning. Instead, their behavior is strange, their physical movements awkward and incompetent, their intellectual and emotional development retarded. What we learn from such studies is that without adequate social interaction, the human animal does not develop normally.

Endocrinal and Hormonal Studies. Studies of hormonal or endocrinal processes in human beings and other animals inform us that many changes in behavior are partly caused by these physiological factors. Injections of male hormones in a subordinate animal may temporarily make it more aggressive, or even dominant. "Mothering" behavior in female animals can be induced by hormonal injections. Unfortunately for the simplicity of our hypotheses, we can also induce *hormonal* changes by altering the *social* situation; for example, by putting a male animal in a dominant position, we can induce the output of more male hormones. Moreover, it is a general finding that as we compare higher and lower animals, higher apes with monkeys, or human beings with apes, we observe that more and more of their behavior is shaped by social experience, so that we should be somewhat sceptical about the one-directional effects of endocrinal secretions.

Weaknesses of the Biological Arguments

As to the logic of proof, it is not correct that if a behavior pattern is universal, we can be confident it is determined by locatable biological factors. As we have already noted, all societies seem to have religious systems, but almost certainly these cannot be traced to some biological trait. All societies have norms or rules that define some children as illegitimate and others as legitimate, but no one has tried to claim that a particular biological factor causes this social behavior.

Even when a trait is biological and universal, it may vary a good bit from one society to another. For example, sexual intercourse is biological and is found in all societies, but it varies in frequency, in rules, and even in modes of performance. We can suppose that visual acuity probably does not vary much from one society to another and is mainly biological, but cultural patterns determine which kinds of things we see keenly. Eskimos could "read" various types of snow with ease, while outsiders might "see" only undifferentiated humps of white. Experienced whalers could "see" traces of a whale on the horizon, when a new member of the crew could see nothing but indigo seas.

The weaknesses of all these kinds of data and logic do not mean that they are simply wrong, or that they are not properly a part of the general analysis of cultural and biological factors. Some of them offer at least persuasive evidence in favor of one or another interpretation. But though biological explanations of human behavior seem simple, they are hard to demonstrate. For example, many people continue to comment that "males are naturally polygynous," or "women should take care of children because they have a maternal instinct." But good counterarguments can be leveled against such statements. For example, if women actually do have a maternal instinct, then there need be no laws or social pressures to persuade them to nurture their children. In any event, the weaknesses of the arguments do require us to proceed cautiously in approaching these two questions:

1.   How much of family behavior can be explained by biological factors?
2.   Which biological traits of human beings determine the range of family patterns?

Definition of Terms

Let us now clarify a few basic terms in this inquiry. *Socialization* comprises all the social processes by which the young human being comes to know about and believe in the norms and values of the sociey, and also acquires the social roles appropriate to his or her position in it. Our total range of behavior is shaped by the interaction of these socialization processes with the particular biological potential of the human animal.

All animal behavior is complex, and is in turn made up of different components. All animals, including human beings, have *reflexes,* such as salivating when food is in the mouth, winking when a moving object suddenly threatens the eye, or (in human and ape infants) grasping any object the hand touches. These are not willed; they are automatic, and they are useful for the survival of the animal. They are innate sensory-motor responses, usually involving one part of the body. Many of them, like the salivating reflex, can be conditioned by learning so that we salivate in response to particular food smells that will be followed by eating. All animals, including human beings, also have *drives,* which are impulses to satisfy some hunger, as for food, water, or sex. A healthy animal experiences such a drive even if no outside stimulus is present, whereas the reflex always occurs in response to a particular stimulus. The drive is a general striving towards some goal, but it does not offer a particular solution for reaching that goal.

In addition to these patterns, some types of behavior appear later in life not because they have been learned, but because the body itself continues to *mature.* For example, many hormones appear in quantity only when the animal moves toward adulthood. Of course, as animals mature, they also learn about their environment, so that sexual behavior, partly due to maturation, is also shaped by learning. Walking cannot properly be called a *drive,* but the human animal does not learn to walk until its body has matured somewhat.

It is especially important that all these elements in animal behavior be separated from *instincts,* since the human biological heritage apparently contains all of them except instincts. Many types of human behavior have been labeled instincts, and fifty years ago it was thought that there were literally dozens of such patterns. The term cannot apply to just any goal-adapted behavior, or all behaviors (such as eating fruit) that are widely dispersed through an animal population. It refers instead to a fairly complex behavior linkage, or chain of behavior, in which the animal moves toward a goal through a sequence of related acts but without much prior learning. The drive is different, because it does not contain the neural mechanisms for its own solution. Almost certainly reflexes form some of the building blocks of instincts, and so do the bodily changes that come from maturation. However, any single reflex is only an automatic neural response to a stimulus. By contrast, the instinct is made up of both the stimulus (temperature, time of year, the presence of another animal) and the internal state of the animal (level of sex drive, hunger) and is executed through a chain of acts linked together somewhat automatically. For example, birds of each species construct rather complex nests each year, different for each species, without ever having gone to school to learn how to do it. Many birds migrate thousands of miles each year, following pathways laid down thousands of years ago, but again without having been taught to do it. From observation, however, we know that all instincts can be modified somewhat by learning.

THE INTERACTION OF BIOLOGICAL AND
CULTURAL FACTORS

Human beings thus depend more on learning than any other animal, and they cannot develop normally without social contact. The family is the social invention that copes with the task of transforming a biological potential into a human being. The family is where most initial learning takes place, and it is where the infant experiences the social interaction that furnishes the content of learning. What the family does and how it operates tells us something about the contribution or the strain created by the physical qualities of human beings when they are pressed into a *cultural* mold. Both sets of factors interact with one another in complex ways, sometimes in harmony and sometimes in great tension.

Indeed, both set limits upon one another. One simple limit that human organic traits place on the culture and the family is that the society cannot ask the biologically impossible of its members. Thus, a religious system may define some people as members of a Kangaroo totem, and thus spiritually as kangaroos, but even in the midst of religious ceremonies these people cannot really *become* kangaroos. Men cannot bear children. Twins may be viewed as semi-sacred, but not every woman can be expected to bear twins. As a second aspect of the necessary but partial harmony between biological factors and the human family, it is self-evident that the society and the family must assure adequate conditions for replacing each generation. Food must be procured and distributed to the young, the old, the ill, and the disabled. Individuals must be protected against predators, marauding bands, and disease. These tasks are the social responsibility of societal or family units.

On the other hand, we must not fall into the sentimental error of believing that under ideal conditions there is some kind of close harmony and balance between biological and social needs, evolved over thousands of generations by some kind of natural evolution. Some harmony must exist, of course, or the species would die out. However, the culture may place great demands on the biological organism. Societies typically expect of adult males that they be willing to sacrifice themselves in battle against their enemies if necessary. Among the North American Plains Indians, young males who sought visions would undergo starvation and self-torture. In many societies people have been required to submit to scarification, tattooing, circumcision, and subincision. Mothers and fathers are expected to protect their young even if they die in the attempt.

Disharmonies also exist because of pressures from the biological organism against the rigidities of cultural norms. That is, biological demands make it difficult to conform to cultural rules. Perhaps all societies require some control over the time, place, and occasion for defecation, urination, coughing, or belching. They also impose restrictions on the satisfaction of hunger, sex, or thirst drives, and of course over the immediate impulses to murder that we sometimes feel. Not all imaginable societies are sociologically possible, and not all are biologically possible, although they do vary over a wide range. The organism itself is not infinitely plastic; it cannot be adjusted to any type of society we might want to create.

Harmonious Patterns

As to the harmony between these two great sets of factors, two broad patterns are visible:

1. The social patterns of human beings are "biologized."
2. The biological traits of human beings are given a social meaning and shape.

Almost everything that human beings do is harnessed somehow to biological motors, for they are the source of all the actions we undertake. We shall discuss this more concretely with reference to the sexual drive, but it is evident in almost all our actions. We do not simply engage in goal-seeking behavior in a cool, uninvolved fashion. Our emotions move us, and these can be traced to the firing of neural impulses, the movement of our blood, the pounding of our heart, and the emotions of rage, love, or exultation that we may feel at different times. Every norm and value, and even such abstract notions as patriotism, are ultimately driven by biological motors—although to be sure the human organism has no specific biological parts that can be called the source of patriotism. On the other hand, we not only learn which foods are poisonous, but we also learn that some foods are disgusting which we know other societies may eat with relish. That is, the body is taught to reject some foods that would be biologically nourishing. It is biologically necessary to take care of the newborn infant, but societies vary greatly in the social actions that are required for that purpose.

It is thus meaningless to assert that the biological is less or more important than the cultural, just as it is meaningless to argue that hydrogen or oxygen is more important in producing the unique qualities of water. Biological traits make family systems possible and set some limits to their variation, though we do not know as yet how narrow those limits are. Human beings have almost no unique biological traits—characteristics no other animal possesses—with the possible important exception that we lack instincts. In all significant biological aspects human beings differ from their nearest ape cousins, the anthropoids, in degree only. The large and complex brain human beings have permits them to make symbols and to reason abstractly, but we know that the higher apes can do this to some extent as well.

General Biological Traits

In the next section, we consider a wide variety of biological traits that have special reference to family behaviors. Here, we first consider the most general of the animal traits.

Like many other animals, human beings are helpless at birth, and would die quickly without care. However, even at several years of age, human beings remain relatively helpless. This biological characteristic is linked with others to form a complex that seems to set human beings apart. Human beings are born with no instincts to simplify their adjustment to the environment, mature later than any other animal, and acquire almost all their skills for coping through the process of social learning. Very likely this arrangement is made possible because they possess a complex brain that is capable of symbolic thought (including language). At what age a human child might survive alone is a subject primarily for speculation. Large grazing animals such as elephants, most whales, or hippopotamuses mature physically rather slowly, but within a few days after birth can forage for themselves, even while living mainly from their mother's milk. If alone, they may be killed more easily, but even at a few months of age they may be able to find their own food. Predators such as wolves or lions of course cannot, since they have to learn hunting skills, but within a year they too could live independently if they had to. Human beings cannot. Their physical equipment is inadequate in all respects, and simple physical maturation does not automatically give them enough skill for survival. They possess no instincts that would lead them to build a shelter, to kill other animals, to grow plants, or to make complex tools. Their hunger and thirst drives would impel them to action and to some accidental solutions, but even at 5 or 6 years of age their physical achievements and endowments do not seem sufficient to ensure survival.

One might, then, view culture itself as an evolutionary adaptation to a large brain and the lack of instincts. Or, we might speculate that instincts were gradually lost because during hundreds of thousands of years our human ancestors were developing a culture that made inborn physical skills less necessary.

The Biological Traits Relevant to Family Behavior

The following biological traits would seem to be the most important for shaping human family roles and social structures:

1. A long period of helplessness in the child.
2. Lack of instincts.
3. A complex brain that creates symbols and abstractions.
4. Sexual characteristics.
5. Sex differences.

Helplessness of the Human Infant.   Since the newborn human being is helpless at birth as well as for years afterward, some kind of social unit must care for it if the species is to survive. However, the biological need does not determine the specific form of that unit, only its general traits. What are they? It must be stable over some years, of course, or there must be a procedure for handing the tasks over to another unit if that one breaks down. If it is to be stable, it will probably contain more than one adult (in case one is ill or incapacitated). Its members must have an emotional or economic stake in the child, so that they are willing to invest years of care in its survival. They must feel some affection for it, since adequate socialization will not occur without love. It must be a production unit, of course, so that its members can satisfy their physical needs.

Societies have universally created family units for carrying out these tasks, but how these units are structured is not determined by biological traits. Many different kinds of families, with different allocations of duties among members, can accomplish these goals equally well. Moreover, other kinds of social units can easily be invented, and sometimes are, to discharge these functions.

Complexity of the Human Brain.   From one point of view, the peculiar human brain is a biological invention to compensate for the lack of instincts (see pp. 23–24 for a discussion of this important point). It does not specify precisely what each family role will be, but it permits human beings to adjust to the wide range of roles that societies create. It can develop complex techniques to cope with harsh or benign environments, physical or social. Because it *symbolizes* (makes one thing stand for another—the word *tree* for a real tree, ritual wine for the blood of Christ) it can link almost anything to family roles. Thus it can link the symbols of family life with a biological drive (wedding rings with sex), just as it can limit the situations in which biological needs are permitted to be satisfied (incest taboos, table manners).

While biological needs are themselves culturally shaped, it is precisely this supreme adaptability of the brain that makes it unnecessary for human biological traits to determine specifically what the family rules of behavior will be: The brain can continue to follow new patterns whenever it finds a new social invention appropriate or needed.

Human Sexual Characteristics.   The sexual characteristics of human beings are more specific in their impact on family roles. Perhaps the most important are these:

1. Constancy of the sex drive.
2. The high sexual level of human beings.
3. Heterosexuality.

A major part of human sexuality parallels the anatomical and physiological traits of other higher animals, from the parts of the genitourinary system to the hormonal system that regulates sexual desire. That heterosexuality is "prewired" biologically seems certain, while the existence of some amount of homosexuality in both human and other animals does not negate that likelihood. However, again it is difficult to point to biological traits that directly explain the special forms sexual activity takes in human courtship and marriage. No animal, as far as we can ascertain, spends any of its time making thousands of moral rules about whether and how to engage in sex.

Two especially human biological characteristics also have a more direct effect on family behavior (aside from sex differences, discussed below).

Human beings, far more than their near cousins the anthropoid apes, have a relatively high and constant sex drive. Their behavior is more pervasively sexual. They are far sexier than is needed for enough births to keep up the population. This has many consequences. First, it means that males and females constantly seek the company of the other sex; or, that both male or female welcome the attentions of the other sex. In turn, human ingenuity attempts to work out rules for controlling sexual behavior (since each individual has at least some stake in ensuring sexual contact with his or her mate or mates, and in not losing that mate to a competitor).

Because it is a potential source of pleasure, human beings build sexuality into ceremonies, symbols, and even onerous chores. It is made into a recurring human "bait" disguised in hundreds of ways. Its connection with the human brain also means, unfortunately, that a wide range of repressions and distortions can also enter between desire and fulfillment. All societies frown on complete hedonism in sex, and instead attempt to confine most sexual pleasure to social roles that contain the other duties of adulthood, parenthood, and maintaining a family. On the other hand, because of the strength of this drive in human beings, social attempts at restraint fall considerably short of success.

Sex Differences.   Still more specific in their shaping effects are the biological differences between the sexes. To the untutored eye these differences are rather obvious, but the overlaps between the two sexes are substantial, especially at the hormonal level. That is, whatever characteristic may be used to distinguish the male and female populations of the world (height, strength), by that same criterion many women will approach or surpass the male averages, and many males will approach or surpass female averages. In short, many males and females are "in between." Moreover, even the average differences change over time: Male-female differences change from one society to another, or from one historical epoch to another. Thus, we must remain suspicious of the claim that all the apparent sex differences in one place and time are only biological. Most of the apparent differences observers fifty years ago took as obvious can now be seen more correctly as the result of differences in childrearing practices.

In any event, our question is the extent to which any such differences directly shape the family roles the two sexes play. The most relevant traits are probably these:

1.   Menstruation, pregnancy, and lactation in females.
2.   Sexual dimorphism, and the greater strength and aggressiveness of males.
3.   The need for orgasm in males if fertility is to occur; the higher sexual capacity of females.
4.   Sex differences in mortality.

Women menstruate and can bear children, while men cannot. It is an unwarranted jump in logic to assert that "therefore" women are biologically disposed toward accepting the tasks of caring for children and the home (or that infants must be nursed by their own mothers). There is no *biological* connection between these two, but surely a strong social link. If all these social duties imposed on women were set in biology, there would be little need for societies to spend much energy on preaching to women about their "womanly duties." Nevertheless, it is likely that in the period immediately after giving birth, hormonal processes in the female do induce an increase of nurturant behavior, along with the flow of milk. In most of human history, women have nursed their infants because that released breast tension and was an easy mode of feeding. This interaction, together with the "burrowing" and nursing reflexes of babies, intensifies the psychological bond between mother and infant. Infants need "mothering," but they do not need their own mothers to do it—fathers or unrelated men and women can do it, too. In addition, women in the later stages of pregnancy and just after childbirth are weaker. For these reasons, even if men and women divided their tasks on the basis of efficiency and comfort, it seems likely that women would have been given the responsibility of staying closer to the hearth and children.

Men and women do not differ greatly in average size; the dimorphism of human beings is modest, about midway between the extreme differences between male and female gorillas, and the near equality among gibbons. Nevertheless, the human male is stronger and more aggressive than the female, and that is very likely one major biological source of the dominance of males in all family systems. Some wives are stronger and more aggressive than their husbands, but on average women rank lower along both dimensions. Men have always enjoyed the additional sociocultural support of social pressure and norms that proclaimed they *should* be dominant. They have enjoyed two additional advantages, based on this biological superiority. When engaged in combat with members of other societies, or in tracking down large or swift animals or navigating treacherous waters, the slightly greater biological effectiveness of men would make them natural candidates for these kinds of activities. They would enjoy only a marginal superiority, but in high-risk ventures, it is wiser to use the best one has. This slight edge, we believe, has had the effect of giving men a near monopoly in such pursuits. Finally, since all young boys were seen as destined eventually to take part in such activities, they were given training in the appropriate skills, while young girls were not. Thus, in nearly all societies women never found out how well they could compete in war, hunting large land or sea animals, and confronting difficult situations at sea. As a consequence, they had even less chance of demonstrating that they could perform these tasks with equal success.

Although women and men are both capable of orgasm, only the male orgasm and ejaculation are necessary for conception. That is, only the male desire is necessary for the continuation of the species. This is probably not even the main *cause* of the different view human societies have of male and female sexuality, but it seems likely that it has had some effect. In almost all societies, the male is allowed more freedom in courtship, and his wishes are consulted far more in arranging marriages. Women have far more often been treated as sexual chattels, and have been subjected to various operations such as clitoridectomy and infibulation (removing the clitoris or sewing up the vagina) as a symbolic denial of the importance of their sexuality. On the other hand, such operations also reveal a widespread fear that the sexuality of women is somehow dangerous and must be controlled. This fear is partly based on a reality, which a few societies have guessed: The multi-orgasmic capacity of women. It is not at all clear why this difference evolved, since it is not necessary for conception, and perhaps no societies have utilized it as a basis for family structures.

One further male-female sex difference has, however, been utilized by many societies: Men can continue to impregnate women almost until the end of life, while women's fertility drops sharply after menopause. As a consequence, older men in many societies have continued to acquire new wives and to sire additional offspring, if their economic and political rank permitted them that luxury.

A final male-female difference is the differential mortality of the two sexes. From the womb to the end of life, men are more vulnerable biologically, except in societies where the birth rate is very high and childbirth itself is dangerous for women. Again, it is not clear that societies have utilized this difference for allocating family roles or for structuring family systems. To be sure, men engage in physically more risky activities, as do young boys, in part because their very aggressiveness tempts them into such situations. Even in modern societies, they are more likely to risk their lives in dangerous automobile driving as well as in industrial jobs where they are exposed to accidents and noxious fumes. Although both sexes live longer now because of modern infant care and more effective medical procedures for all ages, women have increased their life expectancy more than men have. Males suffer more than females from a large number of biological defects, including a lesser resistance to disease. This range of differences probably arises from one set of chromosomes, the XY pair in males, which is genetically deficient compared with the XX pair in females.

One small consequence of this sex difference in mortality is that although males outnumber females slightly at birth (the sex ratio is about 103:100), the two sexes are closer to equality at the time of marriage. On the other hand, this difference has apparently not shaped any important family patterns. In most of the world's populations, female infanticide has been accepted far more than male infanticide. Older men with rank and power have married women far younger than they. And since women past the age of childbirth were likely to be given a low value, their greater ability to survive was not seen as a biological trait that needed to be utilized by family systems.

In the first edition of this book, we expressed scepticism of the widely held belief that "girls mature faster than boys" and are thus ready for marriage at an earlier age. So far, the evidence confirms that skepticism: young boys produce their first viable sperm as early as girls produce their first viable eggs. On the other hand, the social definitions of maturity in the two sexes refer to very different spheres. In most societies, as soon as (and sometimes before) the first secondary characteristics (breast and pubic hair, widening of hips) appear, girls have been viewed as sexually desirable, and at least potentially available for marriage. Their primary sphere was to be the wide range of feminine roles, which they had been practicing from their earliest years. By contrast, boys at the same age were still "unformed" for the most part, since they had much more learning to accomplish before they could be treated as male adults, and therefore able to discharge adult responsibilities. Clearly this difference is determined not by any "early" biological maturation of females, since girls were harmed by early pregnancy and boys were not. It is determined by social definitions of what is expected of the two sexes at the same or different ages.

BIOSOCIAL FACTORS

Sociobiologists consider certain factors as obviously biological, although they have not succeeded in locating the neurological or hormonal pathways that determine the execution of these patterns. Several of them may well arise from social interaction. They are also to be found among most of the higher mammals, which are of course social animals as well. In any event, they are observable in human families, and they are these:

1. Territoriality and spacing.
2. K-strategy of reproduction.
3. Hierarchy.
4. Jealousy.

Territoriality.   Much research over the past two decades has disclosed that almost all family groups of animals occupy a definite space, large enough for an adequate food supply. For large predators, of course, the geographical space is large. Where food is especially abundant, animals occupy a smaller space. Those who occupy a given territory usually defend it successfully against invaders of the same species, and indeed they must do so if they are to survive. Invasion and defense usually consist more in threatening behavior than combat, but when invaders seriously attempt to intrude, the defenders become savage fighters. Here, biological needs are linked closely with the needs of the family unit. Each species requires a varying amount of space, and each family grouping learns the location of different foods in a given area as they mature or become more available over a period of time. They would be handicapped if they were displaced. Usually, the adult male or males engage in defense of the territory.

As ecologists have pointed out, this need for territory and its defense results in the spacing of animals in a way that benefits the survival of the species over long periods of time, though simultaneously it may push less aggressive animals into environments where they may not be able to survive at all. As family groupings or as societies, human beings exhibit this same defense of territory and the resulting dispersion of population over wider areas. Among the anthropoid apes, gibbons are most aggressive in their defense of territory. Gorilla groupings may mingle casually for a day or so, with only a few gestures of latent attack between the great silver-backed adult males. On the other hand, modern studies of housing conditions suggest that human beings can adjust to extremely small living areas.

The K-strategy. Human beings, like most large animals, have followed the K-strategy of reproduction. That is, instead of producing a large number of offspring, (the clam, the salmon) who are then left to fend for themselves, the larger animals produce a much smaller number of offspring, and then give far more care to them. Human beings do not bear litters of infants, but usually only one. Of course, family life would be very different if each pregnancy typically resulted in five or six infants.

Hierarchy. Both within the family unit and within small or large societies, the social interaction of human beings creates a pattern of hierarchy. This pattern is common to other social animals. In some it takes the form of a "pecking order": animal A dominates animal B, who dominates animal C, and so on. Among most mammals, this dominant animal is an adult male. Changes in the hierarchy occur from time to time, as a result of old age or a crucial fight. Some females are more dominant than some males. Dominant females are more likely to rear male offspring who become dominant in turn. And, of course, an adolescent subordinate male may eventually become dominant.

Although some part of this hierarchy results from the greater fighting capacity and aggressiveness of particular animals, it is also the result of learning and social interaction. In its crudest form, one animal learns that if he stands his ground or will not yield a bit of fruit or meat, he will be slashed or pummeled by another. One result is more order, if less justice. If the dominant silver-backed male gorilla starts to leave the others follow, since the group follows only the dominant animal. If juveniles make a great disturbance, a dominant animal may cuff one or both, again often without much justice in the action.

Needless to say, the ability to win in a physical battle is not the same as the culturally approved authority patterns of the human animal, although the biological factors should never be ignored. Social order in the family is partly the result of the fact that parents can typically win in a fight with their children, but in all societies parents are supported by other adults, even if the individual parents are themselves not very effective at physical battles. Children are taught to pay respect to parents, as females are taught to defer to males and wives to husbands, whatever the specific fighting capacity of each. Nevertheless, it seems reasonable to suppose that even if there were no such cultural pattern, some form of hierarchy would arise just the same, and in most cases the dominant animal would be the male parent. As against this harsh view, it must be emphasized that the widely varying value patterns in human societies do *not* permit the male to use all possible force to subdue others in the family. He enjoys the authority derived from cultural norms and social pressures, but he is also restricted in his use of coercion to control others in the family.

Jealousy. Whether jealousy is biological in origin is as unclear now as it was decades ago. Family systems vary widely in the place given to jealousy. In many peasant societies in different parts of the world, it was and still is taken for granted that justified jealousy excuses murder. That is, if a young male besmirched the honour of a young girl, the adults in her family had the right to kill him; an erring wife might well be killed along with her lover; and adultery was perhaps the most widely accepted justification for divorce in many societies.

On the other hand, in many societies and in many subgroups within larger societies, jealousy is viewed with amusement and some condescension, where it is not simply condemned as immature behavior. Modern marital counselors often try to teach clients that they need not be so psychologically dependent on their spouses, and should not exhibit the extreme possessiveness of jealousy: after all, the spouse is not their "property." In societies where one woman is married to two or more men, female jealousy is less common.

Jealousy varies in time and place. It is a complex set of cultural reactions partly based on the notion that one's mate is at least symbolically one's possession. But it also grows from deeper psychobiological roots. The behavior that induces jealousy is, after all, genuinely threatening: One *is* more likely to lose one's mate if he or she engages in very intimate behavior with another person. It is unclear whether the feelings of jealousy arise from the childhood experience of losing intimacy with one's mother, or from the common life experience of losing intimacy with a mate or friend because another person takes one's place. We cannot draw analogies from our anthropoid cousins, for they differ among themselves: the gorilla exhibits very little jealousy, but both male and female gibbons are savagely jealous.

Its importance for family systems is that each society defines which degrees of intimacy permit or justify a given type of jealousy reaction, and both norms and social pressures enforce to some degree the range of that response. The jealousy reaction warns the spouse (or sweetheart, in the courtship phase) that his or her behavior is unacceptable, and thus puts pressure on the wayward mate to conform or risk reprisals of some kind. In puritanical cultures, the spouse who goes too far may also risk losing public esteem. And, since these definitions of impropriety are much narrower for women than for men, in many societies women have been cast out from respectable society if their behavior went too far. Thus, even if the underlying emotional response has strong psychobiological roots, how it is expressed is shaped substantially by the cultural norms and social pressures of each family system.

SOME CONCLUSIONS

We noted earlier the difficulty of creating a research design that would clarify just how much of family behavior is controlled by biological factors. That amount appears much greater if we focus on gross behavior—a family of chimps at play does seem much like a family of human beings at play. It is also great if we examine the physical structure of the higher animals: all clearly share a common pattern. On the other hand, the human solutions for a wide range of family problems have been cultural and social, not biological. Even when the solution is the same for almost all societies, it still may be cultural and social. Our parents first, and then other human beings, tell us what to do and how to do it; our biological impulses do not give us much specific direction. For example, our sexual impulses, even when strong, do not tell us whom we should marry, and they do not tell us what constitutes an acceptable wedding ceremony. Moreover, if we wish to understand the *differences* between patrilineal and matrilineal family systems, or among responses to illegitimacy, our biological knowledge cannot enlighten us much. Doubtless succeeding decades will yield a better grasp of how biological factors help to shape some family patterns, but our advances in sociological knowledge will also enlighten us about the dynamics and structure of family patterns.

CHAPTER 3
THE PROCESSES
OF ILLEGITIMACY

The moralistic focus of nineteenth-century family analysis is evident in its preoccupation with the oddities of sexual behavior in human societies, whether ancient, tribal, or contemporary. They were fascinated by incest, illegitimacy, "wife capture," child marriage, adultery, and various forms of sexual mutilation. All that now seems outmoded in an era when people are urged to explore their own sexuality, middle-class high school youngsters take for granted their right to engage in sex, couples live together openly without marriage, and some nations proclaim that all children, whether born in or out of wedlock, have the same rights. But though the sexual attitudes of Western societies have become more permissive over the past century, no new social agency has taken over all the tasks families perform. Until that happens, societies will be concerned with what is to be called a family, who is allowed to form one, and what kinds of behavior will be condemned as violations of family rules.

Sexual permissiveness does not alter the crucial role of the family in determining whether the society itself will continue. The human infant cannot survive unless adults have already been socialized by their parents to care for it. Usually these will be its parents. This is the key three-generational link between the biological survival of the individual organism and the social system of the family; between the biological survival of the human species and the transmission of culture from one generation to the next. The culture will not continue unless it can cope with the problems of biological survival. The child is taught not only to want to rear children when it grows up, but also to rear children to feel strongly that they in turn want to take care of *their* children. The *biological* chain is secured through the *cultural* transmission of patterns needed for survival.

How is this link established? Social control over child care and thus over the social unit responsible for it became more important when the human animal in its evolution came to depend increasingly upon the *culture* and not on its biological heritage. That is, the human community and its culture came to depend on the effectiveness of socialization—how well the child acquires the values, attitudes, and behaviors of community and family. Because of this dependence, the community must try to shape or guide the unit that passes on social values to the next generation.

When that evolutionary shift occurred, we shall never know; very likely, it was hundreds of thousands of years ago. It was a shift from little or no group concern about who mated with whom, or the effectiveness of child care, to *systems* of marriages arranged by parents or the larger community. It seems clear, however, that increasing dependence on culture rather than the biological heritage, and thus dependence upon socialization, required a human community to control more fully the choice of mate as well as the subsequent family behavior of the couple.

One form this control took was the disapproval of casual sexual unions that created a child without a family unit responsible for it. Those who formed such a unit would have to be mature enough to support themselves and their children. If very young, they would have to form part of a larger family unit such as an extended household, which would contain enough adults to care for the next generation of children until the couple became competent to do so. In some past epoch, long before any written history, the increased dependence on culture pressed human beings to establish *rules of legitimacy*—regulations that define who has the right to procreate and rear a fully accepted member of the society. Those rules determine the social placement of the child. Until that decision was made, no particular persons could be made responsible for its physical care or socialization. Consequently, legitimacy (and therefore illegitimacy) is a basic characteristic of the human family shared by no other family grouping. It is a central concept for understanding family behavior.

Legitimacy Rules and Role Obligations

The rules of legitimacy determine the social placement of the child, and thus partly define which adults have which obligations to the child. The infant also requires important role relations *among* adults. It indicates an intimacy between parents, and its existence makes continuing demands on other adults. Adults in turn—that is, parents and other kin—make demands on one another because of the child. If the child has no acknowledged father, or a "socially wrong" father, these obligations may be ambiguous or unmet, or they may run counter to already established duties. For example, the already married father of an illegitimate child cannot easily take care of it without failing to some extent in his obligations to his own family. Children whose parents are not married do not belong to the father's family, and the families of the father's parents do not have to meet any legal obligations to the child. The child's position is likely to be ambiguous, and its socialization inadequate.

In short, it is the consequences for *adults,* for the society, more than for the child, that the rules against illegitimacy are supposed to prevent. For these reasons, societies disapprove of illegitimacy more than of premarital sexual intercourse, even when the latter is also considered improper. Every society controls to some extent who may mate with whom, and has some rules against bearing children casually or as the accidental result of a sexual encounter. Phrased differently, societies exert control over courtship *not* primarily because of the possibility of sexual activity, but because children may result. This is true even when a substantial segment of the adult population is living together without marriage. A focus on illegitimacy, then, does not betray a moralistic bias on the part of the social analyst; rather, it is required because of its importance for family structure.

Although we have used the terms "rules" and "obligations," we are most successful in teaching children to want to become parents not by underlining the *burdens* they must assume some day, but by emphasizing the pleasures and benefits of parenthood. In almost all societies, parents view their children as a desired link in the succession of generations, and thus as part of their continuing identity after they are dead. In many religions, sons (and daughters to a lesser extent) play an important role in the ceremonies after the death of a parent, especially a father. Children are expected to become part of the social insurance on which parents rely in their old age. It is to be noted that these and other benefits are typically obtained only if the child forms an official part of a publicly recognized family line.

This pattern was emphasized more than a generation ago by Bronislaw Malinowski, who enunciated a Principle of Legitimacy, according to which "no child should be brought into the world without a man—and one man at that—assuming the role of sociological father. . . . " That is, every society presumably has a rule stating that each child should have a sociological father. It should also follow that when there are violations of the rule, various people will suffer from it—the child, the father, the mother, or all three. The focus of the rule may be seen more clearly in the fact that about 60 percent of the societies for which data are available permit premarital sexual relations, but even these sexually more permissive societies do not approve of childbirth outside the marital relationship. Marriage, then, bestows legitimacy on the *parents.* Consequently, Malinowski's Principle should properly be extended to *motherhood* as well.

Of course, the social responsibility of the mother is less often in question, since the child is more obviously tied to her from the beginning of its life than to the father. That link is also emphasized by social pressures. That is, refusal to take that responsibility would be viewed as more "unnatural," a more serious violation of role obligations, than a similar refusal by the father. The mother is less likely to abandon the child. On the other hand, if she does disappear, or refuses maternal obligations, once more the child has an even more ambiguous social position. Note, too, that Malinowski's Principle focuses on social placement, on the location of the child in the kinship structure, and not on whether the child is fed or nursed. If the child is given a position in a social structure, it will very likely be cared for; but merely caring for it will not necessarily give it a social position.

Whether or not we extend the basic legitimacy rule to include motherhood, it must be amended in a more important way. As soon as we try to specify just what we can mean by "sociological father," it is clear that this is a matter of *degree,* or more or less. There are, as we shall see, many specific rules defining illegitimacy. According to some of them, a biological father may be only a short step away from being a sociological father (he is about to marry the mother), or instead an impossibly great distance away (the mother is also his daughter). These various rules attempt to specify *descent,* the location of the child in the kinship network. Where descent is less important socially, people will also be less concerned with illegitimacy. We could then expect that illegitimacy will arouse less social concern in the lower social strata. Where the main descent is through the father's line, the absence of the father is likely to be critical, for then the child cannot be properly placed in the family system. By contrast, in a matrilineal system, in which descent is traced through the mother, there is likely to be somewhat less concern about the exact identity of the biological father as long as the mother is married.

Thus, the rules of marriage (who is permitted to marry whom) determine the social placement of the child, ensure its socialization, and define both illegitimacy and legitimacy. The society usually views the illegitimate child as a burden. It is expected to yield little benefit to the mother's or father's kin, since its obligations to them are not firm or definite. Mother and child will receive no gifts from the father's kinship line, since there has been no marriage. In addition, in some societies the child represents a violation of the elders' power to decide on the marriage itself, and in some it is proof that the mother engaged in forbidden sexual behavior. That is, the prohibition is based on specific rules and consequences.

Because of all these rules and consequences, Kingsley Davis comments that one reason for illegitimacy is marriage.[1] If there were no rules, of course they would not be violated. The historian Crane Brinton offers a more fanciful judgment;

> Bastardy and marriage in this world are quite supplementary. You cannot have one without the other. In another world, you may indeed separate the two institutions and eliminate one of them either by having marriage so perfect—in various senses—that no one will ever commit fornication or adultery, or by having fornication so perfect that no one will ever commit marriage.[2]

1. Kingsley Davis, "The Forms of Illegitimacy," *Social Forces* 18 (1939), 77-89.

2. Crane Brinton, *French Revolutionary Legislation on Illegitimacy 1789-1804* (Cambridge, Mass.: Harvard University Press, 1936), pp. 82-83.

LEGAL AND SOCIAL ILLEGITIMACY

The Five Rules of Childbirth

Davis has outlined the major *structural* forms of legitimacy—that is, the five rules of childbirth, which if violated make the child illegitimate. The first rule is that the child should be born after a marriage. The union may be the result of a casual sexual relationship or the result of an engaged couple. The second rule forbids adulterous procreation. In such a case of illegitimacy, the man may be married, or the woman, or both, thus creating three subtypes of adulterous illegitimacy. Third, rules against incest may not be violated: an illegitimate child may be born from the union of mother-son, father-daughter, or brother-sister. A fourth broad rule forbids childbirth to a man and woman of different castes. Finally, a rule of much narrower application prohibits childbirth to those who are required to be celibate, such as priests.

Not all these forms of illegitimacy are possible in every society. For example, most societies have no celibate statuses whose members are simply forbidden to marry. In most African societies of the past, before industrialization and urbanization undermined tribal rules, the second and third types of adulterous illegitimacy would hardly be possible; that is, the cases in which the woman is married. In those societies the rules of kinship were organized to guarantee legitimacy to the child born of a marriage. (In English and American law, too, it has typically been very difficult to prove illegitimacy if the woman was married). In Africa, children were highly coveted, and inquiry into their biological paternity was unlikely. The mother might be punished for her adultery, but the social position of the child within its kinship network was usually clear. For example, in a *matrilineage* (a descent grouping that reckoned ancestry from a known person, through the female line, and acting at times as a collectivity), the child would of course have belonged to his mother's lineage.

Davis's fourth type of illegitimacy rule, the prohibition against cross-caste unions, applies to a number of societies in which people have been defined as born into a specific social rank and obligated to remain there until death. The black-white division in the United States is one such type of caste system, although the lines have become more blurred in recent years. The laws forbidding such cross-caste unions have now been struck down as unconstitutional. In India, thousands of subcastes still exist, and their interrelations are defined by myriad rules aimed essentially at preserving ritual purity. The rules define whose touch is polluting, who may marry whom, and so on. These regulations specify, for example, who may hand what kinds of food to whom (because a Brahmin is at the peak of caste, he can usually be hired as a cook, since anyone may eat any kind of food from his hands.) A few sections of subcastes permit intermarriage with certain others whom they deem acceptable (for example, two subgroups of Brahmins). This relationship is not egalitarian, since women are defined as marrying "up" the small caste distance to the higher subsection or subcaste. Most crossing of caste lines is still forbidden socially, though it is now permissible by law.

Caste-crossing in marriage or outside it is thus feared as highly improper. But of course that disapproval is only a more extreme version of the disapproval an upper class family in a rigidly stratified society feels when one of its members marries "downward." Such a case would not, within the definitions of this chapter, be viewed as an instance of illegitimacy unless the marriage were forbidden by law, by a monarch, or by very strong social norms. At present those who marry cross-caste in contemporary India may come to be *outcaste,* but most simply find other social groups in cities who are not so traditional in their attitudes.

Changes over Time

If we continue to think of illegitimacy as a matter of degree, and wish to look at a wide range of types, we must also consider how changes in attitudes toward illegitimacy alter over long periods of history. As contrasted with modern permissiveness in some social circles, respectable middle-class Victorians in England viewed as improper almost anything having to do with sexual activity. Illegitimacy in these circles was both rare and scandalous. Daughters of such families lost all their chances for a proper marriage (along with their very position in society) if they had a child outside wedlock. At the present time, by contrast, all those unfortunate consequences are much less likely to occur. But it is not true that as we go back in history we can expect lower and lower illegitimacy rates, and stronger attitudes against illegitimacy. Both can rise or fall over time. Illegitimacy becomes more common, for example, during periods of social disorganization, such as during a long, drawn-out revolution, famine, epidemic, or war. The normal social controls of the society and the family are likely to weaken, and to focus on other types of violations and problems. People care more about personal survival, and less about the fate of their family line. The social meaning of illegitimacy becomes somewhat blurred. Leaders become less concerned about rising illegitimacy rates.

Let us consider another type of historical case. In a society with clear lines of demarcation between classes and with strong barriers against social mobility, as in seventeenth-century France, a nobleman might have children by his mistress. He could not simply make them legitimate, but he could recognize them socially, and give them some place in the social structure. Only rarely were such fathers able or even willing to obtain noble rank for their illegitimate offspring. But these children did not necessarily take a lowly position in the society; sometimes their fathers protected and helped them. Thus, if we think of a wide range of illegitimacy types, this kind of case clearly creates less social disruption and arouses less disapproval than many others.

A Rank-Ordering of Types

These examples suggest that although illegitimacy can be defined with *legal* precision, in fact the various types make up a wide range of *socially* very different patterns, under different intensities of social disapproval, and with very different consequences for the social structure and for the individuals themselves. Here we present a range of these types. As Table 3.1 shows, the rank order follows roughly the degree of apparent disruption in the social structure caused by the illegitimacy. This tentative ranking must be tested by empirical research. Particularly, we need to know *who* or *which* classes disapprove less or more of each type of illegitimacy, and the social conditions under which different forms are more or less approved.

The list forms a basis for several steps in the analysis of illegitimacy. First, a birth can be *legally* classed as definitely legitimate or not, but *socially* there may be many gradations or degrees between full acceptance and strong disapproval. Second, whatever disapproval a child and mother may bear, and whatever ambiguity there may be in the social placement of the child, both have to be placed *somewhere* in the society, under varying degrees of disapproval or disadvantage. Societies vary both in their degree of disapproval and in the extent to which the stigma of illegitimacy pursues individuals throughout their lives. In a modern industrial society, very few people will ever have a stake in continuing to label anyone as "illegitimate" as the years pass on. By contrast, in societies based on land ownership, and in which almost everyone's place is well known to others in the locality, it was more likely that a person's illegitimate origin would be part of his or her identity. Indeed, in Western history until the modern period, several notable figures carried the nickname "The Bastard" throughout their lives.

We have already noted the tentative hypothesis that the amount of disapproval seems to be correlated roughly with the amount of social or kinship disruption created by the illegitimacy. We should also note a further implication of this general rule: disapproval will vary, depending on who the offending parties are, and who does the judging. This may mean more simply whose social position or interests are disrupted by the illegitimacy. Note, for example, that the upper social strata generally do not disapprove much of the illegitimacy occurring among the lower classes; to them, that is no more than an expected characteristic trait of the lower classes, generally deplorable but not specifically offensive. On the other hand, the upper social strata have always disapproved intensely if one of

Table 3.1   Types of Illegitimacy, in Rank Order of Increasing Disapproval

1. Consensual union
2. Concubinage where it is institutionalized (traditional China and Japan)
3. Lower-class illegitimacy
4. Liaison of nobleman with mistress in preindustrial Western society
5. Childbirth during betrothal
6. Casual relationship, followed by marriage
7. Adulterous, only the man being married
8. Union of a person in a celibate status, with another celibate or a noncelibate
9. Adulterous, only the woman being married
10. Adulterous, both parties being married
11. Union of upper-caste woman with lower-caste man
12. Incestuous, brother-sister
13. Incestuous, father-daughter
14. Incestuous, mother-son

the offending parties is an upper-class woman. After all, in that case, there may be a threat to their property interests. If her liaison is with a lower-class man, then the offense and the disruption are even greater, for in addition to the property threat, there is an insult to rank. By contrast, in this last instance, no doubt lower-class men would feel little moral disapproval of *him* (but some envy), and considerable disapproval of *her*.

Incestuous Illegitimacy.   The most intense social disapproval is directed against incestuous illegitimacy. It violates the incest taboos, which are found in every society. These are complex, and vary from one society to another. However, aside from special statuses (such as the Inca rulers in pre-Hispanic Peru, or Egyptian royalty,[3] sexual relations are forbidden among members of the nuclear family, except for husband and wife; that is, sexual relations between father-daughter, brother-sister, and mother-son are forbidden. Some additional types of unions between kin (cousins, nephews, nieces) are also forbidden in some societies; the prohibition is most likely to extend to *closer* rather than distant kin, and the *social* definition of close kinship (along line of descent) is more important than biological closeness.

The incest rules within the nuclear family have several consequences. Since individuals must not find spouses or lovers within the family, even if it is a large one, they must leave the nuclear family each generation in order to find mates elsewhere. The society is thus made more cohesive, for many kin links are forged between families that otherwise might turn inward on themselves, or found a community of their own. The innovations as well as the quirks of a given family are ironed out or distributed more widely within the larger society. Sexual competition is not, of course, eliminated from the nuclear family. Both in India and in Western countries, the seductiveness of mothers toward their sons is described in literature, just as it can be noted in real life. Some fathers still become upset when they must face the fact that a young man is going to carry off their daughter. Nevertheless, such sexual competition is frowned upon, and is not allowed physical expression in actual sexual intercourse and thus possibly illegitimacy. Otherwise, such competitive relations, such as daughters and mothers competing with one another for the sexual favors of the father, would reduce the effectiveness of the exchange of sons and daughters for purposes of marriage among people in the same class. It would also split open the conjugal family itself, or reduce its effectiveness as a production and socialization agency.

As many analysts have pointed out, the child of an incestuous union creates several special problems. First, the problem of its placement cannot be "solved" by a marriage between the two partners, since that marriage is illegal and in almost all societies is scandalous. Second, its status is confused, and thereby the status of its parents. If the child is born to a union between daughter and father (the most common type of actual incest), then its mother is also its sister (half-sister). Its father is married to its grandmother,

---

3.   At least some Roman census data reveal that this was not confined to Egyptian royalty. It appears that brother-sister incestuous marriages were not uncommon in Roman Egypt.

and its father is simultaneously its grandfather. Its brother (half-brother) is also its uncle (the brother of its mother). Other status discrepancies arise if the child is the offspring of a brother-sister union, or a mother-son union. We can have some verbal amusement with these double statuses, but it should be kept in mind that each status is defined by a set of obligations and rights, and these are blurred or violated by the incestuous relationship.

Class and Illegitimacy.   Since the placement of the child is of central importance in understanding illegitimacy, it follows that lower-caste or lower-class illegitimacy is of less concern to the society's leaders than illegitimacy in other social strata. The lower social strata are less focused on lineage and family honor than are other social strata, while higher social strata consider the family honor of the lower classes of almost no concern. "Respectable" people in most large societies think of the lower classes as physically dirty and morally promiscuous (and sometimes the lower classes return that compliment). For the most part, the ruling strata in all societies have limited their concern to the simple question of the *cost* of caring for the illegitimate children of the lower classes. That concern was expressed as charity in seventeenth-century England, and as social welfare in twentieth-century United States.

In the lower social strata there is usually no property to inherit, and thus none to protect by making certain that the proper families are united. Since people are already at a relatively low rank, the families of the young man and woman lose less rank if an illegitimate child is born. Since, typically, illegitimacy is a relatively common event which has touched many lives in most neighborhoods, it is not viewed as quite so improper as in the upper social strata. Moreover, lower-strata families control their young less strictly than do those of the upper strata. One consequence of all these factors is that the illegitimacy rate is higher among the lower social strata. Let us consider this matter for a moment. Although of course the class position of parents is not recorded on a child's birth certificate, indirect evidence in all countries supports this general conclusion, that there is an *inverse* correlation between class and illegitimacy rate. In the poor areas of American cities, for example, the average proportion of illegitimate births to mothers in those areas has been about three times higher than in the higher-income areas. Similarly, the illegitimacy rate among blacks is higher than that among whites. Among both blacks and whites, the rates are higher among the lower social strata.

It should be emphasized that we are not talking about poverty itself, but the social characteristics that are generally correlated with lower social rank: lesser social controls over young unmarried adults, somewhat lesser concerns about family honor and rank, less wealth whose inheritance might be complicated by illegitimacy, and so on. Consequently, we *cannot* expect that poor countries will have higher illegitimacy rates. We are not comparing *countries*, but *classes* within the same country. Thus, both Greece and India will have a much lower illegitimacy rate than most Western countries, though they are much poorer than Sweden, the United States, or Germany. But *within* each country, the lower social ranks will show higher illegitimacy rates.

Because an illegitimate birth is more scandalous in the upper or middle social strata, more effort is expended to hide a pregnancy when it occurs, and to prevent a subsequent birth. Middle-class girls in the United States are better able to avoid an illegitimate birth altogether by paying for an abortion. In the past as in the present, girls of this social rank are more likely (if they decide to bear the child) to travel far away from their homes, and to turn the child over to an adoption agency. In any event, with adequate foresight and money, none of the girl's friends need know that she was even pregnant. For all these reasons, not only is the illegitimacy rate higher among the lower social strata, but the illegitimate birth is more likely to be visible. Because of typical class disadvantages, these illegitimate children are likely to experience a somewhat higher disease and death rate, to receive less adequate education (just as their mothers did), and to obtain less satisfactory jobs. They are also more likely themselves to produce illegitimate children when they in turn become young adults.

SANCTIONS AND CONTROLS

The Disadvantages of Illegitimate Birth

The disadvantages suffered by the illegitimate child are a combination of the legal rules about illegitimacy, the probable class position of the child, the lack of adequate parental care, and the social disapproval that creates obstacles to job opportunities. In the United States, as in many Western countries, laws over many centuries were aimed simply at preventing the child from becoming a charge of the state, and placed the primary obligation on the mother. Only in this century has legislation been directed at seeking to find out who the father is, and at forcing the father to accept some financial responsibility for the child.

New laws have removed the fact of illegitimacy from the birth record in many states, though not yet in a majority. In recent years, the child has acquired the right to inherit from his or her mother (and in many states to inherit from the father as well). In many ways, modern social legislation now attempts to protect both mother and child. At the same time, it is an illusion to suppose that by some combination of liberal social welfare laws, the child will somehow be given a position exactly equal to that of the legitimate child. The laws that aim at protecting the illegitimate child must by legal definition treat that child differently, just to meet his or her peculiar needs. Special laws for a given status simply emphasize the fact that the social position is different.

How much disadvantage the child suffers because of illegitimacy will, of course, vary with the type of illegitimacy, being greater for the more disapproved types. To weigh the disadvantages, we must compare the child's position to that of a legitimate child of the same social class. The lower-class child born of a consensual union in Jamaica, for example, will suffer very few disadvantages compared with his or her playmates. Most of them either are or were illegitimate, and their lot is only somewhat worse than that of youngsters born of equally poor but married parents. By contrast, an illegitimate child born to a middle-class couple in the United

States suffers far more disadvantage if we compare its position to that of a legitimate child of a similar couple. It is likely to lose the benefits of that class position. Of course, in a cross-caste or cross-class union, the problem is more difficult: With whom should the comparison be made? The child is usually the responsibility of the mother, who is likely to be lower class; thus the child will likely be a member of the lower social strata. In the United States, the child of a union between black and white will be treated as a black socially. He or she may suffer fewer disadvantages compared to other blacks of the same economic position, but his or her position will be less favorable than that of the white parent.

Historically, there are many instances in which the illegitimate child of a cross-class or cross-caste union received support and protection from the upper-class father, and thus the position of both mother and child was better than that of others in a lower social stratum. Of course, again, they did not have the still greater advantages that a legitimate union would have given them. For the parents there were also dangers: In the American Old South, death was the social penalty for the black male involved in a cross-caste sexual union, if his identity was discovered. In India the same result was likely, along with the deaths of the mother and child. If not put to death, mother and child would be outcastes.

Social and Internal Controls

As in other areas of possible deviant behavior, most people are not kept from illegitimacy only by fear of its consequences. Internal controls make individuals feel it is morally wrong to run the risk. In addition, social controls warn the person long before any intimacy occurs. Friends and kin caution the woman, and sometimes the young man as well. Even in societies where the cautions are not directed against sexual activity itself, they take the form of warning young people that they must use contraceptives. In most parts of the world, a young woman is still surrounded by a network of people who set the conditions for her interaction with a young man. They can bear witness if the couple was seen together, and they may later pressure the young man to marry the girl if she becomes pregnant. A couple may be alone on a date, but they are not alone before and after the date, so the situation is not anonymous. Finally, friends and kin, along with various officials, may also put pressure on the young woman to have an abortion.

The laws on abortion have not all moved toward permissiveness over the past decade; the leaders of some nations have tried to make abortion more difficult because they feared it would slow down the population growth rate of the country, and thus reduce its political importance as a world power. Nevertheless, on balance, the past decade has seen a more widespread use of abortion than ever in the past. There has been a greater demand for it; as a medical procedure its safety has been greatly improved; and in many societies an increasing percentage of the population believes this is a personal, legal right of women. That is, women should not be required to bear a child simply because they have become pregnant.

Class Differences.   In the past, the Western upper and middle classes used a *dueña* or chaperone system to prevent all males (except perhaps close kin or respected old men) from ever being alone with an unmarried nubile girl. Although Chinese, Japanese, and Indian society have always given adult women less freedom than in Western countries, in all these areas married women were given somewhat greater freedom than unmarried but marriageable girls. This difference arises in part because the focus of attention in most societies is on premarital illegitimacy rather than adultery. In addition, of course, common sense has always supposed that young, unmarried women were more likely to inflame the passions of others, and more likely themselves to respond intensely, while married women in the privileged classes were unlikely to have much opportunity of being alone with any adult male. In Western nations until perhaps the late nineteenth century, many young women expressed the view that they wanted to get married simply to obtain more freedom, for the married woman had responsibilities of her own, was socially defined as an adult, and could move about more freely. In any event, in almost all marriage systems it has been assumed that any child of a married woman was legitimate, unless reasonable proof to the contrary was possible.

The lower classes could not, of course, afford the cost of a special person to guard unmarried women, who after all were working in the fields or as domestics. But though lower-class women have generally enjoyed more freedom than upper-class women, in most countries they were likely to be jealously watched just the same. In some of the less urbanized regions of the West, such as rural Greece, Sicily, southern Italy, and rural Spain, this jealous guardianship still persists. The Puritans in seventeenth-century New England emphasized strong moral repression, defining any sexual behavior as sinful. If we are to believe their personal accounts, they were troubled by temptations that arose in their hearts or heads, and by guilts about their moral lapses. To be sure, they were not so foolish as to suppose that a deep inner conviction would be enough to eliminate illegitimacy. They also watched their women carefully—and indeed in Puritan society almost everyone spied on everyone else.

Cultural Differences. In a majority of preliterate societies, premarital sexual intercourse was permitted. Nevertheless, this apparently high-risk situation did not lead to a high rate of illegitimacy. Instead, a combination of negative factors kept the rate low. First, menstruation typically occurred later than in Western societies. For example, in the United States the average is between 12 and 13 years, as against 14 to 16 years in tribal societies for which data are available. (Dietary and general health factors create these differences). Second, present evidence suggests that for a period varying from one to three years after menstruation, young girls are relatively infertile, so that in societies where early adolescents engaged in sexual relations, the risk of pregnancy was still not very high. Finally, marriage took place earlier, and of course was still earlier if the girl became pregnant. Consequently, the illegitimacy rate was likely to be low.

Both contraceptives and abortion are available in the United States, but pregnancy precedes about one fourth or more of all marriages. This fact suggests a fairly high rate of premarital sexual intercourse, some carelessness, and perhaps a partly conscious decision to risk pregnancy as a symbol of continuing emotional intimacy. We can suppose that at least a substantial (but unknown) percentage of those who become pregnant and go on to have the child are emotionally attached to one another to some degree. Faced with what seems to them a difficult problem, many either make a decision to marry, or move ahead the date of an intended marriage.

Because the disapproval of illegitimacy is much greater in the United States than in Denmark or Sweden, American couples who conceive and then marry are likely to marry very quickly after conception—not very many weeks after making sure that a pregnancy is under way. By contrast, in countries where the disapproval is much less, people do not show the same haste in getting married after they learn that the woman is pregnant; whether the marriage occurs before the birth or slightly afterward is not considered quite so serious a matter.

We have been considering social controls that reduce illegitimacy in various countries. We have especially noted class differences. Let us consider rural-urban differences as well. Lay opinion is inclined to believe that rural people are more moral than urban people. Since the world is becoming urbanized, it must be more immoral, and thus illegitimacy rates will rise.

Rural-Urban Differences. The evidence on the rural-urban differences is at best unclear. The supposed high level of "rural morality" may be only a widespread myth. In much of north and central Europe, and in rural regions of France, Holland, and even Scotland, a widespread pattern of courtship during the eighteenth century and (in many areas extending back through time for many centuries) included premarital sexual intercourse and in some areas a relatively high rate of illegitimacy (about 20 percent or more). That is, fairly serious courtship in rural regions was likely to be associated with sexual intercourse.

The participants were not young children, as in modern times, but late adolescents or young people in their early twenties (the average age at marriage was likely to be 25 to 28 years). The marriage "pools" were usually small farming areas, and casual outsiders were barred from this courtship pattern. After all, they belonged to different communities and in case of pregnancy could not be held to account afterward. Friends, kin, and parents observed the pairing-off process, and also took part in it by expressing their own opinions. Young men could not escape their responsibilities for pregnancy without leaving the region, and thus abandoning their sole means of livelihood, the family farm. Marriage often postdated the birth of a child, but the couple was eventually united legally. Both church and state denounced the pattern, but in some regions it continued until well into the nineteenth century. It permitted some sexual freedom among young people, but maintained close social control over marriage selection.

A similar pattern also existed in rural Japan until long after the Meiji Revolution in 1868. These practices have gradually disappeared, so that in such areas the formal rate of illegitimacy (the official percentage born out of wedlock) has decreased. It must be kept in mind, however, that social controls under the old system were strong, and almost every young mother did marry the father of her child eventually, and with the approval of both parents. Consequently, the social placement and care of the child were certain. There was a sociological father and soon after, or even before, the birth of the child, he became a legal one as well. Thus, under the old system, in Japan as well as in Western Europe, the rate of *social* illegitimacy was low.

A LOOK AT THE PRESENT AND THE FUTURE

In order to analyze illegitimacy in contemporary nations, we must understand an important technical definition: What is popularly known as an *illegitimacy rate*, but which is properly called an *illegitimacy ratio*. This refers simply to the percentage of all children who are born out of wedlock (the *ratio* between those born illegitimate and all newborn infants). True illegitimacy *rates* refer to the number of illegitimate children born to all women of a given age in one year. This is usually expressed as the number of illegitimate children born per 1000 women in the childbearing years 15 to 44.

These two rates normally rise and fall together, so that a high rate of the former means we can expect a high rate of the latter. However, this is not always so. It can be seen that if the legitimate birth rate itself is low, and thus the number of legitimate children born is small, a high percentage of all children may be born out of wedlock, even though the number of illegitimate children born to 1000 women in childbearing years is low. An extreme case illustrates this relationship. Since few girls 15 years of age in the United States are married and have children, they have only few legitimate children. If girls of this age have children at all, they are likely to be illegitimate. Consequently, their illegitimacy *ratio* is high (the number of illegitimate births over 1000 births). However, if we looked at the number of illegitimate children born per 1000 girls in this age group (the illegitimacy *rate*), we know that figure will be low: after all, girls at this age have very few children anyway.

Population experts prefer to use the latter figure (the number of illegitimate children per 1000 women in some age group) because it is not confused by changes in the legitimate birth rate. This distinction is of great importance in understanding the trends of illegitimacy among U.S. blacks as well as whites. If blacks have been increasingly integrated into American society, their *rates* should have been dropping (as the author predicted more than a decade ago). In fact, that drop did begin in the 1960s. However, the percentage of black infants born out of wedlock (the illegitimacy *ratio*) has continued to rise and was 49 percent in 1975.

Present Trends

We may summarize the most important trends in illegitimacy over the past generation in the United States:

1. The absolute *number* of illegitimate births has been rising since 1940, simply because the number of women in the childbearing ages has continued

to rise. This increase was marked in the 1970s, when the children born during the "baby boom" of the 1950s entered maturity.

2.   The percentage of all infants born illegitimate (the ratio) has increased during this period because the legitimate birth rate decreased.

3.   The percentage born illegitimate, and the real illegitimacy rate, *both* began to rise after 1940.

4.   However, the real illegitimacy rate among blacks began to drop in 1961, and that of whites in 1970, while the percentage born illegitimate continued to rise (49 percent in 1975 for blacks, 7 percent for whites).

5.   Sexual activity among women 15 to 19 years of age has risen substantially during the past generation, and the absolute number of women in that age group increased by 65 percent in the period 1960–1975, while the marriage rate did not increase by much; consequently, about half of *all* illegitimate children in the United States are now born to these teenage women.

Modern Political Concern about
Illegitimacy: The Welfare Burden

Most Western nations have exhibited a rise in illegitimacy rates in recent decades. This trend is the focus of much political tension in the modern welfare state because typically the disadvantaged urban ethnic groups have the higher rates (just as our theory predicts), and the "respectable dominant" groups complain about this welfare burden. Let us analyze that change.

Since World War II, with perhaps few exceptions, family systems worldwide have lost much control over individuals, and especially the young. At the same time, the values and norms themselves, the standards that social control efforts aim at satisfying, have become more permissive. This means concretely that far more people are engaging in sex outside of wedlock, at earlier ages, and at a higher frequency (number of times per year). This, of course, increases the risk of pregnancy. These changes also mean that the scandal of illegitimacy has become far less in most countries. To be sure, these rates are reduced by abortion, which is increasingly legalized in both Western and Eastern countries, and both Communist and non-Communist ones. (Among the Japanese, it was always viewed as a normal option.) People have also come to use contraceptives both in and out of marriage. However, women in the lower classes do not resort to either one so effectively as do middle-class women, and this difference is especially strong before marriage. In the United States, one result is that black women experience a higher rate of unwanted pregnancies than do whites. Both black and white lower-class teenage women are likely to feel they must run the risk of pregnancy if they are to engage in dating at all, or to increase the chance of eventual marriage.[4]

Thus, several contrary factors affect the current rates of illegitimacy in different parts of the world. On the one hand, both the technology and

4.   For a good study of this risk-taking process, see Kristin Luker, *Taking Chances— Abortion and the Decision Not to Contracept* (Berkeley: University of California Press, 1975).

the knowledge available for controlling unwanted births have become more widespread, especially in industrialized countries. On the other hand, far more people, especially among the young, are at risk, because more engage in sex outside marriage. Class differences remain important, in that the lower classes (of whatever ethic group) are less likely to use effectively the available means for avoiding childbirth, while middle- and upper-class parents control the courtship behavior of their children more than do lower-class parents. Doubtless the class differences will diminish over the decades ahead, and we suppose the worldwide trend toward lower birth rates will continue. Thus, some speculations about the future of illegitimacy are in order.

The Future: Legitimation of Illegitimacy?

Because illegitimacy continues to be important as one aspect of family theory, we must come to terms with a new social pattern in the modern era—that is, sexual permissiveness and illegitimacy in the socially respectable strata of Western industrial societies. If the line of theory we have presented here is correct, it should follow that under certain conditions the social disapproval of illegitimacy would be much reduced. What are those conditions? Here are some of them:

1.   The most fundamental change would be that an illegitimate child did not create any problems for the larger society or the kin network. Conceivably, this might occur if the kin line itself becomes less important, and therefore people would be less concerned about whom their children married.

2.   The problems created by an illegitimate child in the past would also be much reduced if the young woman had the ability to support herself, with possibly some small support from the state.

3.   In a highly bureaucratic government, where very few fathers could ever escape their responsibilities and everyone had a known location in the society, an illegitimate child would have a clearer position.

4.   If the absolute number of illegitimate children born were very low, then the burden of illegitimacy would also be much smaller.

5.   If the divorce rate were very high, there would be many other children who would be reared by a single parent.

6.   If, finally, a high percentage of mature young people lived together for extended periods of time, with or without marrying later, the normative significance of formal marriage itself would be much reduced.

It is much too soon to argue that some modern countries are moving steadily in this direction, although both Iceland and Sweden seem to exhibit such a trend, and the United States is not far behind them. We cannot know as yet whether these are really emerging patterns, or no more than a passing change. If all these social patterns were to become widespread in the future, illegitimacy would become much more a private matter between two persons, rather than a local community scandal. That decision can become a more private matter because the larger society would have reduced its disapproved consequences to a modest amount: the burden of the illegitimate child would not be great.

Although this state of affairs may seem unlikely, it should be kept in mind that the larger society has already given up its control over some types of unions. For example, legally and socially, cross-caste marriages in the United States were once a public matter, and forbidden because of the supposed consequences for the larger society. Now, such marriages are a private decision. At least legally this is true for cross-caste unions in India. The permission of parents, and often the elders of a clan or lineage, was once necessary for marriage in almost all societies; it was not simply a private decision of the marrying couple. In all societies, marriage has become increasingly a private decision, because the larger kin network as well as the larger society have come to believe that they no longer have a stake in that decision, and the consequences are no longer threatening. In Western countries, a sexual relationship between two unmarried people has moved in the direction of becoming a private activity, not subject as much as it once was to the punishment of neighbors, kin, and legal authorities. This trend has been stronger for living together than for having children outside marriage, but the trend is nevertheless observable. That is, many types of unions whose offspring would once have been "illegitimate" have come to be viewed as appropriately the decision of the two persons most concerned.

A set of trends as complex and widespread as these cannot be ascribed to a single cause or even a precise set of causes. We suppose that the primary factors are these: Parents cannot control their children as much as in the past, particularly because kin and parents no longer control their access to jobs and land as they once could. (Parents can control the higher education of their children, but they receive little social support from other members of their class if they use that threat.) Second, family lines themselves have come to be viewed as of far less importance than in the past. Third, as we pointed out earlier, the experience of the past century in Western countries and in some non-Western countries since World War II suggests that the greater freedom of courtship young people enjoy does not lead to as many catastrophic unions as parents would once have believed, since in fact most do occur between young people close to the same class level, within the same religious and ethnic groups, at about the same ages. Both contraceptives and abortion are increasingly available.

Should these informal, pervasive social controls weaken, and an illegitimate child result, respectable modern parents are not likely to witness what would almost certainly have occurred in the nineteenth century, the social ostracism of their daughter from their social network, and the abandonment of any plans for an acceptable marriage afterwards, because the norms and values of all industrial societies have moved toward greater permissiveness. Since less control has not lead to widespread family catastrophe, more people believe a wider range of actions should be left to individual decision. At the present writing, however, we do not believe there will be a strong, *continuing* trend toward viewing illegitimacy as no more than an unimportant, private decision. Rather, living together may become still more common as a phase of courtship, but having a child will remain an event in which the state, the grandparents, and the kin network believe they too have a stake.

CHAPTER 4
MATE SELECTION
AND MARRIAGE

Members of the family see one another as individuals, in unique relations with one another. However, in all societies they are also linked as a group with still larger networks of kin and friends, and thereby with the institutions of the whole society. Family systems are shaped, then, by the individuals in each family, and also by the pressures of other social structures. It is for this reason that the larger society is typically interested in the processes of individual mate selection.

The larger society is linked with this apparently individual choice in several ways. The two family networks of the marrying couple are thereby linked, and thus still more distant kin networks are also involved. In larger societies, both family lines have a high or a low rank in the stratification system and are likely to be interested in either maintaining or improving that rank. Indeed, one can usually take for granted that families consider themselves to be roughly equal economically or socially if they believe it is acceptable to join together in a marriage.

We can see the importance of these links more clearly if we consider them concretely. Within the families themselves, usually one gains and the other loses a member. For example, in most societies of the past, the woman moved to the location of her husband's family, a system that is called *patrilocal*. In some, the man moved to the location of her family, and that pattern is called *matrilocal*. When they both establish an independent household, the system is called *neolocal*. The latter pattern is becoming more widespread in the world. Location is important, because it determines to a large extent how frequently the members of the new couple will interact with one set of kin as against another. Marriage forges a new social link, and may add some resources to a given family, but it may also mean the loss of a productive worker. In some societies, the loss of a woman as a worker is compensated for by a "bride price" or by the man working for a period of time, called "groom service." Entrance of the new bride or groom into a family creates numerous new role obligations, and necessarily some adjustments and strains.

Consequently, a marriage sets in motion a host of consequences in which many kin are concerned, not just the husband and wife. In all societies, complex rules guide the process of mate selection and eventual marriage. Marriage itself is likely to be a public event, signaling its importance to outsiders as well as to the kin network. The ceremonial is a ritual of passage for the couple, for both pass into adult status, with its new rights and responsibilities. It also proclaims the society's approval of the union. People in the kinship network thereby accept new role obligations, and of course now have a new set of expectations. In Western nations the state has for centuries played a larger part in marriage law than in most nations of the East. But marriage is a public matter in all societies, since at least the local community has a stake in its consequences.

But though the ceremony of marriage is sometimes complex and the celebration lavish, it is only the culmination of many processes that are subtle as well as important. In this chapter we consider some of those processes, many of which are not always visible to the bride and groom themselves. They shape our behavior, however, even when we do not understand them fully. We focus here more on Western nations than on others, but we will not lose sight of the similarities among mate selection processes in different parts of the world, which at first glance seem very different from one another.

THE MARKET STRUCTURE OF MARRIAGE

Some analysts have divided mate choice systems into two great types. In one of these, *preferential marriage* is the rule; and in the other, a much wider range of partners is at least permitted. Possibly this may be called a *free marriage market*—although, as we shall see, in most societies it has been the elders who negotiated, not the bride and groom.

In the first of these, a given individual is supposed to marry within a very narrow range of partners. For example, a young man is supposed to marry his mother's brother's daughter (matrilateral cross-cousin marriage). In that case, of course, only rarely would there be much range of choice. The individual knows from childhood whom he or she is likely to marry. The primary decision about marriage is *when* it is to take place, rather than with whom. Of course, systems vary in how specific these preferences are, and in their definition of the preference itself (for example, the proper wife may be father's brother's daughter, or a second cousin specified by some other kinship calculation). On the other hand, common sense will tell us that sometimes there is no such person available. Societies take kinship lines seriously, but they are not so foolish as to leave their young people unmarried simply because the preferred spouse does not exist. Consequently, in all societies the rules are sometimes bent or ignored to make certain that a proper marriage takes place. Families with higher social standing or power are more likely to be successful in following the rules, but the important goal is to make wise alliances, not merely to follow an anthropologist's kinship chart.

As a consequence, even in societies where preferential mate choice is the rule, elders must take part in various negotiations leading to an acceptable marriage. In no society have these rigid patterns of mate preference completely determined who married whom. Haggling and market patterns have always entered into marriage arrangements. Personal preferences of partners do so too, for they determine in part how much each is willing to sacrifice in order to obtain the other as a spouse. Thus how much negotiation will occur, and who does it, will vary from one society to another. What is viewed as more or less desirable—chastity, learning, courage, grace—will vary, and so will the terms of exchange. Among the upper-class Japanese and Chinese of the past, these transactions were controlled by the elders— formally, legally, and publicly by the eldest male, though elder women often made the real decisions. According to the rules of traditional Arab societies, a man's family paid a bride price for the woman, while in the Brahmin castes of India her family paid a groom price or dowry. If the bride's family pays a dowry, it is very likely that the groom's family will also contribute to the union in some form. Indeed, in most societies when the families are close in rank, and especially when they are friendly, it is likely that the amounts given by one side may be equal to those given by the other. Nevertheless, negotiations may focus on dozens of detailed agreements as to who will do what for whom when marriage occurs.

To think of mate-choice processes as a market system does not mean that both sides are trying to get the maximum profit in money. Indeed, that is uncommon. Only rarely, in great poverty, have families truly sold their daughters to the highest bidder and pocketed the gain for their own benefit. Instead, elders may be trying to increase their political influence, achieve greater security, or maintain relations with friends and allies of long standing. Parents usually see themselves as "seeking the best for their children." Young people who date will usually reject the notion that they are engaged in marketing at all, and many do not consciously base their decisions on any calculations of profit or loss. Nevertheless, whether in a system of relatively free courtship or one of carefully arranged marriages, peoples' actions show that they are guided in part by an awareness of advantages and disadvantages.

Bargaining and Homogamy

We shall offer concrete illustrations of these processes, but let us first emphasize that all mate-selection systems press toward *homogamous marriages* (unions between people of about the same class level) as a result of the bargaining process. In general, like marries like with reference to a wide variety of traits. This general result is evident from ordinary observation. If a girl comes from a wealthy family, her family associates with other wealthy families, and because of her wealth she can command a good "price" in the marriage market. That is, other wealthy families will find her to be an acceptable bride for their son. Families who rank high in prestige and power do not need to ally themselves with lower-ranking families in order to find acceptable spouses for their children. The untalented, homely, poor man may *dream* of a bride with highly desirable qualities, but he cannot offer enough to induce her or her family to choose him.

In simple supply and demand terms, through the inquiries of elders who arrange marriages or the experiences of dating, people do find out how valuable they themselves are in the marriage market. They may initially aim higher or lower than other people believe they should aim, but they do aim. If they aim too high, their success will be small. If they aim low, they will find far more candidates, and thus learn they are worth more. Their friends also tell them whether their choices are wise. Thus, the gradual process of selection moves potential spouses toward others with similarly valued qualities.

Homogamy is also supported by various rules of *endogamy*. This is so by the very definition of group membership, since endogamy means simply marrying within the group, such as a religious faith, a caste, or even a village. These are simply one set of many rules by which groups try to maintain their unity. Very likely, most people who see themselves as a real group (Basques, Catholics, Swedish nobility) "feel better" if their members find spouses within the group; and some actually threaten any likely violation with strong penalties. Typically, then, people exert pressure on one another to marry others like themselves. So homogamy is also achieved partly against some rules of *exogamy* (marrying outside the group), for all societies have *both* kinds of rules. The two sets of rules, endogamous and exogamous, obviously refer to different kinds of groups. Most of the rules of exogamy require that the individual marry someone "outside" certain kin boundaries, or outside the village. Incest rules, for example, are rules of exogamy, for they forbid a person to marry anyone within the kin boundary of the immediate family, as well as some members of the kinship network farther out from the family (for example, certain first cousins). Where lineages are of importance, it is the rule that individuals may not marry anyone in their own lineage.

Thus we say that people with similar traits are more likely to join together in marriage, both because their groups press them to find mates like themselves and because market processes will move them to see that their best marriage opportunity is with someone who has similar qualities. However, we must keep in mind that not all social traits have the same market value; and the same trait may be differently valued in the two sexes, or at different ages, or in different societies. The ability to swim fast and gracefully or to dance well (especially among young people) is given some value, but not so much as family prestige. If a woman's beauty and charm enable her to marry above her class, there is some grumbling among the eligible women in her husband's circle, and some envy among those in her own. But among the larger public, the marriage is likely to be viewed as an appropriate exchange (not necessarily as a wise one). On the other hand, the rich woman who marries a lower-class man for his handsomeness is laughed at, while he is classified, even if erroneously, as some kind of gigolo or fortune hunter. Women enjoy greater freedom in their sexual choices in the 1980s than in prior decades, but these evaluations have not changed greatly. Beauty and charm are still thought of as a socially appropriate part of the female bargaining position, and increasingly in Western countries occupational achievement is too. On the other hand, beauty and charm are still not thought of as being traits that should be important in choosing a husband.

Social Controls over Love

The importance of love in the United States has been exaggerated in popular accounts. These usually argue that it is a poor basis for marriage, while failing to take account of the extent to which the selection process actually leads to pairings between persons of similar backgrounds. Nevertheless, compared to others the marriage system of the United States does give love greater prominence. Here, as in all Western societies to some degree, the child is socialized to fall in love. Falling in love is a common topic of family talk, as it is a theme in movies, television and radio programs, and advertising. Children tease one another about it, and adults engage in mock or serious conversations with youngsters about their "sweethearts." It is taken for granted that eventually almost everyone will decide to marry on the basis of a romantic attachment.

The Institutionalization of Love.   The main connections between the element of love and other social structures in the industrialized West are the following: First, the family unit is relatively independent of the larger kinship group, so husband and wife are free to love each other without serious competition from kin. In many other societies the husband-wife tie is accorded less emotional prominence. Second, the parent-child tie is strong, and falling in love permits the young person to free himself from this attachment in order to enter the independent status of spouse. Third, the American variant of the Western cultural patterns gives considerable freedom to adolescents, thus increasing the likelihood that they will fall in love. And, of course, love may be viewed as a mechanism for filling the gap left by the decline of arranged marriages. Young people who in another marriage system would be pushed into marriage by their elders are motivated to marry because of love.

Since the marriageable population of the United States (and increasingly as well in other countries) is gradually segregated into pools of eligibles with similar social-class backgrounds, even a free dating pattern with some encouragement to fall in love does not threaten the stratification system: That is, people generally fall in love with the "right kind of people." In fact, there is never a completely free market in courtship or mate selection. Rather, as in some economic exchanges, there are many smaller markets in which only certain people are eligible to participate. It is within each such market that the greatest freedom is to be found.

However, this last proposition may be turned around: In a system of arranged marriages, various social patterns exist to prevent love from disrupting the arrangements made by the elders. To understand this relationship more clearly, we can think of the world's societies as ranked along a continuum or degree of *institutionalization* of love as an element in the mate-selection process. At one extreme is the United States, where the individual has to give a good reason for marrying *without* being in love. ("I am too old for that sort of thing"; "I was poor; he was a good man, and rich"). At the other extreme might be placed the upper classes of traditional China or Tokugawa Japan, where love was viewed as a tragedy or at best irrelevant to the elders' choice of the individual's mate. In all societies some individuals do fall in love, but in many this behavior is not regarded as part of the ordinary process of mate selection.

At one extreme, then, is the United States, but many other societies are close to it in their acceptance of love as an important (but not adequate) reason for marriage. Here we would include the industrialized Western nations and all or most Polynesian societies of the past. A different set of cases are those societies in which love is still less institutionalized. That is, many or most young people will become very attracted to one another during the courtship process, but being in love is not viewed as necessary for marriage. Under these systems, elders did take part in the decision and had almost a completely free hand in the financial arrangements for the marriage. Young people usually associated with one another prior to marriage, and decided to marry someone with whom they had fallen in love. They could not control the financial arrangements, and thus their love might be thwarted, but parental or kin refusal was not typical. This pattern was widespread among the peasantry of Europe prior to industrialization. A substantial number of Melanesian and Papuan societies exhibited such a love pattern, which was also found here and there in Africa. Doubtless, a large percentage of tribal societies of the past fitted this description. In them, love was kept under some control, but young people did have a considerable amount of freedom within a narrow group of possible mates. In China, India, Japan, most of the Islamic countries, and among the Western upper classes, however, love was kept under far more control. That is, in much of the world, love has *not* been given much institutional support, and it has been kept under strong controls. Why has this been so widespread a pattern?

Patterns of Strong Control. Love is potentially a threat to the stratification system, for it may impel some young people to marry those whom their elders view as inappropriate spouses. It can disrupt the elders' plans to unite two lineages or family inheritances; it can link a high-ranking family with one of low rank, to the embarrassment of the former. Property, power, lineage honor, totemic relationships, and other family resources in all societies flow from one generation to the next through the kinship lines, linked by marriages. Mate choice thus has many consequences. People who fall in love have braved storms of anger, violence, ostracism, and their own inner fears in order to marry the one they loved. To avoid all this, love and mate choice are controlled, so that marriage is not left to the whim of youngsters.

The fullest possible control can be obtained, of course, by arranging marriages before love can appear. One such arrangement is *child marriage.* The Hindu prescription was, until very recently, that all girls should be married *before* puberty, and this was the practice as well. In 1891 the average age of females at marriage was 12.5 years. This figure did not rise at all until the 1930s. It was 14.7 years in 1941, and by the 1970s, 18 years. Under that system, the young girl had little opportunity to fall in love, and no resources for getting her way if she did. Living with her husband before the marriage was physically consummated, she was more likely to fall in love with him than with anyone else.

A second pattern for controlling love through early choice, and some-times linked with the preceding one, specifies rather closely which status is to be linked in marriage with which. This is a form of preferential mar-riage. For example, the traditionally approved marriage among the Be-douin Arabs was between a young man and his father's brother's daughter (*patrilateral parallel-cousin marriage*). In most of Arabic Islam this was not the usual type of marriage, but in some outlying regions where political power flowed from family linkages, this form made up a majority of marriages. The young man had the right to marry his patrilateral parallel cousin, and would have to pay only a token bride price if he entered that kind of marriage. A more common type of preferential marriage has been *matrilat-eral cross-cousin* marriage, in which the boy marries his mother's brother's daughter.

There are many other types of such specifications. When the popula-tion of a tribe is small, as noted already, there may actually be no one in that "marriage cell." Indeed, computer analyses of the likelihood of there being appropriate spouses for every person, with the proper age, in the proper status, given the usual facts of fertility and mortality, show that most highly specific preferential marriage systems could not continue to operate over many generations. Thus, since elders are likely to be realistic, more distant cousins may be treated as "equivalent" and also appropriate. In many societies *child betrothal* or engagement was easily combined with the system of preferential marriage, since everyone knew who was to marry whom.

Very common in all Western nations of the past, and continuing into the twentieth century in many Latin nations, is another method of control-ling love relationships: *strict chaperonage,* so that young people were simply never permitted to be alone together, or in intimate interaction. Social segregation can best be achieved by physical segregation—for example, the *harem* system of Islam. In much of Arabic Islam the peasants were too poor to be able to keep their daughters and wives in separate quarters, but they could stay near them and watch them carefully. Women were and most still are required to wear one of a variety of costumes that hide their faces and bodies from scrutiny. Bedouin Arab girls, on the other hand, were ordinar-ily permitted some interaction with marriageable men, but since they were nomadic desert groups they were always under close observation anyway. In China, potential spouses were usually selected from families in a dif-ferent section of a city, or in another village. Most of the young men a girl met would belong to the same clan (*tsu*) and would be ineligible for mar-riage. Upper-class girls were, of course, chaperoned more carefully.

Overlapping with strict surveillance is the Puritan system of love control. It called for severe self-examination and high self-control over all the appetites, with special attention to the sexual. Both adults and children were constantly exhorted to beware of and to suppress all sensual desires outside marriage, and children were told to obey the commands of parents. This was not a "loveless" social pattern, as so many books suggest. The more ascetic Protestants (of which the Puritans were one part) did believe in love within marriage, but children were told never to give way to their personal desires or wishes without the approval of their parents. Since this system was accompanied by a constant pattern of family and community supervision (as well as gossip), not many young people would feel strong enough to marry for love, and parents would have felt justified in disinheriting them if they were so foolish.

By now it is also clear that the Western system of *formally* free courtship also controls where love will appear, and how people will respond to it. In this system, falling in love is actively encouraged, and people are likely to view being in love a necessary part of getting married. However, most of the people we meet as possible dates are likely to be of the same class. If an individual falls in love with the "wrong sort," and wishes to marry him or her, friends and kin will express disapproval. Finally, we noted earlier a related system of control, common among European peasants for centuries, but also in other parts of the world: *within* a pool of eligibles, couples were likely to pair off, to become emotionally attached to one another, and to marry, but it was always understood that they could do so only with the permission of their elders. The elders held the control of property in their hands (cattle, land, or other rights), and they had the power to choose a partner for the young adult.

In general, as might be inferred from the preceding discussion, families with a higher social rank grant less freedom in courtship than do families of lower rank. They have more to fear from the disruptive effects of love, have more resources for controlling it, and expend more energy in avoiding some of its consequences. By channeling love or keeping it under some control, the family elders can be freer to make marriage bargains with one another. Only where they do have the authority to give their sons and daughters in marriage is it possible to maintain a traditional bride price or dowry system. It becomes pointless or expensive to make an agreement whose execution cannot be guaranteed. Let us now consider this element in the process of mate selection.

Bride Price and Dowry

Just why one society has a bride price and another a groom price is not fully understood, but some relationships can be discerned in these kinds of marriage exchanges. Let us first see what each of the relevant terms means. A *dowry* is a sum of money or property brought to the marriage by the girl. It is given by her family, but to whom it is given varies from one culture to another. In Western countries it was generally given to the groom, who could use it under certain restrictions or even have (under some circumstances) the full disposal of it. In rural Ireland the dowry was in effect given to the groom's father, who then handed over his land to the groom and his bride. The dowry itself was used to secure a marriage for the groom's sister (*her* dowry) or sometimes (if there was no sister) to help a brother get started in an occupation. Thus, so long as a family had two children or fewer, and no more than one daughter, it could handle the financial problems of marriage.

In many Western countries, a large dowry was sometimes used to marry a daughter into a higher-ranking family. Generally, a girl would be considered only if her social skills were adequate for a higher position, and the amount demanded would of course be greater, the higher the rise in rank the family sought. In eighteenth-century France, the amounts needed for a given type of alliance were much discussed. In the late nineteenth and early twentieth centuries, many American heiresses married into English or European nobility by furnishing large settlements to their husbands. In contemporary European middle-class society, a dowry becomes less and less necessary, but it may still smooth the path toward marriage.

A *dower* system does not substitute for a dowry system, but is often a part of it: a dower was a sum given to the bride by the groom's family, as a kind of social security when her husband died. Under the feudal system of Europe and England, she had no right to her husband's property after his death. However, in England it was common for men who made wills to include some provision for the widow's care through her lifetime. In addition, it could be expected that if she had a son, he would take care of her. Generally, she would not have any rights of property from her own family of origin. (Some women were heiresses, but they were special cases). In contrast to the dowry is the *bride price*, now more commonly called *bride wealth*. This was a sum of money, goods, or cattle given to the family of the bride, often at certain of the many steps that were part of the marriage process. Several general principles can be noted in such marriage exchanges.

First, one may suppose that the direction in which the greater value flows will express the relative evaluation the society places on the new spouses, and what they do for the family line. In patrilineal African societies, for example, the *lobola* or bride wealth is paid for the children to be born of the mother, and for other wifely duties. Since children belonged to the mother's line in matrilineal societies (*not* to the groom's family), only a nominal or modest amount was given by the father's lineage. If payment was in the form of groom service, the amount of cattle given in addition would be small. (Brahmins in India had to pay a groom price or dowry in response to a set of forces we discuss below.)

Second, no matter which direction the greater amount of wealth flows, the elders who make the rules will arrange them so that all such exchanges must even out over time among families or lineages in the same marriage pool. Since most marriages occur within the same economic stratum, the stratum as a whole neither gains nor loses. On the other hand, in a particular line, bad luck (having many daughters in a noble English family) might create much financial embarrassment or distress in that generation.

Third, the family receiving more wealth typically reciprocates with other gifts. Indeed, among the well-to-do, it is usually a point of honor to make the countergifts about equal in value. Such exchanges are publicly known, and they express both the social rank of the families and their pleasure in the event. This may be observed in the many exchanges that occur upon the occasion of a marriage between well-to-do families in the United States. People do not label these gifts "dowry" or "bride price," but very likely a visitor from tribal Africa or classical China would! The bride's family in the United States is expected to bear the costs of the wedding, and many other costs as well, but the groom's family is also expected to be generous in helping the young couple get started in their new life.

Fourth, when a dowry or bride-wealth system exists, some room for haggling is found within the marriage arrangements. If a rich French noble-man fell in love with a beautiful, charming girl from another French noble family, her family would probably not have been required to furnish a large dowry, while his kin would have expressed their pleasure through generous gifts. On the other hand, it has often happened that a young nobleman in a Western country had to seek an alliance that would bring in a large dowry, since his elders continued to remind him that the family estate was nearly destitute.

Expert haggling can drive as good a bargain as possible, but the terms will always be limited by social evaluations of the traits of the young spouses. If by the standards of the society the young man is not attractive, clever, or of a desirable rank, haggling will not transform him into a rare bargain. It is clear that as love begins to play a larger role in courtship, these arrangements become less explicit, or they are dropped. Young people in love are much less disposed to haggle about such matters in this generation, and do not wish to risk delaying the match by driving the best possible bargain for their family line. In addition, as already noted, when young people are independently making their own decisions, elders no longer have the power to guarantee the arrangements they make. Consequently, they are less willing to make this kind of family investment, and the dowry and bride wealth become less important.

On the other hand, where such exchanges do remain part of the general cultural pattern, the combination of modern affluence and infla-tion in most parts of the world increase the apparent *monetary* value of whatever is exchanged. Moreover, marriage is likely to be the occasion for many gifts and countergifts, even when (as in the United States) most people would deny that a dowry or bride price system exists. Each system is somewhat different, since each grows from a particular history. For exam-ple, among Indian Brahmins the groom price or dowry is taken for granted as a necessity, the amount being higher if the man has been well-educated or has a profession. In Hindu society the pattern was enforced by the traditional prescription that a girl must be married before puberty. Con-sequently, the girl's family was under some time pressure, while the boy's family could wait. In addition, some small amount of hypergamy was per-mitted, and the girl's family would have to pay for such an upward step. In the Bengal region in the nineteenth century, a Kulin Brahmin man might marry scores of girls from a slightly lower-ranking Brahmin caste, receiving gifts with each visit to each wife in addition to the original dowry. A bride-price system was the pattern followed in China, Japan, Arabic Islam, and most of sub-Saharan Africa.

MATE CHOICE: A SUMMARY OF GENERAL PATTERNS

The pattern of homogamy, that is, marriage between people of similar traits, is the result, as we noted earlier, of two major sets of processes. One is rooted in the marriage market, specifically the interaction between aspirations toward obtaining a spouse with more desirable traits, and the real market value of the person who seeks a spouse. The second major process is made up of the social pressures and individual evaluations which affirm that the manners, tastes, religion, or ethnic membership of one's own group are all superior. For example, whatever the individual's aspirations in a marriage market, that person as well as his or her friends and kin are likely to feel that a potential spouse from the group is more desirable, other things being equal. Thus, a German Catholic family would be more pleased if their son chose as his spouse a young German Catholic woman, if she were not undesirable in other ways.

Although this set of evaluations may be labeled as nothing more than simple *ethnocentrism,* that is, a feeling that one's own group is superior, it also contains a widely accepted folk belief that couples of about the same cultural background, education, style of life, or rank will make a more satisfactory marriage. The amount of personal adjustment each has to make to the other will be less under those circumstances, and both political and domestic arguments are likely to be fewer. Although our analyses of what causes family disharmony are not strong, they do not suggest that this bit of folk wisdom is incorrect. It also seems likely that if homogamy typically led to more domestic conflict or bitterness between spouses, it would not have become so widespread a social pattern. Adjustment in marriage is not assured in any family system, but it does seem to be a more likely outcome of similarity between spouses than of dissimilarity. Consequently, when religious sects or ethnic groups press their members to seek spouses only within the group, it is not only because of their ideological narrowness, but also because they believe that outsiders with dissimilar attitudes and backgrounds would not adjust as easily in a marriage as one of their own members, and would not help to maintain the traditional ways.

Since the success of people in the marriage market, as well as the control their groups or families have over them, will vary by their position in the social structure, it is useful to consider together a wide range of homogamous patterns. Here are some of the more common ones.

1. A generally *increasing* homogamy will be observed as we move from casual dating to serious dating, and then from engagement to marriage. That is, casual dates are less likely to be homogamous, but among people who become increasingly committed to their partners, there will be

a higher percentage of couples of similar social rank and background. Even within the Western system of dating, we can expect to observe certain regularities of homogamy. Most young people in their late adolescence will date others who belong in the same general social class. If a boy crosses a class line, he is more likely than a girl to date a person in a lower class, while the girl is more likely to date "upward." Those who date *upward,* whether boys or girls, are more likely to have special qualities such as being very popular, attractive, or outstanding in athletics. Because of the age differences, most people in school or college are likely to date others within the same school class, while again the boys who date girls in other school classes are more likely to date those who are younger.

2. Both cross culturally and historically, women are more likely to be controlled by kin or family in their choice of mates than are men. This applies to ethnic groups as well as to social class; young men are more likely to expand their range of eligible mates by reaching out beyond their own membership groups. On the other hand, as we noted earlier, in general families in the higher social ranks achieve greater control over the mate choices of their younger members, and thus maintain a homogamous mate choice more often.

3. The preceding two patterns usually mean that women are somewhat more likely to move upward when they marry (*hypergamy*) than men are. In the past, this has meant that women with higher education were much less likely to marry at all than men of a comparable education. That difference remains, but it is much smaller.

4. Because of the complex social definitions of adulthood by sex and age, those who marry are close to one another in age. When there is a difference, in almost all large societies, the groom is older than the bride. In the United States, the average age of grooms was 24.2 in 1977, while that of brides was 22.1. On the other hand, in the older age categories, the age of the bride does not increase equally with that of the groom, but lags somewhat behind. For example, although a man 40 years of age is more likely to marry women who are older than the national average, he is not likely to marry a woman only two or three years younger than he.

5. All studies so far show that people who are likely to marry are also likely to live close to one another. That is, people are also homogamous with respect to place of residence. Living in the same area is usually indicative of class similarity, since those who live close to one another are also more likely to be of the same class, and of course much more likely to meet one another. In this relationship, class is also a differentiating variable, since those from higher occupational groups are likely to marry people who come from great distances. In part, this is a simple result of the fact that so many spouses are first encountered in colleges away from home. In some societies (China was an important case), however, people did not often find their spouses within the same village, because they were supposed to marry from a different clan, and very often a large percentage of the population in the village was of the same clan. That is, *village exogamy* was common in some societies.

Residential propinquity is not explained only by class, however. Living close by is a little-noticed but powerful factor in the development of social relations, whether friendship or marriage. Its social importance is that it increases or decreases the likelihood of unplanned, social encounters between strangers or acquaintances. This affords them more or less opportunity for easy social interaction. If people have traits that might attract them to one another, propinquity increases the possibility that they will find this out. People who live close together are more likely to attend the same schools, shop in the same store, or simply greet one another on the street as familiar strangers. This apparently spatial factor, then, is an unmeasured part of our social interaction. Residential closeness also has a time and energy meaning. A young man who is deeply in love may be willing to travel far to see his sweetheart home; and in the modern era of relatively easy transportation, some people even conduct transcontinental courtships.

Thus, both variables are important. People who live far from one another are less likely to meet, to become attracted, or to continue a relationship long enough to be that deeply committed. On the other hand, it is obvious that people with more money will find that the costs of travel as well as the cost of long distance telephone calls are a smaller drain on their pocketbook than they would be for people with less available money. This, of course, is one of the causes for the social pattern noted above, the greater tendency of people at higher class levels to find spouses in a wider geographical range.

6. Other things being equal, the larger the membership group, the more likely it is that members of that group will find spouses within it. That is, homogamy is partly a function of simple relative *size*. If the group is very large, then almost anyone can ultimately find a congenial partner within it. If it is smaller, those chances diminish. This latter effect will be reduced, of course, if the smaller group is very intense in its disapproval of out-marriages, engages in a great deal of matchmaking, or is looked down upon by the larger group.

7. Most marriages, in this and other countries, are homogamous with respect to race. People marry overwhelmingly within what they view as their own race, if the marriage pool is large enough, and does not have a highly skewed sex ratio (number of men for each 100 women). Such a sex skew has often been observed when males migrate long distances to places where few members of their own race have moved. At the turn of the century, for example, there were large numbers of Chinese, Japanese, and Filipino males on the U.S. West Coast, but very few women socially defined as Oriental. Few whites and blacks cross the race line to obtain spouses now, and they rarely did so in the past. Most of this homogamy results from race prejudice, on one or both sides (for example, U.S. whites have generally disapproved of anyone who married a Chinese person, but the Chinese thought that no proper Chinese would marry outside their group either). Nevertheless, both within any ethnic or racial group, as well as among such groups, various patterns of marriage exchange have been reported.

Black-white marriages are still rare in the United States, although they have been increasing. Social rules and, in some states, caste laws used to forbid such marriages. Almost everyone believed that they would fail, or would be tragedies for the resulting children. Those laws have been struck down, and the accompanying attitudes have weakened a good bit. Most available data suggest that such marriages have mainly been hypergamous as to class (the woman marries upward in class). In 1977, three-fourths of the black-white couples were reported to be made up of a black husband and a white wife. That pattern has been observed over many decades, and is generally thought to be the result of a particular type of social exchange: in it, the white wife was marrying upward in class position, for she was marrying an occupationally successful black man; the black man was marrying upward with respect to caste. Thus there was a kind of exchange in which both gained somewhat. This pattern was suggested by both Robert K. Merton and Kingsley Davis over a generation ago.

Whatever may have been true of the past, it is clear that description is not now correct. First, it seems likely that the increase in black-white marriages has occurred mainly among college couples, for whom caste has lost much of its importance. Both spouses are likely to be in a middle or higher class, and both partners assert their freedom from caste prejudices. Aside from this important change, at least some data suggest that in southern rural areas the more common pattern is the marriage of a black woman to a white husband. It now seems doubtful that we can ever be sure of the facts about the past, since the data were not always recorded, and many people had good reason to hide their race affiliation. Data about the present are also open to question, and seem to be inconsistent.[1] If the facts themselves are not clear, we should not be hasty in trying to explain them. Thus, we offer no new interpretation of the data. Equally important, since laws forbidding interracial marriage have been struck down by the courts, while caste prejudice against blacks has been diminishing (changing their value on the market), a much larger number of such marriages has been occurring, and very likely a different set of exchanges may now take place. We shall instead suggest a different line of speculation about out-marriages generally.

First, as much research has reported, out-marrying people who belong to a less prestigious ethnic group are likely to have achieved a higher rank (in prestige, power, or wealth) than members who did not marry upward. Second, among members of the higher-ranking ethnic group as well, those who "marry out" will also have achieved more than the average members of their group—and, of course, so will those whom they marry. If this speculation is correct for most interracial or interethnic marriages, then caste and class factors may play a lesser *direct* role in mate choice bargaining than has hitherto been supposed. Instead, one might guess that a simpler set of processes occurs: Those who marry earlier will achieve less, and will also marry within their own group, since they interact mostly with group members. Those who marry later are more likely to meet far more

1.   Here I draw upon a personal communication from Lewis F. Carter, as well as his article, "Racial-Caste Hypogamy: A Sociological Myth?" *Phylon—The Atlanta University Review of Race and Culture*, **29**, (1968), 347-350.

members of other ethnic or racial groups on the job, at college, or in military service, and thus increase the likelihood of an out-marriage. By then too, they have had a better chance to rise somewhat occupationally. Moreover, in the new social setting, the ethnic or racial background of both persons will be of far less importance to them personally, as well as to the people in their social network. Thus, their mates are likely to be of a similar class position, education, or style of life. These speculations may also apply to cross-racial marriages of almost all types in the United States.

8. The pattern of homogamy also extends to marital status. Most who marry are of course single, but within each marital pool the widowered, the widowed, and the divorced also marry within the same marital status in a higher proportion than could be attributed to chance alone.

Finally, a large number of studies, over many decades, have shown that husband and wife are more alike in a wide range of traits, often apparently irrevelant, than could be accounted for by chance. It cannot be supposed that young men and women spend much thought on whether their date or fiancee is similar in such matters as hair color, height, weight, eating patterns, and so on. Rather, homogamy is for the most part the product of other social processes we have been describing, especially the differential association of people in groups or networks that are more or less homogeneous; the process of finding one's own level in the courtship market; and obtaining more pleasure from others with similar traits and habits.

One technical point needs to be made with reference to the amount of intermarriage that occurs within specific subsects or religions. Although it is common to calculate the amount of out-marriage as simply the percentage of a given group, such as Catholics, who marry members of other religions, that is only a crude measure. It is also necessary to calculate the number of potential spouses within the marriage pool. Thus, if Catholics make up one-fourth of the population of the United States, and they pay no attention to religious affiliation, one would expect that three-fourths of all Catholics would marry non-Catholics. The actual figure is about one-fifth. Thus, Catholics are more than three times as likely to marry Catholics as might occur simply by chance. If we recalculate figures in a similar fashion for Jews and Protestants, it is clear that Jews are far more endogamous than Catholics or Protestants. It is more difficult to obtain exact figures for smaller religious groups, but in each case it is necessary to relate the number of out-marriages that would occur by chance alone to the number of out-marriages that actually occur. Finally, it should be noted that even when individuals do find spouses in other religious denominations, it is likely that such people feel much less allegiance to their nominal religious affiliation. Thus, they are closer in religious attitudes than their apparent affiliation might suggest.

As a further comment on homogamy of religion, it should be noted that the pressures on individuals to find mates within the same religious denomination mask social traits other than simple religious beliefs. At least in the United States, few Americans even know what these beliefs are, or feel strongly about them. More important is the social or ethnic background correlated with the religion. For example, Jewish families will ordinarily have no objection to a young man who never visits the synagogue, if he is at least nominally Jewish. Protestant families often object to their children marrying Catholics primarily because they object to a union with a lower-status ethnic group, since Catholics in the United States are likely to be identified with ethnic groups whose prestige ranking is lower.

CHAPTER 5
ROLE RELATIONS IN FAMILY AND SOCIETY

Any general theory of society must consider the links of the family system with all the other institutions that organize human action. By contrast, most people pay little day to day attention to how the outside society affects family behavior. Instead, they focus on the specific acts and feelings of each member of their own family. What each member does is partly shaped by the rights and obligations (the usual definition of *roles*) of each person to each other, and still more by all the influences each can use to move other family members toward desirable acts. These factors, in turn, are affected by the larger society, because many of the resources we use to control one another come from the larger society. Thus, for example, how the larger society defines the *mother* (using her talents as an artist, physician, or clerk; or instead refusing to give her an education) will determine in part what her roles within the family are.

In this chapter, then, we consider especially the major patterns of social interaction between the two sexes, the relations between husband and wife, and the changing roles of parents and children. However, we continue to note the many points at which the larger social structure affects the actions or attitudes of individuals within the family. Since all of these will vary considerably according to the stage of the *family cycle*, we first present some descriptive facts about these stages.

THE LIFE CYCLE OF THE FAMILY

Social analysts, whether Marxist or mainstream, often use the metaphor of the *system*, viewing the society as a kind of social unit or organism, which presumably is born of conflict, matures, and eventually dies. It is an appealing imagery in apparently all cultures. Family analysts have often advocated its use, pointing out that many behavioral patterns are more closely tied to life cycle stage than to chronological age. For example, it is likely that the daily schedule of a young woman is shaped more by her life cycle stage of being wife and mother, than by her age of, say, 23 years.

But the realities of family life in an industrial society are too complex to fit the imagery of a "cycle" or a "marital career sequence."[1] Some people do not marry at all, and some of these people may remain with their parents. Some live with someone, but do not marry the partner; or they marry only after a child is born. Many marry but divorce before a child is born. Still others marry, but one spouse dies while their children are young, and the surviving spouse goes on to marry again. In the United States, less than half of all who marry will have children and remain married until the "completion" of the cycle—the death of one or both spouses. On the other hand, some of the characteristics that have been viewed as "stages" can be used fruitfully as variables to describe or explain family behavior. For example, we can ascertain whether the family behavior of people who go through a formal marriage is different from that of couples who do not marry; we can compare the behavior of couples with or without children, or families with or without adult children (a later stage). We thus avoid the futile task of trying to fit each couple into an ideal but unrealistic set of family stages and instead are led to analyze the structural differences among different types of family units.

The notion of family cycle also can suggest the likelihood that although the large extended family may not be the most common type at any given time, it may be very common as a *phase* of the family unit. Thus, both the Arab and the Indian family may, for a while, contain at least one married son (with or without offspring) before the married couple breaks off to form an independent household. This also suggests a broader question: Under which conditions are families more or less likely to complete what is viewed as the model family cycle of their culture? The events of the life cycle and the family cycle are parallel, of course, but *where* in the life cycle a specific famiy event occurs may also make a difference. For example, in Western families over the centuries, husbands and wives were close to the same age (about 30 percent of the wives were somewhat older) and were mature adults in their mid-twenties. Would this make their relations more companionate than, say, in Hindu marriages, where the husband was considerably older? Note too that Western families might need less ideological support for a mother's authority over her children, who would be much younger, as contrasted with the lesser age difference between many Hindu mothers and their first children. It seems likely that we gain some understanding of the Indian family at the beginning of this century if we know that most girls were married at about the age of puberty (ideally, at about 12 years of age) and that their husbands were about nine years older. Their

---

1. See the uses of the family cycle approach in Jean Cuisenier (ed.), *The Family Life Cycle in European Societies* (The Hague: Mouton, 1977).

first child came several years after marriage, and their life expectancy (at birth) was probably less than 30 years.

We note how different the family system of the United States is from most others of the past when we understand that it permits a wide range of personal choice of events in the life cycle, so that at many points these do not form a simple sequence. Let us consider some family cycle events in American society as a framework for the description of family role relations.

Family Patterns in the United States

The median age of the husband at first marriage in the United States in 1977 was 24 years; the age of the wife was 22. Both figures had risen during the 1970s. Although 95 percent of the population marries eventually, only about 38 percent of men and 53 percent of women in the age group 20 to 24 had not married. These figures are lower (and thus the age at marriage is higher) in other Western countries. Table 5.1 gives some comparisons.

Children.   In the intact family, the wife will bear her first child within about 27 months after marriage, an average figure that includes any births that may have occurred prior to marriage, as well as the approximately one-fourth of all marriages in which the wife is already pregnant at marriage. This time period is slightly longer than two decades ago, in conformity with the general rule that when fertility is lower in a population, the length of time between births is longer. If a couple intends to have three or four children, they are likely to have their first child sooner after

Table 5.1   Age at Marriage for Selected Countries

COUNTRY	AGE AT MARRIAGE		PERCENTAGE MARRIED, AGE 20-24 YEARS	
	Men (mid-1970s)[a]	Women (1980)[b]	Men (mid-1970s)	Women (1980)
United States	24 (1977)	21	38 (1976)	58
Sweden	28 (1975)	26	9 (1975)	24
West Germany	28 (1975)	22	22 (1975)	51
France	26 (1972)	23	27 (1972)	49
Spain	27 (1970)	24	9 (1970)	31
England/Wales	25 (1974)	23	35 (1974)	62
Finland	25 (1975)	23	23 (1974)	41

[a] Calculated from group data in the *1976 United Nations Demographic Yearbook.* For Spain, a midpoint of 17.5 was assumed for the 1–19 age group; for all the countries, a midpoint of 65 was assumed for the 60+ age group. Percentage of men married is from the same source.

[b] Age at marriage for women is estimated singulate mean age, calculated from the Population Reference Bureau, *Family Planning and Marriage, 1970–1980 Data Sheet,* 1980. Percentage of women married is from the same source.

the marriage. With the spread of abortion, this event may be seen as at least common in courtship and marriage. In the United States, as in other Western countries, the laws and rules against abortion have been eased considerably. In the United States, for every 1000 live births, there are about 250 legal abortions. In some countries, the number of total abortions may be as great as the total number of births.

Parallel to the general decline of the birth rate in the United States is a decline among both blacks and whites in the percentage who bear three or more children. This, then, is a change in the family cycle experience. About 25 percent of wives aged 18 to 24 can be expected to have three or more children eventually. Women now complete their childbearing, on the average, by the time they are 30. This is about three years younger than women in the United States in the early 1900s. At the present time, the female population is bearing about 2.8 children per person during a lifetime. If, however, we consider only the younger age group, 18 to 34, black women are expected to bear 2.3 children over their remaining years, and white women are expected to have 2.1 children.

Independent Households.   Most young people set up their own households at marriage. This is less likely for young black women who bear illegitimate children without marrying, and who are more likely to continue living with their relatives. On the other hand, because an increasing percentage of young people go through a phase of *cohabitation* (living together without marrying) and because the age at marriage has risen, it is likely that most couples who marry have already established an independent household, at least as a single person, before embarking upon a marriage career. Very young couples are more likely to live with one or the other set of parents for a while. This pattern of doubling up is more common in the American South, and of course also more common in Japan and India.

Working Wives.   Holding a job must now be viewed as a normal part of the marriage career of American women, and a large majority of women work just before and after marriage (more than three-fourths). More than one-third of women with preschool children have outside jobs (37 percent of whites, and 54 percent of blacks). More than half of all adult women are in the labor force, and that figure has been increasing. The increase is especially high among mothers. There is a drop in employment from the initial period of marriage through the first few years until the children are in school: 82 percent of married women age 25 to 34 without children were in the labor force, contrasted with 40 percent for those whose children were all under age 6.

After the children go to school, there is a rise in wives' participation in the workforce, though in the late 40s the curve begins to drop off again and continues downward from that point on. However, the drop is not precipitous; in the age group 45 to 54, about half of all wives are still in the labor force. In general, a higher percentage of black then of white women have jobs, but this difference has been decreasing.

Divorce and Remarriage.   Divorce may happen at any time in the life cycle of the family. Indeed, it is estimated that some 12 percent of married women who are 65 years and over will eventually divorce. The median age at divorce (1978) was 30.3 years for the husband, and 28.2 years for the wife. This is about two years after their separation. However, since it is estimated that about 40 percent of all current marriages will end in divorce, a slight majority of marriages will endure until the death of the husband or wife—the end of the family cycle.

Although divorce must be viewed as one of the expectable contingencies in a marriage career in the United States, we must note that the majority of people who divorce will also remarry. The average age of *remarriage* for women is about 29 years, and 38 years for a later divorce (if it occurs) from that second marriage. The median duration of a first marriage is seven years.

One consequence of a relatively high illegitimacy rate and a high divorce rate is the likelihood that one phase of the "family cycle" will be that of the female-headed family. (In most divorce cases, custody is awarded to the wife). At any given time, more than one-third of all black families are headed by women (1975), and about 10 percent of white families. In about half of all divorces, there are one or more children.

Older Women Alone.   By the time her last child has married, the wife is about 55 years of age. Because women have lower mortality rates and are usually younger than their husbands, they are more likely to be the survivor when one spouse dies. Almost two-fifths of women over 65 live alone.

Among the 11 percent of the U.S. population who are elderly (aged 65 years and over), almost one-fifth live in the same household with one of their grown children (1975), and three-fourths live within a half hour's driving distance. In one survey in the mid-1970s, about half had seen one of their children that very day. Although the elderly see fewer of their kin than do younger people, most (and especially those who still form married couples) continue to visit with close kin or descendants on a regular basis.

Contrasts and Comparisons

Such family cycle data reveal several differences from other cultures, as we have been noting. The most obvious is that in a relatively free marriage system there are far more choices at every phase: late or early marriage or none at all; a stable marriage or a divorce; divorce, remarriage, and redivorce; living close to or apart from kin; and so on. Second, although the divorce rates of most nations are rising more rapidly than in the United States, in many countries only a small percentage of couples ever take this step as a part of their marriage career.

Furthermore, some members of the lower classes in the New World, especially blacks and mestizos in the Caribbean and Latin America, have for generations formed unions that were not formal marriages, but it is only recently that a sizable segment of the middle classes (about a million couples in all classes) have cohabited in the United States without first marrying. That percentage is rising in the more advanced industrial countries of Europe, too. In addition, a higher percentage of households in the United States are female-headed than in other nations. Finally, even though most of the elderly are not socially isolated in the United States, far more live in their own households than in other countries, while both the elderly and their grown children approve of this independence. By contrast, in Japan both generations still believe it is more appropriate to live together, but that attitude is now weakening a good deal.

In each phase of the family cycle, the obligations and rights of each family member to every other will change. For example, when a couple is young, it is likely that their parents will help them financially and in other ways. As the parents become elderly, they are more likely to begin *receiving* gifts or aid from their grown children. When kin or friends give advice about proper family behavior, it will differ depending on the age, sex, or marital phase of the individual. It is taken for granted, for example, that a mature father does not owe the same obligations to his unmarried brothers or sisters that he once did as a younger single person. Thus, the phases of the cycle do affect behavior, even if we cannot discover a simple set of sequences into which all family units can be neatly fitted.

SEX ROLES AND THE DIVISION OF LABOR

Earlier, in analyzing the biological bases of family behavior, we considered various regularities in family roles. Our conclusion was that biological factors make certain social patterns more likely, but do not fully determine the complexity of family behavior. In this section, we examine in more detail how societies allocate various rights and duties to the two sexes.

In any analysis of sex roles, perhaps the first point to be kept in mind is that not everyone in the society, whether it is industrial or tribal, will fit the gender roles that the society tries to impose. Even where women are socialized to be nurturant and docile, some will not be. As soon as we observe particular husbands and wives in biographies, diaries, or field studies of the past or present, we see that always there are some exceptional men and women who do not fit the rules. A second caution is that all sex roles are complex even as a set of ideal roles, not just as a particular reality. Masculine role prescriptions in even a strongly male-dominant society often *approve* certain patterns of nurturance and tenderness between males, or between older males and children; a common subcategory of the female role in the Mediterranean nations, for example, is the strong, commanding matriarch. A higher percentage of black women than of white women in the United States have better jobs than their husbands, and this increases their influence in the family in spite of the male ideal of dominance.

Nevertheless, the general regularity in the sexual division of labor is clear. In all societies a range of tasks is assigned to females and another set is given to males, while still others may be performed by either sex. Both sexes are socialized from the earliest years to know what these tasks are, to become competent at doing them, and to feel that the division of tasks is proper. Although these assignments by sex are considered "natural," they differ a good bit from one society to another.

Some division of labor by sex is universal, but much of it does not seem to be required by the biological peculiarities of the two sexes. To be sure, a man cannot bear a child or nurse it. On the average, men are stronger and can run faster than women, who are in turn somewhat handicapped at times by pregnancy and menstruation. On the other hand, women usually command enough strength and speed to perform almost all tasks in every society. Equally important, what is defined as a man's task in one society may well be classed as a woman's job in another, thus indicating that some of the division is culturally defined.

In any event, in very loose conformity with a biological view, in three-fourths or more of societies for which information is available, women mostly carried out these tasks: grinding grain, carrying water, cooking and preserving food, repairing and making clothing, weaving (of cloth, mats, and baskets), gathering food (nuts, berries, herbs, roots), and making pottery.[2] All these tasks can be carried out while remaining close to the children or the hearth. In most societies men are assigned these tasks if they are done at all: herding, hunting and fishing, lumbering, mining and quarrying, metal-working, making musical instruments, manufacturing ceremonial objects, woodworking, and housebuilding. Some of these require strength or speed, and others demand some wandering from the hearth. Some demand neither strength nor absence from the home. Notice that the tending of crops calls for endurance and some strength, but it is as likely to be a female activity as a male activity. It does not take either to make musical instruments or ceremonial objects, but men do that. That the division is not based only on a rational judgment of capacity is seen from the fact that men can perform all the women's jobs, but do not, whereas the jobs that are strictly male do not generally take all the man's time. The division of labor seems to be based neither on biology nor on simple equality. Another factor to be noted is that whatever the strictly male tasks are, more of them are defined as more *honorific*.

This relationship between male tasks and men's status may be seen most clearly in the societies in which the interaction between men and women was less marked by male dominance than in other societies. These are classified as gathering and hunting societies. First, modern reports prove that life was relatively easy in most of these groups. Only a few hours a day was needed to obtain an adequate supply of food. Any adult could feed himself or herself without the help of others. Women furnished a high percentage of all food consumed—from 35 to more than 50 percent of the total. On the other hand, the two sexes did cooperate. Both sexes ate as they wandered, but both brought food back to wherever the family camped for the night. This pattern is very likely primeval, dating from long before the dawn of history. Men engaged more often in the high-risk high-return activity of hunting, a task in which the payoff may be relatively generous if luck is good, but zero if it is not. Women, in turn, more often brought back vegetal foods (nuts, berries, roots). Note that this pattern *requires* coopera-

2.   George P. Murdock, *Social Structure* (New York: Macmillan, 1949), p. 213.

tion. Neither would have had reason to bring back food for the other, without an understanding that *both* would do so. Note, too, that in such an economy neither was completely dependent on the other. Just as the male could gather and eat vegetal foods while walking about, so the female could catch small animals while she was away from camp.

But though in general the gathering and hunting societies known to us from anthropological field studies were more egalitarian, men nevertheless commanded greater authority and higher rank than women did, and their hunting contributions were given greater social attention. Meat was, as it is in modern society, given a higher valuation, and more often was the occasion for sharing with other families. These facts emphatically do *not* permit us to infer that men's higher position can be deduced from their ability to supply meat. The more important point is that even when women furnished almost as much food as men did, in societies where almost no wealth was accumulated (and thus no real class system developed), men still kept a near-monopoly over the major tasks that were viewed as more honorific. In warlike societies, of course, courage and skill in battle yielded more prestige, and women were excluded even more from the male realms of authority. In societies with large accumulations of wealth, property was in the hands of men, who had still greater resources for the domination of women.

Many modern analysts argue that the sexual division of labor is an obvious case of biological determinism. Just which sexual differences are emphasized varies, but these are common: First, as noted above, women are not as strong or as speedy as men. Second, when women are pregnant or nursing, they are handicapped; they are less useful on the hunt or in a battle. Third, they are physically or psychologically less aggressive. Fourth, the biopsychological ties that develop between mother and child make it more difficult for women to travel far from the hearth for any great length of time. These factors doubtless have some explanatory power, but perhaps not in the direction the biological determinist might wish. The general argument suggests that human beings were sensible and worked out a rational division of labor based on the most efficient allocation of the talents of the two sexes. Had this been so, the division of labor would not be based on sex, but on individual talents. We would not then observe that the same tasks may be given to men in one society, but to women in another. We might also find that many more tasks of control, management, decisions, appeals to the gods—the higher-level jobs that do *not* require strength, speed, or traveling far from home—would be given to women. Let us summarize what we know:

1. The biological differences in capacities or talents between the two sexes that might affect how well the two sexes could carry out various tasks are much too *small* to determine the large differences in sexual allocation across a broad range of societies (or to explain the curious doctrines that serve to uphold it).

2. The overlap in talent among men and women is so great that a majority of men (or women) could do almost any task as well as could members of the other sex.

3. The biological differences are too fixed in anatomy and physiology to account for the diversity of sex role allocations we observe in different societies over time and cultures.

No general explanation of the sexual division of labor is likely to account for all its complexities. Nor could we test it by comparing egalitarian and inegalitarian societies, since we do not find any of the former type. It seems clear, however, that an adequate explanation very likely has to include at least the following general points:

1. We do suppose that the biological differences between the two sexes give some advantages to men in a few activities, although not in most. However, even a small but continuing advantage would be enough to create a division of labor by sex.

2. The marginal utility of men in certain types of activities gave them, throughout history, a greater value in the eyes of both sexes, since it was and is felt that women cannot substitute for men in those particular tasks. That is, men were indispensable at certain crucial points (notably battles and hunting large game). Societies can operate very well at low levels of efficiency, but using less than the best talent at certain points might mean extinction. No woman's task is that highly evaluated across a wide range of societies, not even childbearing or lactation. In any event, people have generally considered these to be indissolubly linked with biology, and not tasks that are allocated by the society.

3. Next, it is highly likely that the greater fighting ability of the average male has, in all societies, helped to support the male claim to a greater share of privileges, including freedom of movement, escape from child care, and a choice of more interesting jobs. That one sex could have a greater command of force and its vague threat and not use it strains one's credulity.

4. Precisely because most societies have not aimed at the greatest efficiency, but a rough effectiveness, *ascription* (ascribing social tasks by birth) has always been a widely used solution for allocating almost any reward or task that was supposed to be handed out or divided. It is common in the technologically most advanced nations as well. Except where the principle grossly violates observable facts—and often then, too—ascription has these advantages: (a) Low cost of seeking information, of testing skills and so on. (b) People can begin training early, and almost any necessary skill can be learned by adulthood. (c) People's personalities and emotional needs can be shaped to the social role thus imposed early, and continued throughout life. (d) Under these conditions, few individuals will be so talented in the socially "inappropriate" skills that they will become a challenge to the system.

These facts suggest that the historical division of labor within family and society has often come perilously close to racial or caste restrictions in some modern countries. That is, the low-ranking race, caste, or sex is defined by birth as not being *able* to do certain types of prestigious work, but it is also considered a violation of propriety for members to try to do it.

Obviously, if women really could not be trained to do various kinds of male tasks, no moral or ethical prohibition would be necessary to keep them from it. They would not be able to do it anyway. It is safe to say, even without making a complete tabulation, that in no society are men and women free to choose whatever tasks they want to do and might be able to do, given the training, if we apply the criteria of efficiency, convenience, and capacity. There is no "free labor market" in this matter. This is true in China and in the Israeli *kibbutz* just as it is in the United States, although women in fact have been given important jobs in all three. That division is justified by various moral precepts and ideological principles, which are part of the socialization experience of boys and girls in the society.

ROLE RELATIONS IN THE FAMILY

Acquiring Sex Roles: Children and Adults

As in all systems of ascription, even though most people have believed that sex role behavior flows "naturally" from biological or inborn differences, societies do not leave that development to choice or chance just the same. Instead, from the earliest years, before they can understand a word, infants are told what their sexual identity is, and are praised for any behavioral evidence of appropriate activity. Western adults—and no doubt Eastern ones, too—will describe an infant as having ideal feminine traits, if told it is a girl (sweet, pretty, charming), and as having ideal masculine traits if told it is a boy (strong, aggressive, rebellious).

What begins in infancy continues through the years. For generations girls have been praised for their maternal behavior with dolls; and boys were told they were sissies if they showed the same behavior. There is considerable uniformity among societies in the role demands that define feminine and masculine behavior. Illustrating this general difference, one study of two decades ago investigated to what extent societies are likely to demand different kinds of behavior from boys and girls, as preparation for the later division of labor. In four-fifths of nearly one hundred societies for which information was available, the socialization of girls emphasized nurturance more than that of boys. In three-fifths, girls were pressed toward responsibility ("being dutiful") more than were boys. In about one-third of these cultures girls were urged to obedience more than boys, but in the remainder no substantial difference could be observed. Finally, in more than four-fifths of these societies boys were more strongly pushed toward achievement and self-reliance than were girls. Although these were tribal societies, it is likely that the findings would not be greatly different if they were drawn from most industrial societies.

Thus, from an early age boys and girls both learn about and acquire the socially approved sex roles, which in turn parallel their roles in the sexual division of labor. These sex roles, as noted before, are more complex than Victorian stereotypes would suggest, but they are fairly clear in almost all societies. *Both* males and females, of course, have "instrumental" and "expressive" duties. Women, for example, are expected to prepare food, which must be viewed as an instrumental duty. Even professional women in "liberated" circles are at least expected to organize its preparation, as well as to manage the household. Men are also expected to show tenderness toward women and children, and on occasion to smooth over family squabbles—and this must be viewed as an expressive duty.

Nevertheless, each sex is expected to lay greater emphasis on one of these two aspects of behavior than the other. Men are expected to focus more on their jobs, on matters outside the family (politics, war, building a dynasty, property), while women are still expected to be more nurturant, integrative, and domestic. Because children come to share these role definitions of feminine behavior, it is very likely still true that a cold, distant, unyielding mother creates more stress in children than does a father with a similar personality.

Sex role differences appear, as Erving Goffman has noted, in a wide range of behaviors, from handwriting to running, even when it is difficult to perceive why the society would approve of the differences, or how it creates them. Males and females are excused for very different failures, as they are approved for very different successes. For example, girls may show a fear of small heights or small animals, but boys should not. Boys are unlikely to be praised for their skill at embroidery; on the other hand, they are more likely to be excused if they break something while engaging in rough physical play. Similarly, adolescent girls in countries with universal education are encouraged to avoid the physical sciences and mathematics far more than boys are, and from that time on they drop behind in mathematical skill. Since the sexual division of labor and sex roles are linked, the lesser willingness of families to invest in higher education for girls is partly based on the lesser likelihood that girls will devote themselves as intensively to a full-time career. Thus, even when girls have had some early success in school, they are less likely to be criticized as dropouts or failures if they follow an undemanding liberal arts curriculum, work for a few years, and then settle down to a homemaker's role, interrupted now and then by employment.

Changes in all these relations are occurring, apparently almost everywhere in the world, but the trends are slow. For example, time-budget surveys in the more advanced nations show that women who hold full-time jobs also work fewer hours at domestic tasks than women who are not in the labor market. But their husbands take on only a small amount of domestic duties as part of their new, male sex roles (in the 1970s their total weekly contribution was about 6 to 11 hours). Indeed, it is possible that much of the move toward sex-neutral roles in the domestic sphere will consist (in the near future at least) in no more than a reduction of the hours wives devote (for full-time U.S. workers in the 1970's, about 25 hours) to household tasks, rather than a large increase in what husbands do at home. In the living arrangements of unmarried student couples at prestigious universities in the United States, one can observe a more conscious effort to share both burdens and decisions. However, even in such "advanced" segments of the population these are new role patterns, not at all strongly supported by the outside society as yet.

It seems clear that ideology, organized effort, social pressures, and economic resources all have some effect on the allocation of sex roles in the family. The women's movement has offered to all females a set of arguments in favor of the freedom to choose sex roles, and against domination by men. Women's groups, legal action, election pressures, public marches, and so on have supported women who wished to reduce their childcare and homemaker tasks. The demands of the outside job, and the resulting changes in the resources men and women have, will doubtless have some impact on the allocation of sex roles in the future.

Other things being equal, the closer the incomes of the man and the woman, the less dependent she is on him and the more mutually dependent they are. Mutual dependence, it can be supposed, is more likely to lead to a less traditional allocation of sex roles. From newspapers, television, or neighborhood gossip, spouses and couples can learn about other kinds of domestic arrangements: the husband who takes a clerical job to put his wife through law school; the husband who comes home to care for the children while the wife works, men who are not embarrassed to embrace each other, or to be nurturant or emotional. The number is large enough to lend some support to the individual's efforts to develop new sex role patterns, while greater economic resources in the hands of women give a somewhat stronger basis for negotiations.

Whatever the present social pressures, women in all parts of the world, except for avant-garde segments of the population in a few countries, are still fulfilling relatively traditional sex roles. They accept more restrictive rules on their own sexual behavior than males do, both before and after marriage. They are socialized to want to bear children, and take for granted that it is their duty to mother them afterward, whatever the men do. If a child is ill, it will be the mother in the family who stays home to nurse it. If elderly parents need temporary or longer-term help, it is expected that sisters rather than brothers will go home to take care of them. In conversations, men will talk more, be given more encouragement to talk, and more often overlap or drown out what the woman tries to say. At the same time, all these and other aspects of sex role behavior are being challenged now and then; some part of the eternal conflict between the two sexes now arises from the fact that individuals can never be certain that the other is going to follow a traditional sex role pattern, or reject some part of it. Consequently, parents and children are likely to engage in more conflict than in the past, when children and wives "knew their place."

Husband-Wife Relations

In most societies the husband-wife dyad has been given less prominence than relations with elders or with the kin network. But though it was not supposed that marital happiness was the prime goal of marriage, that relationship was never unimportant to the members of the dyad. In the world's great cultures, both East and West, the flow of advice over the centuries (how to please, how to rule) suggests that even in arranged marriages most people thought these relations might lead to contentment or to bitterness, and they were not trivial.

Although thousands of studies have attempted to ascertain the factors that cause marital contentment, the dominance of the wife or husband, or the many different forms of adjustment between the two, we are far from understanding these complex processes. These investigations have not yielded a solid body of knowledge. Perhaps the causes of these different forms of interaction between husband and wife change over the lifetimes of the two persons, just as they probably change over the centuries; and almost certainly the standards by which we evaluate those relations change as well.

Throughout world history until recently, most people earned their living from agriculture. It is possible that good relations between spouses were more dependent on their competence at these tasks, and almost none at all on whether they felt much love for one another, or communicated their thoughts and aspirations clearly in intimate conversation. In societies in which divorce was rare (and even in Japan and Islam where it was common), few would have supposed that romantic love or intimate communication were ideals to be taken seriously. In most traditional societies people would have supposed that almost any marriage should be lived with, unless it was extremely hurtful. It seems likely that modern people have a lower threshhold for marital discomfort, and complain about it or reject the marriage because of it at a level that once would have been viewed as quite bearable. Indeed, at least some men in the past were not so dominant in their relations with their spouses as we might expect from the marital norms, because wives who were strong by temperament could be certain that their husbands could not divorce them, however intense the domestic conflict might become.

Western fairy tales often ended with the formula, "and they lived happily ever after," but Western plays, poems, and history all contain innumerable cases of hostility or conflict between spouses. There is no way to find out how content the average wife or husband was in the past, in Asia, Africa, or Europe. Nevertheless, sociologists have generally supposed that the following statements are true of most great societies of the past. First, where divorce almost never occurred, spouses had little choice other than to accept each other as they were. Second, where a lesser intimacy between husband and wife was expected, conflict was less than in modern societies. Third, where both spouses grew up in the same traditional culture, very likely they did not have to do much adjusting anyway; both knew what to expect of the other. Fourth, where spouses married early and spent their first years together in the house of (usually) the young groom's parents, both spouses would have been prevented from engaging in much conflict; that is, elders as well as kin would not have approved of fighting. (Most Western marriages of the past, by contrast, took place between adults in their twenties, and they lived in households apart from kin). Finally, where both society and kin supported the authority of the male, the bride had little choice but to adjust to her husband, and she received little support from anyone if she wanted to oppose him.

If these suppositions are correct, it seems likely that most marriages of the past were not marked by great happiness, but they were also not full of daily conflict. Modern marriages are different. As many analysts have commented, contemporary marital unions are being asked to carry too large an emotional burden. Spouses expect more from each other than either can give in happiness, fidelity, freedom, and even personal service.

Literally thousands of studies in many Western countries have been devoted to marital adjustment itself. For well over a generation, sociologists and psychologists have tried to define and "measure" marital happiness and to ascertain which traits might best assure this blessed state. The most important early work was done under the influence of Ernest W. Burgess, and some variation of his and Leonard S. Cottrell's Marital Adjustment Scale has been used on a wide range of populations. These scales were developed by finding which background traits (age at marriage, religious affiliation, and so on) and which current behavioral patterns (expression of affection, willingness to give way to the other, and so on) are associated with marital satisfaction. Items that exhibit no correlation with adjustment or "happiness" are discarded. Such an instrument can be used as a basis for counseling couples who plan to marry, and as a diagnostic tool for locating problem areas in an engagement or marriage. Obviously, if we can make predictions of this kind, we might be more rational in ordering our lives. Indeed, such instruments are no more than a formalized or impersonal way of making the same kinds of predictions kin and friends always make when a couple plans to marry.[3] Some critics have argued that it is not possible to measure marital adjustment, and doubtless some people might call "reasonably contented" what others might call miserable. However, how we feel at any given moment is no secret to ourselves. We may report incorrectly to others, but few persons will tell themselves they are happy in marriage when they are not.

The discriminating power of the various instruments used for measuring and predicting marital adjustment has, however, never been impressive. It would be wrong to say that it is no more useful than common sense, for one clear result of these researches is that few of the intuitive "truths" about who should marry whom are secure enough to be trusted as guides. That is, many of the traits people would suppose are strong predictors of marital happiness have only a modest power. Such studies do suggest that a similar background is more likely to lead to marital happiness, if we exclude such obvious negative but shared traits as drinking or hanging around bars. A similar religious background or commitment to religious activities, ethnic background, age, class, and so on are all slightly

---

3. For recent summaries for research on these topics, see Wesley R. Burr et. al., *Contemporary Theories about the Family*, vol. 1 (New York: Free Press, 1979), especially "Theorizing about the Quality and Stability of Marriage," by Robert A. Lewis and Graham B. Spanier, pp. 268-294.

associated with expressing contentment in marriage as well as marital stability.

Similarly, if both partners are inclined toward "altruistic behavior," i.e., if both give way to each other in conflicts; if both have similar definitions of the other's proper role behavior; or if both find much value in interaction with each other, again we can predict that their marital relations will give them more happiness. This does not mean, of course, that the pleasures also eliminate the areas of tension. As in other studies of happiness, the satisfactions people feel in one area seem to be modestly correlated with the dissatisfactions or tensions in other areas. In at least one study, it has also been suggested that being able to take the role of the other, or guess accurately how the other is feeling, does not have a simple relationship with marital satisfaction: If the *wife* is empathic (makes good guesses about how her husband feels), there is more marital satisfaction, but not if the husband is empathic. Almost certainly this finding applies only to the present. If the wife is very empathic, she may be able to adjust better to his needs. On the other hand, if the husband is sensitive enough to understand the hostilities or angers his wife feels, he may simply become unhappy or hostile.

The most general finding of such studies is that individuals who have more traditional backgrounds are more likely to be contented in marriage—or are more likely at least to say they are contented. Thus, if the individual comes from a contented family and has a long acquaintanceship and engagement with the spouse, the marriage seems to be a better risk. On the other hand, diagnostic instruments that merely distinguish between traditional couples and the rest of the population are not as useful as one might wish in a time when an increasing percentage of the population comes from marriages in which there was a divorce or continued conflict, and marriages often occur between people of very different social backgrounds. Whether research on marital adjustment will be able to surmount this difficulty is as yet unclear.

Power and Authority Relations

Even the happiest family may be viewed in part as a system of power, for at all times each member is trying to move others to do something (or not to do it) against the wishes of the others. Power in all its various senses—influence, authority, domination, coercion—has become a more frequent subject of study in modern times, because those who possess it have been challenged more than in the past. In politics as in the family, those who once enjoyed unquestioned obedience can no longer be sure of it. Social analysts therefore pay far more attention to conflict than they did in the past. Family researchers now try to learn what factors determine who rules over *what*, as well as over *whom*, in the family.

Generally, sociologists use the term *power* to refer to getting one's way even though others would prefer not to conform. *Authority* refers to the extent to which other individuals believe it is right or proper that a given person exercises command. In most family situations, the individual acts in certain ways both because of his or her commitment to what is right or desirable, as well as the various social pressures from others who support that conformity. If the wife believes, as she did in many societies, that she should not eat until her husband did so, and others in the village or group felt the same way, it is likely that she would conform. On the other hand, in this case she would probably not *feel* that she was being forced to do so because of her husband's power. In many decision situations she would bow to his authority, without questioning it. That is, in most familial interaction, members simply take for granted who has the right to ask for help, command, or act without asking permission.

On the other hand, when there *is* conflict between husband and wife, or parents and children, then in addition to norms and social pressures (these pressures amount to punishments and rewards), an additional set of variables comes into prominence: The *resources* of the parties in conflict. It is in such conflict situations that we are more likely to view the outcome as caused by the *relative power* of the two spouses—for example, the wife's political support from her kin, whether she controls any independent wealth, the willingness of the parents to engage in conflict with their children, and so on.

The exact norms that define the authority and privileges of spouses differ from society to society. We can suppose that in general they grow from the advantages of the two sexes—in law, in politics, and in the economy. Thus, where men operate plows, devote themselves to war or to herding large animals, or control all the land, they have more power. We have no way of understanding how that allocation of power once arose. At best, we can seek to understand the social factors that maintain the norms of spousal authority. Moreover, an exact cross-cultural analysis of the *relative* power of spouses, and thus the factors that are associated with those differences, has yet to be carried out. But without pretending to analyze that problem fully, we can at least see that in almost all societies the traditional norms and pressures give far greater authority and privilege to husbands over wives, and parents over children. In most societies, this is also expressed by a wide array of gestures of deference, including the requirement that the wife follow behind the husband when walking along the street. More important, legal and socioeconomic arrangements in most societies put far greater resources in the hands of fathers and husbands, should any conflict about authority arise.

Except for some gathering and hunting economies, the means of livelihood will be under the control of the husband or male elders. Even in gathering and hunting societies, which are more egalitarian, if husband and wife engage in a physical fight, others will (if they enter it at all) help the husband, not the wife. If there is private property, most of it will be in the legal possession of the husband, or controlled by him. In matrilineal societies this control is weaker, even though social norms and pressures support the husband. The means of livelihood for his own conjugal family are not in his possession, but in that of his wife's brother or her lineage elders. A husband may work on his own land and give food to his sister's family (Trobrianders); or he may work on the land of his wife's lineage.

Thus his control over his own wife does not have as strong an economic base as in most agrarian societies.

On the other hand, almost all men are fathers and husbands in such societies, too. Thus they do not have a general stake in weakening the social support for the authority of husbands or fathers. All are substantially in the same position: Although they have some lineage authority over their sisters' children, and have a stake in her welfare, all have a considerable interest in maintaining the authority of their sisters' husbands, because otherwise their own authority as husbands would be threatened.

Most people, in any event, have lived in peasant societies until recently in world history, and in those societies husbands and fathers could and did control their wives and children by virtue of social norms, social pressures, and the legal and economic command of most resources available to them at their class level. Within this broad social pattern there are of course many variations. That is to say, not all husbands have controlled their wives, or parents their children. Although history has mostly been written by men about their own activities, it is replete with portraits of strong wives who dominated their husbands. Nor was the influence of wives confined only to their gifts at persuading or nagging their husbands behind the scenes. After all, some women have also been queens and empresses, owners of mercantile enterprises, or land owners in their own right. Thus, because of differences in temperament, normative patterns, and position in the social structure, some women have not simply agreed in a docile fashion to whatever their husbands commanded.

Another set of tensions has also prevented the complete domination of wives by their husbands, or children by their parents. There are inherent socioeconomic contradictions in any attempt by males to dominate or to exploit fully the members of their families. Doubtless many men have wished to rule absolutely over their families, many have tried to do so, and in every society some make an effort in that direction. However, women who are permitted no rights or voice, who are kept isolated from the world of action and skills, are also (like anyone else in that situation) not likely to be productive, useful, or even pleasant companions. At the other end of that set of choices, wives (and children) who are freer, and also in command of productive skills, as in gathering and hunting societies and increasingly in modern industrial ones, simply contribute far more to their household and to the comfort of the husband. However, they are also more resistant to domination.

Since husbands/fathers are like other people, they would prefer to rule through the domination of love. If one is loved absolutely, making others conform to one's wishes is easier. On the other hand, that is not likely to occur unless they reciprocally care about the joys and sorrows of their wives and children. If they feel much love and caring in return, then they are forced to stop short of the harsh, arbitrary rule that laws and socioeconomic resources might give them. Thus, the resources for domination are not entirely in the hands of a male tyrant.

As traditional authority has been increasingly questioned over the past several decades, family research has focused more on the *relative re-*

sources of family members. To make such comparisons, researchers have asked members of the family (wives, husbands, children) to make certain kinds of decisions, and then observed how initial decisions are changed after discussion. Other bits of evidence may also be used, such as who handles the money, whether most of the money is spent for the pleasure or comfort of the husband, or how authority is given to different members of the family, depending on which kind of activity is being considered. With reference to such comparisons, we must keep in mind that we obtain somewhat different findings if we observe different *kinds* of decisions in different areas of family action. In day-to-day activities, some wives may seem to control almost everything, but when a more important decision arises (buying a house, making investments), their husbands take control. Thus, the *weightiness* of the decision may affect who makes it.

The freedom to act is not the same as compelling others to go along. In Western societies of the past (as in the present period), well-to-do wives often had considerable freedom in their leisure time, in making small purchases and household arrangements, without being able to influence their husbands much in other areas. Third, the apparent possession of resources should not keep us from looking for who really controls. For example, in the early stages of capitalism in Italy and Japan, thousands of women worked for wages in spinning mills, but they actually had very little autonomy. The decision about hiring them, as well as how the money was saved and what it was used for, was usually in the hands of their fathers.

Another set of complexities has to do with *class*. In general, the authority of the husband is correlated with social rank. Very likely this is true of all societies with class systems. In Western nations, women in the higher social strata have more money to spend as they choose, and generally enjoy more freedom, but they have less influence over their husbands than do wives in the lower social strata. Lower-class husbands are more likely to claim authority simply because they are males, but actually they have to concede more voice to their wives. In the higher social strata, husbands are less likely to assert the values of patriarchal authority, in part because education weakens that conviction, but in fact they manage to have more power anyway. They command more resources *relative* to those of their wives. Their wives are somewhat less likely to work, but even if they do, the discrepancy between the two incomes is greater than in the lower social strata. Husbands in the upper ranks are less dependent on wifely services, and can more easily purchase them. Since these differences in resources are not as great in black families as in white families in the United States, it follows that black women enjoy somewhat more influence in the family than do white wives. This is also true in the upper social strata, where a higher percentage of black wives than of white wives have more education or income than their husbands.

This class pattern is also influenced, as just noted, by education. Increasingly, in most societies, as husbands are influenced by the egalitarian values of higher education, they feel less willing to assert their traditional authority. Thus, education may counter in part the greater resources husbands command at that class level. Similarly, within some industrializing countries (for example, Yugoslavia and Greece) some well-to-do men still live in a traditional or even agricultural setting, and thus exert far more authority than other men at the same income level but with somewhat less education and somewhat less exposed to modernizing influences.

Within this general area of relative resources and normative differences, we can assert several further relationships that are likely to be observed in most modern nations. As already suggested, the greater the education of the woman or the man, the more likely it is that one or both will agree to some extent with egalitarian norms—with the general belief that husbands and wives should share equally in both goods and authority. Moreover, under those circumstances, the woman is more likely to express her opposition to the traditional allocation of authority. She is also more likely to challenge the exercise of the man's power if she is employed full-time, and especially if she has a job that yields a high level of prestige and income. Note that in this case, the relative resources of husband and wife are more in balance.

Adolescents in modern society have far more autonomy than in traditional societies of the past, East or West. This simply confirms the general explanatory power of relative resources. To be sure, adolescents do not often command a means of livelihood, and thus are dependent on their parents. On the other hand, modern parents can no longer produce jobs for their children. Typically they do not have productive land to pass on, and thus a means of livelihood that could be taken away from the children if they did not conform. In the past, when most made their living from the land, parental control of land gave them great power. Modern parents do pass on a means of livelihood to their children by assuring them an adequate education, but very few parents gain much power thereby. Parents do not feel they can threaten to take away this major resource in order to enforce their authority, because the norms of all industrial societies are strongly against carrying out this kind of threat.

A further complexity in power relations in the home may be observed in the slightly increased participation of husbands in domestic activities. On the one hand, this is a move toward greater equality, to the extent that husbands share a slightly greater part of the burden of house care and children. On the other hand, to the extent that men increasingly enter a domain where women once had full control, women lose some of their autonomy.

Among the relative resources a spouse can have is other kin. Thus, if a husband must spend alternate years in his wife's village, or must spend a year or so working for his wife's kin (to pay for the wife), he is likely to achieve fewer victories when he has conflicts with his wife. Similarly, in most large, extended households (as in India or China), the wife is surrounded by *his* relatives, and in the present as in the past the wife in that situation has less influence. Of course grandparents were usually part of any extended household, and in general could be expected to support their grandchildren, not the in-marrying wife. However, grandparents play different roles in different societies. Even in some traditional societies, grandparents were not always authority figures, ruling all members by virtue of their privileges as elders. For example, there were often informal or "joking" relations between grandparents and grandchildren.

Although that pattern is not standardized in the United States, it is evident that at the present time many grandparents strive to make a kind of easy-going coalition with their grandchildren, against the seeming authority of the middle generation (the parents of the grandchildren). The prime differentiating factor between these two types of societies, the one in which there is an informal or playful relationship between grandparents and grandchildren, and the other in which the elder generation are authority figures, seems to be whether the *grandparent continues to rule the parent*. That is, in many traditional societies the elder generation continues to direct the daily conduct of the next generation, often in the same house. In that situation, custom does not permit a relaxed, permissive relationship between grandparent and grandchild.

PARENT-CHILD RELATIONS AND SOCIALIZATION

Throughout history, parents have complained that their children were not as obedient or helpful as *they* were when young, but at least they could expect that moral authorities, their elders, and tradition would support them in any conflict with their children. Moreover, the cohorts of children did not become a group, a social force in their own right. In most major countries, by contrast, new knowledge about how to rear children, the undermining of traditional authority, and new social problems persuade many parents that the socialization of the young is difficult, and they can no longer be sure their parental opinions are best. Since daughters and sons will usually not follow the occupations of their parents (although almost all daughters will become housewives, part-time or full-time), they are not even dependent on their parents for farming land or a specific job. Thus, the forces that once put great power in the hands of parents are much weaker than in the past.

Although the specific customs and social skills each child must learn will vary greatly from one culture to another, many of the social psychological processes that affect socialization are similar. Here, we shall focus on only three aspects of this family task. The first is simply what it is that societies demand of the younger generation. The second is how some biological patterns affect socialization; and the third is the main factors that increase or decrease the extent to which children do acquire the patterns of their social system. In almost every chapter of this book, we have commented on the relations between parents and children. Here we focus on the specific processes of socialization.

What parents try to teach their children is whatever the society views as necessary to behave adequately as an adult later on. All this social behavior has two main aspects or modalities: children must learn to be *competent* at ordinary skills, both social and physical; and they are also expected to *feel* appropriately about goodness or evil, family ancestors, and a wide range of other events, actions, and objects. The importance of the second modality is clear: The costs of social control are much lower if people actually have negative feelings about forbidden things and positive feelings about approved ones. If people are led to *want* to do the things the society wants done, it is easier to get them to do those things.

The Content of Socialization

The content of socialization may usefully be seen as made up of several types of learning, some of which are more difficult than others. Certain skills must be acquired if the person is to become a part of the society at all. These include learning how to eat and drink correctly, how to talk, control one's toilet behavior, and so on. Children are rewarded as they learn these skills. Parents spend much time in encouraging these first beginnings of competence, but almost all children acquire these elementary skills sooner or later as part of growing up. Physical and neurological maturation makes these tasks easier with each passing month, and children themselves take pleasure from their increased skill.

The second set of skills is somewhat more difficult, since it includes some complex bits of knowledge or ability to cope with the physical or social environment. These include such capacities as spearing a seal through the ice, driving a giant trailer truck, or using a computer. Typically, these skills will yield intrinsic pleasure as well as some material and social rewards. Many societies do not succeed in persuading their members that they should work extremely hard at acquiring the highest level of skill possible, but all do manage to socialize the younger generation to master enough of these complex skills, both social and physical, to permit the society to continue to operate reasonably well.

It is the third segment of socialization that is more difficult to teach or learn, and that is the source of much of the conflict between parents and children in any generation. This segment is made up of the *obligations* family members owe to one another: how elder children should protect their younger brothers and sisters, paying respect to parents, helping with chores, and so on. Socialization for this third segment is somewhat more difficult because many of the rules seem arbitrary and without any obvious justification, but still more because what one is told to do or forbidden to do is a burden or a self-denial. What is a right for one person is an obligation for another and what one family member wants is obtained at the expense of another. Children do not easily absorb the rules of fairness or equality, for that may mean giving up a toy to another child. Most of the interpersonal rules parents try to teach children have this disagreeable quality, which makes children somewhat less than enthusiastic about such obligations. Consequently, the role prescriptions taught to children are always under some strain: One or the other person must yield or obey, or give some service, and children (like adults) often feel no strong allegiance to the rule when it applies to themselves. That is, norms are always under some strain when they violate the individual's self-interest. Children can get some benefit by ignoring or violating the rule, even though this risks parental threats, persuasion, or punishment. Much of parent-child interaction focuses on this area of socialization, and contains very few social rules that require children to enjoy themselves, to do what pleases them. Instead, parents spend much of their energies trying to persuade children that though the rules may be somewhat costly at times, they are desirable in themselves. What determines how successful parents are at achieving this goal?

Factors in Effective Socialization

Let us consider some of the family patterns that seem to have the greatest effect on the extent to which children come to accept the norms of their family and society, and to adjust to the demands of others. The first important point is that both children and adults vary greatly, and that the child is not simply molded by overpowering parental forces. Just as some parents are more sensitive and understanding than others, so some children are more competent at expressing their needs or molding their parents to fit their own needs. Thus, although parents and children are biologically connected, they do not necessarily adjust well to one another. Some parents never learn how to reward their children wisely, so as to elicit the kind of behavior they desire. Even if they do learn, sometimes they feel they ought not to offer bribes or rewards for behavior the child should carry out without any special payment: The child *ought* to be good anyway. In addition, even when parents are wise enough to know how they should interact with their child or children, they may not be able to change their own behavior that much. They may be simply unable to be patient, to give a great deal of love, or to devote a great deal of time to the child.

In tribal as in industrial societies, parents try to socialize their children to live according to the norms and values of the society. In both Communist and non-Communist countries, child-care organizations seek the same goal. Which factors are especially effective in achieving that goal? Systematic observation and research have suggested that these are most important:

1. Warmth, nurturance, and affection from parents or other persons (teachers, peers) who are trying to socialize the child.
2. Identification of the child with the parent or socializer.
3. Authority of the parent.
4. Consistency.
5. Giving freedom to the child.
6. Giving explanations and reasons.
7. Punishment.

Warmth and Nurturance. If those who socialize the child are loving, the child is likely to reciprocate that love and to care about their wishes or feelings. Warm parents are more likely than others to be alert to the needs of the child, and to offer rewards that will reinforce what they consider good behavior. If the parent is warm, he or she can more effectively arouse guilt or concern in the child by withdrawing love; the hostile or abusive parent cannot use that threat as easily. The child who frequently experiences coldness or anger has much less to lose by disobedience.

Identification.   A warm, nurturant relationship is also more likely to motivate the child to identify with the parent or parent substitute. Thus, what hurts the parent will also hurt the child. When the child identifies with his or her parents, he or she gets more pleasure from good behavior. Through the process of identification, the child accepts the wishes of the parents as his or her own, so that those role patterns become part of the child's personality.

Recognized Authority.   Social commentators have frequently complained that modern parents and teachers have lost their authority. That is to say, young people do not accept their right to command. The combination of love and authority has a great impact on the child's belief in or commitment to the values of the group. This does not, of course, imply physical punishment. The use of naked force by parents or parental substitutes does increase simple obedience out of fear, but it is likely to decrease the child's moral commitment to the rules. Perhaps the most important element in parental authority is the ability of parents to convince the child that they stand for the moral community itself, that the rules they have laid down are not viewed as whimsical or selfish, but are part of the moral order of the society itself. Obviously, this process is most effective when the parents themselves obey those rules.

Consistency.   Consistency is of great importance, but the reader will recognize that parents cannot always be consistent. After all, parents may not even know of some of the child's rule violations. In addition, each parent may punish or reward for different kinds of behavior. Often, parents do not praise or reward when the child is being good. In addition, much experimentation in learning has suggested that one type of inconsistency, being rewarded much of the time but not all of the time, may be especially effective in creating a deeply held belief or attitude. This social pattern is fairly common in childhood. One of its consequences is a continuing expectation or hope that if one is good *this* time, one will be rewarded; or an inner anxiety that *this time* one will not get away with the violation.

Freedom.   Although giving freedom to the child suggests a laxity about the rules, this social pattern—very common among tribal societies—increases the child's inner commitment. We can observe much behavior in support of this general fact. For example, we are much more likely to believe in a rule, and to follow it, if we have chosen it ourselves than we are if it has been imposed upon us. Members of a group who make a decision together are also more likely to believe in it and to follow it with action.

Thus, the pattern of very strong punishments or lavish rewards that leave little choice or freedom is not as effective a learning situation as being gently induced to conform. A third alternative, complete laxity, in which the child is allowed his or her own way almost entirely, does not create much inner commitment to rules either. Then the child does not even learn what others believe is desirable, and sees no great reason to care about conformity at all. Some permissive parents may persuade their child that they simply do not care what the child does.

Communication.   Implicit in this discussion is the view that all the patterns of socialization are reinforced by *communication*—that is, by the explanations and reasons parents or teachers may give the child. Both adults and children are much more likely to accept rules as their own if others explain why the rule should be followed. This result is partly caused by the simple fact that giving reasons requires more social interaction, and more caring, between the person being socialized and the person doing the socializing. Thus, the child comes to see that he or she is part of the rule-making process. Giving explanations also links the specific rule or situation with the larger system of moral rules the society upholds. This pattern helps the child to see the social situation through the eyes of the other person, for explanations usually show how the rule might affect other people. In addition, of course this process gives some respect to the child, because she or he is treated not as a helpless person being commanded, but as a person whose opinions are being considered.

Punishment.   The results of punishment in socialization are complex and even contradictory. Punishment has a strong, lasting, crude, and negative effect. It does not teach the child to explore or to create, but of course much childhood learning consists in prohibitions: not to start a fire in the house, not to break things, not to hit one's younger brother. Punishment is somewhat less precise than rewards, for the child does not easily learn what is *right*. One can be punished many times for doing something wrong, without ever learning exactly what is right, or how to do it. On the other hand, in much of social learning, authority figures do not want the individual to learn just how closely he or she can come to a violation or wrongdoing. Punishment helps to create an attitude of fear, anxiety, or rejection as the individual approaches the possibility of violating a rule.

Much experimental evidence about animals, and observation of abused children, demonstrates that severe punishment is not effective. It arouses resentment, and often a rejection of the parent or parental substitute. It teaches the child that it is dangerous to do certain things, but the child may simply become clever at hiding a violation, without ever making the rule a part of his or her own personality. Moreover, extreme punishment, like extreme social deprivation, may eventually cause the child to develop neurotic or psychopathic behavior.

Parent-Youth Conflict

In industrial societies, parents want their children to be emotionally dependent when young, but adults are expected to be relatively independent. Thus, both parents and teachers attempt to motivate the child to make his or her own decisions, set up an independent household, and become competent in some kind of occupation. Adolescent or adult love relationships also motivate the individual in many societies to move out into the world. In most industrial societies, *peer groups* in the adolescent period have become increasingly important, for they help to set nonfamilial norms, which are generally at variance with those of the young person's family. Indeed, it is likely that whenever the surrounding society makes demands on individuals that are very different from those within the family, some type of age or peer group will arise to help in this sometimes difficult transition between the two types of social patterns, dependency in youth and autonomy in adulthood.

It is especially in Western societies that the phenomenon of "adolescent rebellion" has been reported, usually with alarm. Most people take for granted the assertion that parents and youth are in more frequent and intense conflict in modern nations than in other regions or times. To be sure, most research suggests that parents and their adolescent children often agree far more than parents believe, and most young people probably move closer toward some of their parents' opinions as they themselves marry. This is evident from the simple observation that whenever any given generation of adolescents becomes adult, we do not see any sharp, sudden break in social behavior. Nevertheless, the conflicts between parents and teenagers are often strong, and their roots are interesting.

In a period of rapid social change, the society in which the child grows up is different from that in which his parents grew up. The parent calls on his or her childhood experience as a guide, but much of that has become irrelevant, and the old standards may no longer apply. To consider an obvious example, young adults in the 1960s were the first generation to grow up under the constant threat of atomic warfare, with the contraceptive pill easily available, with television constantly suggesting a limitless material abundance to be seized, with the threat of world pollution and the exhaustion of natural resources, with the loss of privacy and the increasing power of national governments. These and other changes have persuaded many adolescents as well as adults that the older traditions are simply no longer an adequate guide. Thus, the two sets of people, children and parents, are not only at different points in the life cycle—one older, and one younger—but at the *same* points in their life cycles their experiences are very different.

In addition, parental roles combine both authority and intimacy, power and love, while the authority of the parent is steadily diminishing as the teenager matures. This group of tensions is seen in all modern societies, in contrast to most tribal societies, because there are no well-recognized *steps* by which various areas of authority are gradually given up by older adults and gradually assumed by young adults. There are few or no rituals by which we recognize that an individual has become "grown-up," and is no longer subject to the authority of his or her parents. In most Western societies there is also a relatively free market in ideas, and considerable profit to be made in being a moral authority, a guru, or a merchant of new fads. Consequently, many adults find it to their interest to convince younger people that they should deny the authority of the parental tradition and take up the newest hobby, philosophy, political program, or clothing style. Young people can, in turn, carry on their conflict with their parents by calling upon alternative authorities to justify their actions.

So it is apparently characteristic of large-scale societies undergoing rapid social change that young people in their late teens rebel against their parents to a greater or lesser degree. Modern revolutionary societies attempt to harness that rebellion by calling upon the new generation to invest all its energies in the creation of a new world. Of course, time carries its own irony, for time eventually stills the turbulence of any given generation, whose members themselves are likely in turn to become parents facing *their* rebellious adolescents.

CHAPTER 6 SOCIAL PROCESSES IN THE EXTENDED HOUSEHOLD

We have been analyzing the household made up of husband, wife, and children because that is a common family unit in almost all societies. However, as we have also emphasized, whatever the elementary family unit (mother and children; father and child; husband and wife), it is always embedded in a network of kinship relations. We shall go on to discuss the consequences of such networks in Chapter 7. Here, we focus on the family relations that are to be observed when one elementary family unit is joined with one or more such units in the same household. We shall not lose sight of the elementary family unit, since we shall continue to compare the larger unit with the smaller.

The importance of the extended family household in its various forms was doubtless overplayed in the research of a generation ago, for it was thought that this was the common pattern in most peasant societies of the past. Analysis of the Indian, Japanese, Arab, and Chinese societies often described their family systems as made up of large households containing several generations under one roof, along with collateral relatives. It became clear, from the author's historical review of nearly a century of world development, that this family form was statistically uncommon. That is, at any given time the family made up of husband and wife, parents and children, or wife and children was much more common. The structural and economic reasons for this are analyzed in this chapter. It is also clear that the extended family was a *phase* of the larger family cycle: for at least some part of the individual's life, he or she might be married and living with parents or parents-in-law. Note that this often happens in the contemporary United States.

Such complex households yield a very different set of family experiences, and thus deserve our attention. It is surely no trivial matter if after marriage a young man could once expect to remain in the household of his father, who would also have the right to make all major decisions for him as long as the father lived; or a young bride could not expect to be in charge of her own domestic unit until her parents-in-law died. People do have experiences of this kind even in industrial societies, though the individual may view these events as accidents of personal history or temporary episodes, as when grandparents come to live with their adult children while the grandchildren are still in the home. More important, a consideration of this range of household types gives us a greater understanding of family dynamics both now and in the past. Let us consider why it does.

First, in many societies, and perhaps most peasant societies, the large family household was probably an ideal. Indeed, it appears frequently in American literature about the family of a century ago: Life on grandmother's farm, with a benevolent elderly couple ruling over married and unmarried sons, unmarried daughters, and grandchildren, all living of course in harmony. When many members of the society accepted that ideal, a man who became successful would try to create that type of household if he could do so. As one might expect with such ideals, such households have been much more usual among the upper strata. We shall analyze later the advantages or disadvantages of complex households. It is also likely that even in modern industrialized countries such households, when they can be administered successfully, can more easily resist the eroding effects of industrialization. In addition, even when the large extended household is not common, the family norms that helped to support that system may continue for generations, in the form of rights and obligations. People who have grown up in that tradition feel more strongly that they have real obligations to their kin, and are likely to engage in more elaborate social exchanges with them than would occur in a modern Western urban setting. Family members who live by such ideals are likely to gain some social esteem from living up to these traditional obligations. But before we analyze the extended family in detail, let us first look at the range of family forms and their distribution.

TYPES OF FAMILY FORMS AND THEIR DISTRIBUTION

Almost all the world's population lives in family units of some kind, but just who lives with whom, and how large these units are, varies not only from one society to another but also from one class to another within the same society. These variations result from many economic and organizational factors, accidents of personal and family history, and different rules or customs about who should establish independent households.

Types of Households

In the United States, about one-fifth of all households are "one-person" units, while less than one percent contain ten or more persons.

Both extremes are viewed as permissible within the society, but neither is considered to be "typical." When most people think of a family, they think of a unit made up of a married couple alone, or a married couple with children. In the late 1970s, about 40 percent of all families were made up of a married couple with children under 18 years of age, and without any other relatives or lodgers in the household.[1] This is the *nuclear* family.

But there are other family forms. *Polygyny* and *polyandry* are the two types of polygamy that may create an extended family. In the first, one man has two or more wives, so that the household is made up of two or more nuclear families, in which the same man is the husband. A common form is *sororal* polygyny, in which a man marries two or more sisters. In polyandry (a much less common form of marriage), one woman is wife to two or more men, but of course there is only one set of children. A common subtype is *fraternal* polyandry, in which one woman is married to two or more brothers. A given household may be enlarged generationally (grandparents, grandchildren) as well as laterally by the addition of other nuclear units, such as by the marriage of the children of the household, who stay there after marriage. Lateral extension occurs because of the inclusion of in-laws, usually the in-marrying brides.

Although the foregoing household forms are also extended families, the term *extended* family is more commonly applied to a system in which the ideal family contains several generations living under one roof. For example, it refers to the family system of prerevolutionary China, in which a man and his wife ideally lived with the families of their married sons, their unmarried sons and daughters, and of course any grandchildren or great-grandchildren in the paternal line. All would live together in a compound, great house, or in tents close together. The term "extended" can also be applied to the *stem* family common in feudal and postfeudal Europe, among some immigrant farmer groups here and there in the United States, and the Tokugawa Japan. Under this system only one child, usually the eldest son, inherited the family property. After marriage, he stayed there with his wife and children. After the father's death, he had some responsibility for his sisters until they married, and for his brothers until they were grown. Thus the property, family title, and responsibility were in the hands of one person.

The *joint* family of India is sometimes called "extended," but it is best to use the more specific term. Its principal members are, *co-parceners*—that is, male persons who have a right to the products of the family property, which was supposed to be passed down intact from one generation to the next. These are the brothers in any generation, together with their sons in the next generation, plus sons of the third generation. The domestic household included all the brothers in each generation in a direct line, *from* a given set of brothers, as long as the unit was still intact, and of course including any in-marrying brides and their children. The emphasis was placed on brothers, since in Hindu tradition a male child from birth had

---

1.   "Marrying, Divorcing and Living Together in the United States Today," *Population Bulletin,* 32, 5 (October 1977), 29.

rights in the family property. It is generally assumed that this type of co-parcenary property has become less common in modern India, although many brothers continue to assert their common rights in farmland, even when they have themselves entered urban occupations. The family members who were supposed to be in the Indian household were not significantly different from those expected to be in the Chinese household, but the social definition of the property was somewhat different: it focused on ownership of the property by the brothers, rather than rulership by the eldest patriarch. Chinese property was usually divided among the sons on their father's death.

Both in modern times and in the past, even when Hindu brothers live separately, many have continued to think of themselves as a joint family if they continue to respect their common obligations. These include a joint budget, authority in the hands of the oldest male, and joint maintenance of the property. They may consider themselves a joint family even if they do not do all of those things but only engage in many social exchanges and share some ownership of property. The oldest male, who is head of the family, cannot dispose of the property if it has been defined as co-parcenary. In modern times, the legal status of this unit was changed to include sisters and widows as being entitled to a share of the property as well.

Of course, rules of residence affect the composition of the household. In Western societies, for hundreds of years in the past, *neolocality* has been the rule. That is, it was considered proper that a young married couple set up a new residence, apart from the parental home, or commonly the newly married couple created their own independent unit by taking over the direction of the farm itself. This often meant that young people delayed marriage until that new home or transference of property was made possible by the elder generation. In patrilineal societies several different types of residence rules could be found. The residence rule that accompanies patrilineality is *patrilocality,* which was the majority pattern in patrilineages. Under those rules, the new family unit was likely to become part of the groom's father's household. More common in matrilineages was *matrilocality:* the couple would reside near the wife's family.

Before continuing our analysis, let us note the importance of residence rules, aside from whether they created extended households. The rules of residence determine in part who associates with whom after marriage. If a man moves to take up residence near his wife and her lineage, the likelihood increased that he would have frequent social interaction with her kin, and of course with her brothers, who were the dominant figures in her matrilineage. Residence rules also affect another set of relations. In any society whose economy depended partly on hunting, trapping, lumbering, quarrying, or fishing, the man who moved far would thereby render less useful some of his localized, geographical knowledge. In most societies residence is patrilocal, but where it was matrilocal, the man only rarely moved to a new community. Instead, he moved to a different part of the village, near his wife's relatives. In a few instances, by contrast, the group was migratory anyway, in a territory which the man knew well. In many societies, the wife's contribution to the food supply was very large, since much of it was simply gathered from hour to hour (fruits, nuts, roots, small animals) while wandering over a specific territory. As long as her residence was not charged greatly, those skills would still be valuable. In societies in which the woman did move, there was more likelihood that a bride price was paid because her group lost a producer. By contrast, in a matrilocal society a substantial bride price was not usual. In that case, her skills would not be lost to her family (as her children were not), and thus no payment would be required.

The Distribution of Household Forms

Before analyzing some of the traits of these various forms of the family, let us first ask how common they are. If we define a society as polygynous when the *ideal* is for a man to acquire two or more wives, then a majority have been polygynous: in Murdock's classic sample of a generation ago, 193 out of 234 tribal societies were polygynous. These were, of course, relatively small societies, some of them numbering only a few hundred members or less. Some societies permit polygyny although it is not an ideal. However, the great civilizations of the world have not been permitted polygyny. Islam did, but China, Japan, India, and the West did not, for most of their last thousand years of history. Murdock also calculated the number of societies in which as many as 20 percent of the unions were polygynous and concluded that about 70 percent of the polygynous societies were above the 20 percent line. Unfortunately, there is no way to test such an estimate, since many ethnographic reports did not contain an actual count of such household units.

Polygyny as an ideal was more widespread in Africa than in any other region. It appeared in about nine out of ten of the sub-Saharan tribes for which data were available. In one evaluation of this phenomenon, it was estimated that one out of three males lived in polygyny at some time, and that the average number of wives per married man was 1.5.[2] We have not been able to find estimates for modern Africa, but polygyny now occurs primarily when a man has a wife in his native village, but also marries a more educated wife in the city. Almost certainly, the percentage of men in such circumstances is low.

Only under very special conditions has it ever been possible for a majority of men in a society to have more than one wife at a time. The primary limitation is that at birth, males outnumber females slightly, about 103:100 (this is called a *sex ratio*), and in subsequent years the mortality rate is higher among males. Females outnumber males substantially only in the later years of life, long after the normal age of marriage. Thus, polygyny is not possible unless a society loses a large segment of its males through war, captures many women, or forces many of its males to postpone marriage. Some part of the discrepancy between ideal and reality is made up by girls

---

2.   Vernon R. Dorjahn, "The Factor of Polygamy in African Demography," in *Continuity and Change in African Cultures,* eds. William R. Bascom and Melville J. Herskovits (Chicago: University of Chicago Press, 1959), pp. 102–105.

marrying early in life, and men marrying late in life. Thus, if females marry at age 14 and males at age 25, a surplus of nine marital years per female is created, which can be distributed among the men who are able to acquire an additional wife. In some of the warlike African kingdoms, young men sometimes were required to spend many of their adult years in military regiments, and were not permitted to marry.

Although the Western view of polygyny is a set of fantasies about harems, in fact additional wives were not typically a garden of delights; they were partly an investment. For example, women in most African tribes worked at agriculture or trading, and usually produced more than they and their children cost. As in other profitable economic enterprises, however, initial capital is necessary, in this case the funds needed for the additional marriage. A man whose kin could not secure an adequate bride price, or whose personal resources were insufficient, could not obtain secondary wives even though they would not be an economic burden.

More important, in most societies it was not considered appropriate for all men to acquire additional wives, even if by some chance they might have been able to pay for them. If a man's social rank was thought to be low, or his power modest, he might have been criticized for stepping out of place. By contrast, an older man of high station, or a politically powerful one, might enlarge his entourage of wives as a validation of his status, or to cement an alliance with another family or political figure. In a precarious hunting economy such as the Eskimo once was, a second wife betokened the prowess of a great hunter who needed more than one wife in order to take care of all the skins and meat he brought home. The general conclusion is clear: In most tribal societies, as in most major civilizations, few men have had to cope with the problems, or enjoyed the possible delights, of polygyny. Since modern family laws in most new nations over the past generation have forbidden polygyny, while economic and social pressures have undermined its bases, here we are necessarily talking about the past, although in some cases that past is only a generation ago.

In China, a man could bring a concubine into his household. Some scholars consider these women to have been at least "secondary wives," since public rituals announced the arrival of some of them, and various laws and rulings defined their social status, as well as that of their children, as members of the family. On the other hand, taking a concubine was close to a genuine purchase, and only the rich could afford one. Japan was also legally monogamous, but there too a successful man might buy a concubine. Thus, he might have in effect two sets of children, although only the children of the legal wife would be viewed as equal in rank to the children of other highly placed families. Polygyny was possible in India, but Hindu law did not support the practice, and few men had more than one wife at a time. More commonly, a man simply put aside his first wife and took another. Under Islamic law a man might have as many as four wives, and even in relatively recent generations many men married more than once. But few ever had more than one wife at a time, and the Koran expresses disapproval of polygyny.

Large households were not, then, typically created through polygyny. On the other hand, large households could be created through residence rules that urged or pressed young men not to leave the parental home when they married. Until very recently, the usual descriptions of the Chinese, Arab, or Indian family systems showed the extended family as the usual mode of living. In fact, the multigenerational household was not common except among well-to-do families. In any event, even with the spotty historical data at our command, it is clear that large-scale, multigenerational households could not have been common in most areas. We know from the simple data on family size that such households must have been rare. Let us look at some examples.

China.   In a 1942 survey, the average household size in China ranged from 4.1 to 6.9 persons in various provinces. If the ideal extended household was to contain a grandparental couple, at least one or two married sons and their children, plus some unmarried daughters, it is clear that the actual numbers are too small to create an ideal extended family. In an urban survey conducted during the 1920s, the average size of a household was 5.8 persons. Modern scholars now estimate that throughout much of the past two thousand years, the average family in China probably included only about five to six persons. Thus, although the patriarch who is surrounded by his married sons and his grandsons was accorded much esteem in China, the ideal was not typically achieved. Doubtless a major cause was simple mortality. In China, as in much of the world until very recently, the average life expectation probably did not exceed the range of 28 to 38 years, which meant that a fairly high proportion of both sons and daughters died before marriage. Mortality also took its toll among the older generation. In addition, sons could demand a division of the property after their father's death, and some wives pressed them to do so.

In addition, a simple economic fact reduces the likelihood of large size still further. If a patriarch had a great deal of land, or a large business, then it would be economically advantageous to his sons or grandsons to stay in the same household and give their labor to the enterprise, since their rewards from that contribution would probably be greater than what they could obtain elsewhere. On the other hand, in a society in which perhaps 95 percent of the population were poor peasants with tiny plots of land, most families would not have enough land to justify the labor investment for even two sons' families. Historically, many were so poor that they had to sell some of their children in order to survive.

The Middle East.   In the Arab family system, both polygyny and the retention of the married sons in the family could have built up very large households. Indeed, it is possible that until the past generation most Arabs lived in such a household for at least some time in their lives, if only briefly. On the other hand, at any given time, most would not be living in a large household. Among the desert Bedouin, a young man was usually given a tent of his own when he married, though of course his new family would still continue to be part of the camp of his father.

The large Arab household was not simply a legend, for even in large cities in Syria, there were a few households of forty or more members in the 1920s. Of course they were not common. Much more typical data are the spotty historical records which suggest that even in the nineteenth century the average family size was modest (in one Egyptian province in the 1880s, 5.5 members). Sixty years ago, only one-third of Egyptian families had as many as six to ten members, while 60 percent had one to five members— again numbers much too small to encompass the great extended household. The few data that are available for Morocco, Algeria, and Egypt of two generations ago give an average size of 4.0 to 5.1 members. These data, combined with other survey and census data, undermine the assumption that most Arab households were made up of several generations of families in the male line.

India.   India deserves special attention, because scholars have debated among themselves for a generation as to how prevalent the co-parcenary or joint family was in India, and especially how much effect the industrializing process has had on the family system.

In the 1971 census, less than 7 percent of Indian families had ten members or more, whereas 25 percent had three members or less, and 43 percent had four to six members. Since 68 percent of the families had six members or less, a genuine joint family (made up of an elder generation of brothers, including any married brothers and their wives and children, plus unmarried sisters) has been uncommon. That small a figure might suggest a change from the past if a large household was once common. One might suppose that change is occurring, since a larger percentage of small households are to be found in Indian cities than in rural regions, and a higher percentage of large households are to be found in rural areas. Interpreted plausibly, these data might show that the joint family has declined. Unfortunately, that easy conclusion is weakened by the fact that the census of 1901 also reported a small average household size of 5 persons, with a range from 4.4 to 6.2 in different regions. In addition, colonial rulers at that time, long before any substantial effect of industrialization could have occurred, were already commenting that the joint family was not so common as had been supposed.

The joint family cannot be dismissed as a myth, however. First, as we noted earlier, to the extent that it is an ideal, men who achieve rank and wealth will establish such a household, and will receive some esteem for it. If the large household is associated with high class position, it should continue to enjoy the esteem of others. Second, some modern Indian scholars have argued that even when members of an extended family network do not live in the same household, they may share a common budget and follow the advice of the same family leader. Third, perhaps a goodly percentage of the population may live in such a joint household at some time in their lives, as their families pass through the phase of being joint. Finally, as we shall note later, under some circumstances the larger extended household offers some advantages in the modern world, as it did in the past. Now let us look more closely at the Indian joint family.

The Indian Joint Family

An examination of the Indian joint or co-parcenary family throws light on the dynamics of all extended families. First, it is based on the relations among adult males, more than on the conjugal bonds between husband and wife. Arranged marriages are still typical in India, and they reduce the chances that an intense marriage bond might break up the unit into nuclear households. Although the sexes are not segregated so much before and after marriage as they once were, segregation is still more widespread than in Western nations, and this again reduces the likelihood that spouses will feel the need to become independent.

The Indian family emphasizes respect between generations, as well as between spouses, rather than an easy familiarity. The husband is not supposed to express romantic feelings toward his wife in the presence of other adult males, and most of the time others will be present. Even the very intense emotional feelings between Indian mothers and sons are supposed to be expressed in privacy, at least after the son grows beyond infancy. Men and women now may eat together, but under traditional domestic norms men ate first. Adult males were not supposed to take care of only their own children, but of all the children of the household. Thus, many rules reduced the tendency of the nuclear family to break away and form a separate household. On the other hand, in any large unit there are many pressures toward fission. Wives who entered a large household did not feel as much allegiance to that unit as their husbands felt, for they were treated to some extent as outsiders until they had produced sons. In the past as in the present, wives are likely to feel that their own husbands contribute more than they receive, that their children are deprived of a fair share, and that adjustment to so many others is difficult. One may say that the joint family, especially as it emerges in Indian literature, was compassionate, for it took care of the helpless; but it was also indulgent, for it also took care of the lazy. On the other hand, a woman with diligent sons might not be willing to take care of the less deserving.

Problems of integration and authority are always created by any attempt to keep many people organized within the same household. The father's authority was not likely to be publicly challenged until perhaps after World War I; nor that of the oldest brother if he was considerably older than the rest. On the other hand, as soon as efficiency or technical knowledge becomes the basis of decision, challenges are more likely to appear. An educated younger brother, or even a younger sister—and the many women figures in Indian government and the professions should be kept in mind—might well be able to give better advice on jobs in schools than the oldest male in the household.

In traditional Indian society, as at present, almost everyone remains at the same caste level in which he or she was born. On the other hand, many people rise substantially in wealth or political position. Sometimes, then, social mobility may decrease joint family solidarity. A man who has risen to a high occupational level may become reluctant to share all his income with the larger family. Note the important experiential difference: When all are roughly at the same level, sharing may mean something like equal exchange; when only one person is well to do, that person may experience "sharing" as paying out constantly. Nevertheless, the ideal of remaining together is strong. One consequence is that men might blame their wives for their decision to set up an independent household, rather than admit they themselves prefer to live separately.

Considering these conflicting forces, it is to be expected that no recent surveys have shown that a majority of Indian families in any region live in joint households. Numerous surveys have shown that many families engage in social exchanges with one another. For example, they may accept to some extent the authority of the oldest male (or at least ask his advice), though they no longer live with him. Or an urban brother continues to maintain an interest in a co-parcenary agricultural plot his rural brother operates, while they exchange food and help; or the urban brother aids his brother's sons in getting established in the city. Present data suggest that most families do not operate jointly, but they are linked by a keener sense of mutual obligation and a more intense loyalty to distant relatives than are families in the West. Public opinion polls show that most people are still in favor of this family form, while a substantial minority is in favor of living separately. As might be expected, the educated are less in favor of the joint family than the uneducated.

BASIC SOCIAL PROCESSES IN THE EXTENDED FAMILY

Now that we understand better how widely distributed the extended family is, let us consider the inner dynamics of the extended household. Several sociological generalizations may be applied to the patterns of interaction among its members. At this point, we are not weighing their advantages or disadvantages for the unit itself, although some of these may seem fairly clear; rather, we are simply analyzing the observable processes.

Behavioral Rules

The most obvious fact is that the number and kinds of social relations increase geometrically with an increase in the number of people in the unit. Each person must take into account not only a larger number of people, but also a larger number of social relations. For example, if the family grows by the addition of a new wife, the others will not only enter into social relations with her, but they must now also take into account all the relations she establishes with others, both as individuals and as smaller or larger collectivities. This is a formal, numerical trait of the extended family unit, but with it will be found several social regularities. One is the increased likelihood of structural differentiation within the family. That is, a greater number of kinship labels, terms, or positions will be found, and a clearer recognition of formal authority. There will be a much more specific, detailed division of labor. Rules of avoidance or reserve are more common. The large household becomes like a small community, and there may be much delegation of authority; for example, the elder female may put one of the wives in charge of a group of wives and children harvesting beans.

Next, an individual cannot spend as much of his or her time with any one person as might be possible in a small conjugal family. Any person's day is divided among far more people. Social analysts generally agree that one consequence of this dispersion of social energy and interaction is a lessened intensity of emotional ties between any two individuals. It is therefore likely that there will be more rules to specify the frequency and type of role interaction that each individual owes to others. Those obligations cannot be left to individual preference alone, to accidental encounter, or simple personal liking. For example, polygynous households are made up of two or more subunits, each being a wife and her children. In such households rules often specify how a man shall spend his nights with his wives.

We noted earlier that there are also likely to be rules of avoidance, a kind of traffic management. For example, a young wife may be required to avoid being in a room alone with her father-in-law, or to avoid speaking to him; or a young husband may be prohibited from speaking to or using the name of his mother-in-law. Rules of avoidance do reduce possible friction in a limited living space. They are also sometimes interpreted as a mechanism for lowering the possibility of sexual relations between certain categories of people.

The members of an extended household are, of course, highly visible to one another; they see each other more frequently than they would if the constituent nuclear families each had their own separate households. More people have the right and obligation to *watch* one another, to be concerned about one another's behavior. Privacy is lacking, which means that any individual who deviates is more likely to be exposed. Everything is everybody's business, and no one can go unscolded or unminded. As a further consequence of that visibility and talk, we should expect greater consensus among the members of the extended household concerning what is right and proper than among the same families if they lived separately. This process of continued reaffirmation of common values partly counterbalances the threatened conflict that is generated by the sheer number of different people, in many different social statuses, who thus have somewhat different interests to pursue. Of course, the differentiation of roles also helps to reduce conflict somewhat.

Being fully surrounded, visible to everyone, and immersed in a kind of social consensus about appropriate behavior has of course a considerable impact on in-marrying affines, who will usually be young brides. If the young bride enters a large extended family unit, she has no support from anyone else for any impulse she may feel toward rebellion or deviation; there is no place to hide; and everyone else agrees that she should adjust. This pattern of social control was of special importance in the socialization of the bride in such cultures as China, India, and the Arab countries.

Child-Switching

The processes of consensus and social control in the large extended family are somewhat more complex in a few societies because of a social custom that has been insufficiently analyzed—the practice of child-switching, the practice of exchanging children, or sending them to live elsewhere.

It was common in medieval England and among Puritans until late in the colonial period in the United States, for parents to send their young children to live with kinfolk, or sometimes allies or friends. English aristocrats sent their young heirs to other noble houses, where they spent their earliest years serving other knights or nobles at table and acquiring the skills of their high rank. The seventeenth-century Puritans thought of child-exchange or handing them over to surrogate parents as a way by which the natural tendency of parents to indulge and spoil their children could be neutralized. The children would receive training in a good family, among kin who would not exploit them. This type of exchange was not confined to large extended households, though of course aristocratic families were more often large-scale domestic units. The pattern did mean, however, that some members of the family were absent because they were living with other families, while some "strangers" were growing up in the family, but were not expected (as young brides might be) to spend their lives as part of the kin group.

This pattern cannot be ascribed to the supposed harshness of Puritan parents, since it grew from an older English tradition, continued among the aristocracy, and indeed the pattern of sending young children away to boarding school in England may have its roots in this older custom. It was also relatively common in Africa, where often the son was sent to live with the mother's brother at about the age of 6 to 10 years. Among the Haida of the Pacific Northwest, a boy might spend his late childhood in his mother's brother's family, and grow up to marry the daughter of the family. Such a system helps to integrate the child into the larger community, but does raise interesting questions about the transfer of affection and identification from one set of adults to another, and of course from one set of siblings to another.

Conflict Situations

We noted earlier the possibility of conflict arising from the simple fact that a large number of people occupy the same living space, but one special type of conflict deserves brief attention. In polygynous systems with a preference for sororal polygyny, the sisters might well live together in harmony. But when wives were not sisters, it was more common for them to be segregated from one another in separate rooms or even separate huts in a larger compound. In either case, the problem of overall authority for domestic processes within the large family unit will necessarily arise. In most systems it was the eldest wife who had the most authority, and there was a greater chance that the family from which she came had a higher rank than the families of other wives. On the other hand, the newer and younger wife might receive more favors and attention from the husband. As the elder wife became older, the husband might delegate some responsibility to another wife, and thus create resentment.

Another common set of conflict processes has to do with inheritance: not merely who is to inherit, but the present use of resources versus what is later to be passed down to the heirs. In most systems, who is to inherit is known and is set by custom or law. However, polygynous households are sometimes rent with intrigue because each mother may attempt to obtain favors for her children, and to persuade the husband to make her son the main heir. Rules of inheritance are often not specific enough to eliminate all threats of conflicts among mothers. The history of African kingdoms is studded with fraternal violence, half-brothers fighting half-brothers for a chieftaincy because neither would accept a subordinate position. Elder males were supposed to care for all members of the family wisely and considerately, but each subunit within a large extended household might attempt to use up more resources than others thought proper; or some might use up resources that the heir believed ought to be kept intact for himself.

Family Childrearing

Socialization patterns are also affected by who is included in the household. A mother-in-law may continue to supervise the training of a young daughter-in-law (since she has entered the household), or a young boy may go off to his mother's brother's house to grow up. A young child in a polygynous household (in which the child's father has several wives) sees a wider range of adult models intimately than he or she could observe in a nuclear family.

Respect for Age

Wherever the extended family system was highly valued, elders, both male and female, were paid much deference and prestige. This was not simply because such societies were nonliterate and thus had no accumulation of written knowledge. After all, they included China, India, Japan, and the Arab world. However, in none of these were daily living patterns regulated primarily by technical or scientific learning. As a consequence, the accumulation of folk wisdom by elders was not thought of as an ornament alone, but as a necessity—the ways of a tiger, how to conduct delicate marriage negotiations, when to plant, or how to approach a high official. The young could not easily outstrip the old in such knowledge, as indeed they do not now. The elders' advantage also came in part from their responsibility for rituals. They were in addition considered closest to the gods because of the imminence of their death; they thus deserved respect and authority. The unit cost of maintaining the old was low under such systems, and the absolute cost to the whole society was low because so few lived to be very old. As a consequence, following their advice was more likely to be sensible, while keeping them around was not very costly.

People at intermediate ages or statuses felt that they had a stake in supporting the old, in maintaining such a system, for they knew that in time they too would grow old. If these intermediate people challenged the family authority of the old too soon, or supplanted them without finesse and respect, then they would undermine the very familial structure which they themselves could enjoy in their own old age. Indeed, the consequences of giving no clear familial status to the old may be seen in our own society, where the problems of the aged are viewed as increasingly difficult to solve. Under all the forms of the large extended household, the aged had a place. They had tasks to do, some authority and resources for carrying out those tasks, and some prestige for serving as wise family leaders. As one consequence, the elderly enjoy less esteem in an industrialized society than in a less developed one, although Alex Inkeles has reported it is not true that *individuals* who are more "modern" or who have had more direct experience in industry feel less respect for the elderly.

STRENGTHS OF THE EXTENDED FAMILY

The extended family may be viewed as a kind of social invention, and thus we may examine its strengths and weaknesses under various kinds of circumstances. A given large extended household grows and declines over the years as it is affected by fertility, marriage and divorce, mortality, residence rules, and the alternative socioeconomic opportunities open to its members. Under modern industrializing conditions, this type of household becomes less common. However, as we shall see, it can still resist the forces of industrialization here and there.

Durability and Continuity

The extended family is most likely to be found in nonurban, nonindustrialized settings. In those settings, it can furnish social services that are typically lacking. That is, each person can obtain help from a larger group of people. When the domestic group is larger, any given individual represents a smaller marginal or extra cost to the group. Consequently, the burden of the aged, the ill, the crippled, and the infirm is less for each member of a large extended family. As an extreme contrast, consider the former custom among the Eskimos, who usually had a small conjugal family. When food was short under the perilous Arctic conditions, the unit cost of any nonproductive person was very high, and the other few members could not shoulder it. The Eskimo would thus abandon older family members, or young infant daughters. In many African societies the social security measure of the *levirate* existed. In a common form, a man inherited the wives of his brother. That is, they became his wives, and he guaranteed support for these sometimes elderly women as long as they lived. Here, in contrast to the Eskimos, the family unit was likely to be made up of several domestic households united in one compound. Consequently, although taking in an additional wife or more might be a burden for everyone, it was not likely to mean more than a small unit cost per person.

Although the extended household loses members through mortality or migration, it is more durable than the conjugal household. That is, as in any other large group, the loss of an individual or two does not change the basic pattern of the group. Even the loss of the eldest male will not change things fundamentally, since there is typically another mature male to take over when that happens. By contrast, in the small domestic unit, the death or absence of the mother or father seriously impairs or even destroys the effectiveness of that family.

Economic and Political Strength

It is perhaps most important that the extended family is better able to amass the capital for an important economic enterprise, whether that is obtaining enough cattle for a marriage, buying land or a governmental office, or paying for the education of a young man of promise. As long as those who receive the benefit of the investment also continue to feel obliged to share that benefit with their kin, the group as a whole can function as a kind of cooperative, or a savings bank. The conjugal family has to apportion its rewards among fewer people, but correspondingly there are fewer people from whom to obtain support when investment capital is needed. One important consequence of this fact is that in the first stages of industrialization in a new country, upper-strata families are likely to become still better off economically than other citizens. Having an extended kinship network to call on, and often an extended household, they are better able to put together the necessary capital for new types of enterprise, or help each other to get better jobs.

In societies where all adult men were at least potentially warriors, the large extended household also had more political influence than the small conjugal family. The threat of violence does not confer legitimacy in itself, but it often bestows some power, at least as a protection against the tyranny of others. A family head who can call on a goodly number of armed followers from his own family is likely to be accorded more attention than the head of a small family unit. One consequence, especially among the upper strata of most societies of the past, and in political circles of contemporary life, is that negotiations leading to marriage are frequently concerned with the possible political fruitfulness of new alliances. Of course, with the establishment of formal agencies of the law and a more effective police system, this protective support of the extended family becomes less important, just as this family form becomes less common.

Rural-Urban Integration

It should also follow, however, if this line of theory is correct, that in industrializing countries we should find not merely that some large extended households continue to exist, but that they continue to exist under certain kinds of favoring conditions. One study of a particular region in the Philippines revealed, for example, that urban families were larger than rural families. This apparent contradiction of the direction of expected change simply confirms the reasoning we have been outlining. The members of these larger, urban families were not only the grandparents and their lineal descendants in a single unit (in conformity with traditional rules); they contained many more distant relatives, such as cousins, nephews, or even younger in-laws. The observed process can also be seen in other parts of the world: Relatively more successful families in urban centers are used by their rural kin as a base of operations. Typically younger people move from the rural region to the city in order to obtain education, training, or jobs, and kinship norms require that they be taken in. Later on, it is assumed, they will themselves contribute to the larger family unit, or will help other members of their kin network get started in the city. The traditional family form has thus often been replaced by a temporary conglomeration of kin.

In contemporary Taiwan, many extended family units have been reported, some with a considerable division of labor. One young man may be sent to the city to earn wages; members of one family may be required to work on a farm; still others may operate a small store. The elder male directs and integrates these enterprises, while everyone can continue to contribute his or her labor and wages, in the knowledge that there will be a fair apportioning of the benefits from this cooperative enterprise. Larger tasks can be accomplished than a small, conjugal unit could accomplish alone; larger quantities of capital can be amassed; and a more efficient allocation of personnel can be made. On the other hand, as we continue to emphasize, most families do not have the skills or the initial capital with which to develop such a common familial activity. Sometimes the sharing may be no more than the exchange of food grown on a rural family plot for family help in guiding an application through the urban bureaucracy.

Sustaining Factors

Thus, although large extended households were very likely not typical in any major civilization of the past or present, they do continue to exist. They rise and decline under the same conditions now as in the past—though to be sure those conditions do not occur as frequently in a fully industrialized country as in one that is undergoing industrialization. And, of course, they are most common in societies that have not industrialized at all.

The particular factors that sustain the large extended family household will vary considerably, but they may be summarized in a general way. If the family has an effective leadership as well as sufficient resources to be exploited, and if the cooperation of its members will yield more output (in prestige, power, safety, or material goods) than each can earn by leaving the family to set up independently, then such families are more likely to retain their members within the household, both direct descendants as well as in-marrying affines. We would also expect that when such conditions are more widespread in a given society—which will be true of less industrialized societies—the large family household will seem much more desirable. It will be more likely to be viewed as an ideal, and more families will try to create or maintain one.

If the extended family household possesses all these advantages, why is it not prevalent in all or most societies? Even in Western societies, it possesses some nostalgic appeal. It suggests a time when people affirmed the familial values of descent and lineage, loyalty and solidarity of kin, and affection and warmth for one's far and distant relatives. However, it is clear that even when societies give a high value to this family form, a relatively low percentage of families actually are able to sustain a large extended household. The reasons lie in the inner dynamics of such a group, and its relation to the larger social structure. Some of these factors have already been stated, but we will review them here.

The fundamental demographic facts cannot be overlooked. In most societies prior to the present epoch of relatively modest death rates, high mortality and the normal ages at marriage and reproduction made it inevitable that most families would not be able to create and maintain a large household. The integration of many people into a single unit also requires managerial skills and leadership, even when most of the members' duties are traditionally assigned. Usually, a strong older woman is needed to organize the internal flow of services and food, and a strong man to assume overall direction of the unit and external relations with other parts of the society. Often, the male head is not able, or not the ablest man in the family, while the latter may be prevented by traditional rules from assuming that post. A strong man or woman may refuse to cooperate with the formal head of the family.

Although such a grouping can take care of the infirm or incompetent, it has no way or ridding itself of this burden, and sometimes the cost weighs heavily on total income. A wealthy family may spoil its sons, who may drain its income, and eventually dissipate the family fortune. Diffuse, strong familial obligations to take care of everyone may also support family members who are essentially parasites. Perhaps most important, the large household can stay together only as long as its land or other wealth can support it and it can offer adequate opportunities to the younger generation. If it grows without a commensurate increase in its control over political posts, jobs, land, or military opportunity, members of the family must go elsewhere to establish families of their own. Children who are heirs to the land do not typically break away from the parental hearth, but junior family members, who will inherit little or nothing, must get out. Since most families do not maintain themselves at a high level of power and wealth from one generation to another, the large extended family unit is likely to break up over time.

If the large household can hold together, it obtains some advantages, but it cannot control all the factors in the larger society that permit it to hold together. Nor can a conjugal family unit without great luck or talent manage to amass the wealth or political power that will permit it to grow into a large extended family unit, even when the surrounding society supports that ideal. Consequently, we should not expect that a majority of families will be of the extended type in any society, even when most members of the society aspire to live in or to found such a family.

THE CONJUGAL FAMILY

It may be useful to consider the general characteristics of the modern urban conjugal family as a way of highlighting the dynamics of other household forms. We may use the terms *nuclear* or *conjugal* interchangeably if we wish to refer to the family unit itself. However, the term *conjugal* is preferable when we refer to the family system as a whole. As noted earlier, no nuclear family *system* exists, if by that we mean a system in which most families maintain few or no relations with their more extended kin. All contemporary studies in the most industrialized countries (Great Britain, the United States, Holland, France) show that in fact each family unit maintains contact with a wide range of relatives. In many studies, the largest single category of "recreation" is visiting with relatives. A majority of the families report that they engage in many types of exchanges with people in their kinship network, and these range from simple services to large gifts.

It cannot be supposed that the maintenance of relations with kin outside the household is some kind of residue from ancient times. These patterns continue to be maintained by both the pleasures and the necessities of exchange with people who are likely to extend to us a relatively long line of social credit, and who are under some social pressure to give help when it is needed. That the *kin network* is closely linked with the small family unit can be seen from the fact that the relatives *outside* the conjugal unit cannot be cut off without hurting or annoying someone inside the family. That is, each person in the family is or will be a member of two families simultaneously, his or her family of orientation (the family we are born in) and his or her family of procreation (the family we found). A son cannot rebuff his father's father or father's sister without angering his father. A husband cannot exclude his father-in-law, sister-in-law, or son-in-law without annoying his wife or daughter. One cannot be hostile toward nephews or nieces without rebuffing sisters or brothers. Thus, it is useful to keep in mind that the family unit is not entirely independent, although a conjugal system is one in which more social emphasis is placed on the conjugal bond.

The fact that the conjugal family is more independent from the kinship network than family units in other kinds of systems has further implications that help us to understand the large extended household better. Since most affinal (in-law) and consanguineal (blood) kin are relatively excluded from the conjugal family's day-to-day decisions, neither these kin nor the small family unit can count on a regular flow of services or help from each other. The larger society does not require much exchange of this kind. Of course, many such exchanges do occur from time to time, depending on how friendly kin are with one another and the kinds of needs they have. But since those exchanges are not societally required and do not occur as frequently as in the past, both extended kin and the nuclear family unit have a weaker basis for social control over one another; they cannot as easily get compliance through reward or punishment. Since these mandatory exchanges are fewer and reciprocal controls are weaker, there are fewer pressures on the new couple to settle near relatives after marriage. This neolocality, in turn, supports the relative independence of the small family unit.

Neither the bride's nor the groom's family is likely to gain much from the marriage, because custom does not demand many social or economic exchanges or formal alliances, and besides the high divorce rate reduces the chances that such investments will pay off in the long run. As a consequence, choice of mate is relatively free. The adjustment between husband and wife is supposed to be more important than the adjustment among relatives, or either of the spouses to their in-laws. Thus, members of the relatively excluded kin network do not attempt to assert much control over who marries whom.

The conjugal system is multilineal or bilineal, rather than unilineal; *neither* the female nor the male line is viewed as the only important line of descent. (In the West, a remnant of the historical emphasis on the patriline is still found in the custom of the wife taking her husband's name when she marries). As contrasted with a lineage system, or any large corporate kin grouping based on a line of descent, in the conjugal system it is the *marital* bond between husband and wife that is considered most important. In any event, neolocality makes difficult the maintenance of any social emphasis on one kin line, since wives and husbands may live too far away from the rest of their kin to be able to take part in many collective activities or rituals.

Equally important is the intensity of emotionality within the conjugal family unit. This type of household is founded on mutual attraction and love. It is made up of a small number of people in close contact with one another. The emotional ties among members of the large extended household are likely to be diffuse and less intense. The higher degree of emotionality in the conjugal unit is accentuated by the fact that custom forbids the individual to go anywhere else in the society for solace. This emphasis creates both the intimacy and the fragility of the conjugal family. If the husband or wife does not in fact obtain love and comfort within the family unit, then both have less motivation to continue to stay in it. Thus, the divorce rate in a conjugal family system is likely to be high.

Finally, since this type of system contains no large kinship groupings that offer various social welfare services, it has no simple way of taking care of the dependent, the helpless, or the aged. If children lose their parents, no corporate kinship unit is responsible for supporting them. When couples divorce, no corporate kinship unit will automatically take care of them. To meet this problem, complex social security measures have developed in industrial societies, along with homes for the aged and the helpless, and specially organized private or governmental programs for the handicapped. Indeed, a wide range of social services of all kinds develop as substitutes for the help once given by the large extended household or the kinship network in other systems. It should not be assumed, however, that the older systems were necessarily *effective* in solving these problems. Often they did not have sufficient resources, and of course in all such systems those who were powerful were much more likely to divert the available goods and services to their own needs, rather than to those of the helpless.

Thus, the conjugal system has many characteristics that set it apart from the system in which a nuclear unit is a less emphasized part of a strong kinship network. The conjugal system seems to fit the needs of an industrial system better than many other family forms. Individuals can more easily follow the opportunities of the labor market, are more likely to focus on the task itself rather than needs of their kinship network, and very likely spend less of their time on kin activities. It should be emphasized, however, that this does not mean that the industrial system fits the needs of the conjugal family. There is no reason why the needs of one institution in a society will necessarily fit those of another. There are recurring tensions between the family system and industrialization, which we explore at length in the final chapters on social change.

CHAPTER 7
KINSHIP GROUPS
AND NETWORKS

To most people in the United States, the term *kinfolk* seems quaint or rural. The term *kin network* seems artificial and alien to their experience, even though they take for granted their obligation to visit with a distant cousin who happens to be passing through their city. No one seems to be given the specific task of reminding others to maintain kin ties, and there are few clear rules that specify just how one should behave toward kin. Nevertheless, kin networks continue to exist in all industrialized societies. In this chapter, we focus primarily on one type of kin network, the organized or *corporate* network. This type is not to be found in the most technologically developed nations.[1]

In all societies, the links of kinship have been recognized beyond the confines of the nuclear or composite family unit. If we accept everyone as kin who is related by blood, through however distant a tie, clearly everyone in any society would be considered a relative of everyone else in the whole world. The network of kinship is indefinitely extensible. If one wished to create various organizations to take care of a wide range of activities beyond the capacities of the individual family, such as maintaining temples, conducting religious rituals, administering a market, or furnishing labor for road-building, people could be chosen to participate in such organizations on the basis of their position in a kinship network. Indeed, this type of social invention has been widespread, and has been identified by various labels, such as lineage, clan, and kindred.

1.   In Arab countries, however, there are formally organized kinship "clubs" or associations, with by-laws, meetings, dues, and so on, as there are "cousin clubs" in the United States.

TYPES OF ORGANIZED DESCENT GROUPINGS

The *lineage* is only one form of corporate kin group. But though there are many kinds of kinship organization, most can be classified among four main types: patrilineages, matrilineages, clans, and (in the Western world) kindreds. They differ by virtue of the mode of tracing descent. The two most widespread modes are unilineal and omnilineal. As the term suggest, in a *unilineage*, descent is traced through one line only (mother's or father's). Since these are likely to be genuine corporate groups, acting collectively, most members will live close to one another. *Omnilineal* descent is traced through both parents' lines, and of course (if our kinship data were complete) could be traced almost indefinitely throughout the society. The kindred is based in part on this mode, but as we shall see this mode can not be used for a true corporate descent grouping, for there are no clear boundaries setting off one set of kin from another.

Clans are like lineages in that the unilineal principle is followed, but the more distant kin connections are somewhat more obscure. Not all the generations between the founding ancestor and the individual can be clearly charted. Sometimes the founding ancestor is a mythical figure, symbolized by a clan name, such as Wolf, Beaver, or Owl. Many clans exist without lineages, but sometimes the latter are united into clans, which contain one or more residentially unified, unilineal kin groups.

Different descent principles could be used to divide the population by kinship position, and some systems are very complex. For example, sisters might be allocated to the maternal line and brothers to the paternal. Notice, however, that what distinguishes most kinship systems from the type found in most industrialized nations is not which descent principle is used, but the fact that certain kin are *organized* and have collective duties and rights.

Since these kinship structures go beyond the family, do they properly belong in an analysis of the family? Traditionally, family sociologists paid little attention to them, and anthropologists are likely to think of them less as a part of family interaction than as the main constituent of the larger social structure itself. But they are important in the study of the family, because families and the alliances they make are the building blocks of the lineage.

The lineage is also important because membership in kinship collectives usually defines who may or may not marry whom. The lineage, for example, is exogamous: one may not marry within it. Another justification for examining corporate kinship units is that the individual family, and especially the husband-wife couple, is less likely to be the prime social unit in social interaction where such groupings are well developed. In that setting, many family tasks become lineage obligations too.

Another reason for considering such larger kin groupings here is that they partly define many family obligations. For example, among the matrilineal Trobrianders, the wife's brother furnished yams for her family. Both were joined in the same lineage with her children. She had some claim to the produce from the land he held, and so did her children, who in turn had no claim to their father's landholdings, since they were not his heirs. Later, we will discuss other features of a matrilineage, but here we are merely noting that some family obligations may be based on kin relations outside the immediate family.

Finally, the family is the source of the loyalties and commitments on which the descent grouping must be able to count. Rights and duties are couched in a rhetoric of the family, and are first taught there. A vestige of this is the former U.S. rural pattern of calling distant relatives "cousin" or "uncle" to express kinship solidarity and friendship.

PATRILINEAGE: A HYPOTHETICAL EXAMPLE

Since it is the rare Western reader who has had any experience of living even briefly in a lineage, perhaps an exercise of the imagination is necessary to understand it. Let us suppose we had patrilineages in this country. Almost everyone would be a member of some lineage. How many lineages there would be would depend on how far back one's ancestry would be traced—with a literate tradition and concern for records, perhaps eventually ten generations or so. The Polynesian Maori did that without writing. The greater the generational depth of a lineage, the fewer the number of lineages needed to include the entire population. Perhaps a few hundred might contain the population of the United States. These might, in turn, be linked in still larger groupings of lineages, called clans. Extensive lineages might be segmented into sublineages.

Who would be included in your lineage? Since it would be patrilineal, you would include all your male ancestors in the direct line. The men's wives are not members, although in some societies they may eventually become assimilated into their husband's lineage. In any event, your father's brothers would be included, and his sons and daughters. Also included would be your father's father, his brothers, and their descendants, the *collaterals*. Only the descendants of the males would be included. The descendants of females would be included in the lineages of the men these women married. In effect, the lineage is composed of all the descendants of a founding father. Most would live near each other, in order to make decisions together. Of course, not every member would be in the same location, since married female members would be living with their husbands.

Would family and kinship behavior be different from what it is today, when the ordinary family head in a Western nation interacts with scores of in-laws and blood kin over a period of months? With reference to most actions within the nuclear family, little change would be evident, although your father would have more authority than at present. With reference to matters outside the nuclear family, however, some changes would occur. Most important, your relatives through your mother's family would play a smaller part in your life. You would expect less help from them, and you might be less anxious about incurring their displeasure. Of course, as in all societies, if they lived very close to you, they would nevertheless be rather important to you emotionally.

If you were old enough to marry, the patrilineage would play a large role in the marriage—setting rules concerning whom you might marry, helping to amass the money for the marriage celebration and setting up the household; perhaps even picking out your spouse. If you were male, you would claim your children for the lineage in the event of divorce, since they would be members of it from birth. If you were female, you would have to return to your family without your children.

At various religious rituals, your lineage might have certain responsibilities, such as furnishing members to carry out the rituals, or helping to pay for them. If you traveled to another town, you would expect to be received with open arms by members of your lineage even if they had not met you before. If you had a serious quarrel with another member, the elders of the lineage would adjudicate the issue rather than permit you to go to court. If your serious conflict were with an outsider, the lineage would support your side of the quarrel.

In general, in your role relations *outside* your own household, you would be treated as a member of a lineage more than as an independent individual. Under such a system you would lose some of your present freedom to make gifts to your kin through your mother's line, or to will property to them. Within the solidarity of your patrilineal kin, you would gain some security and protection. Finally, many important activities of the society (maintaining temples or roads, repairing irrigation canals) would be the responsibility of one lineage or another. They would not be carried out by employees of the ruler or state.

THE MATRILINEAGE

Another way to understand the lineage as one type of descent grouping is to look at one particular kind. Let us now consider a type far removed from ordinary American experience. Here we simply trace out the consequences of a matrilineage for a range of kinship role relationships,[2] and through the contrast see still more clearly the traits of a patrilineage. One caution applies here, as in all analyses of descent groups. In no society is the sole emphasis placed on a single descent line. In all patrilineages, for example, many rights and obligations tie an individual to the mother's kinship line. Moreover, the frequency of social contact based on common residence often outweighs the day-to-day importance of lineage ties. Families that live close to one another may call upon one another for help far more often than they call on members of their lineage.

The essential structure of matrilineage can be described simply: An individual is part of a descent group whose members are linked through

2. This section is based on David M. Schneider, "The Distinctive Features of Matrilineal Descent Groups," in *Matrilineal Kinship,* eds. David M. Schneider and Kathleen Gough (Berkeley: University of California Press, 1961), pp. 1–29.

the successive generations of females. A boy and his sister are members of their mother's lineage, and she and her brothers and sisters are part of *their* mother's lineage. Since no society is a matriarchy, every lineage contains men (brothers and sons of the women through whom descent is traced) who will hold the most important positions. At the same time, since almost every individual eventually marries, any lineage is composed of both men and women who are married to *nonmembers*. This situation results from the fact that members are linked by descent, but lineages are exogamous. Everyone marries outside the lineage, but everyone in the society is a member of *some* lineage. A given matrilineage, then, excludes the women who are married to the male members *in* it, as well as the "outside" men who have married its female members.

Naturally, then, not all members of a lineage *as a whole* will ever reside all together. Its members are found in many families, some of whose members are part of one lineage, and the rest of whom are part of another lineage. If they are in the same village, of course they can consult easily with one another, and in any case the men who are the leaders live close to one another. Figure 7.1 illustrates this structure. In Figure 7.1, the connections of one generation with another can be seen. A, B, and C are three matrilineages, each exchanging wives and husbands with one another through the common pattern of matrilateral cross-cousin marriage (a man marrying his mother's brother's daughter). A more complete but very complex diagram would show all the members of the lineage within a given society; it would include all the collateral relatives who are part of the same lineage. Notice from the diagram that in a matrilineage, when a man marries he does not produce children for his matrilineage. They belong to his wife's lineage. His sister, however, marries and produces children for *his* matrilineage. Although male members of a lineage produce children, as it were, for other lineages, over time the exchanges balance out. Since each lineage depends on others, the society is thus more closely integrated.

MATRILINEAGES (*)

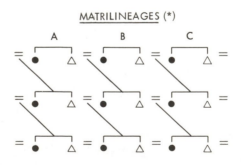

Figure 7.1 Matrilateral Cross-Cousin Marriage (Matrilineal Society)
Source: George C. Homans and David M. Schneider, *Marriage, Authority, and Final Causes—A Study of Unilateral Cross-Cousin Marriage.* (New York: Free Press, 1955), p. 11.

Although a matrilineage is sometimes described as the mirror image of a patrilineage, close study of the relevant descent charts discloses further important structural differences. One lies in the fact that the matrilineage must restrain and control the in-marrying males, who by the status definitions of the society will have considerable authority as husbands and as males. In a patrilineage, on the other hand, there are no in-marrying males, and the in-marrying females can be controlled simply because all members of the society agree that women should be subordinate. In some patrilineages the wives are eventually assimilated to a considerable degree into their husband's lineage, but even if they are not, they form no threat. They produce no sons for their own lineage, and cannot assume much authority in their own right.

Because the mother's brother is an authority figure—the representative of the family in ritual matters, and the man from whom a boy (brother's sister's son) inherits—these two statuses are closely linked, but in a different way from that of the patrilineage. In the latter, a father is supposed to be *both* an authority figure and a source of tenderness. In a matrilineage a father can be a source of tenderness (as a mother's brother often is in Western society), but his authority must be limited at certain points by the lineage. Indeed, since his property goes to his sister's sons, and he must spend a great deal of time with them as they become older, he has less grounds for demanding obedience from his own sons. On the other hand, because he loves his sons, works with them, and interacts with them daily, one type of additional strain is evident. He may wish to help them, to offer them gifts, or even to bequeath some possessions to them, to the annoyance of his nephews specifically and his lineage generally.

Since the position of the in-marrying male is under some strain, and the rights and duties of the wife with reference to domestic affairs (where she is clearly under his authority) must be closely defined, the divorce rate is likely to be high in a matrilineal system. The children remain with the mother, since they belong to her lineage. In some types of conflicts with her husband, she can obtain support from her kinsmen, and especially from her brothers. The available data confirm this prediction. In general, strong, durable, intense links between husband and wife are less common in matrilineages than in patrilineages. One consequence of this is that the bride price in a matrilineal system is likely to be low. It is the elders of a family or a lineage who put together the property and gifts that make up the bride price; and they will not invest much in a union that is not likely to endure. Besides, the lineage of the *male* does not receive children from the union. A patrilineage, on the other hand, will not only receive the services of the in-marrying woman, but also of the children she bears. Moreover, she gets less support from her kin, in the event of a domestic quarrel, so that divorce is less likely. Thus the bride price is likely to be more substantial in a patrilineage.

Matrilineal systems can be found in many parts of the world, but make up only about 15 percent of the world's societies. A great belt of matrilineal tribes runs from West Africa eastward across the continent. The Navajo and Zuñi of the southwestern United States are also matrilineal.

The subcontinent of India once contained many matrilineal groups, of which the best described are the Nayars who reside along the Malabar Coast. Some are also found in Melanesia in the South Pacific. One of these tribes, the Trobrianders, is analyzed in the classic field work of Bronislaw Malinowski. Clearly, they are not common in the least industrialized societies, nor are they prevalent among societies that are highly advanced in technology. Matriliny seems not to be, as once was thought, the "primeval" kinship pattern, created before human beings learned of the connection between sexual intercourse and birth. Matriliny is most likely to be found in societies that engage in gardening but do not use the plow (in horticultural societies) and in which women thus play an important role in food production. In societies that demand large-scale cooperation among males, or that assign central societal tasks to political or economic organizations *not* based on kinship, matrilineages are nearly absent. And as most tribes become gradually incorporated into modern economies, matrilineal systems begin to disappear.

THE CHINESE CLAN

The Chinese clan system was most fully developed in the southeast provinces, such as Fujian, Guangdong, Guangxi, and Jiangxi, but the general pattern shaped much of family life throughout China. This system continued until 1949, when the Communist regime assumed power, although it had already gradually declined in significance in the cities, toward the northwest, and of course in the spreading areas under Communist control from the 1930s on.

To the Westerner it was symbolized most dramatically by the considerable number of villages, in both southern and northern China, in which almost everyone had the same surname. From the administrative point of view, its significance may be seen in the fact that under the empire the administrative apparatus did not reach down to the village level, where the strength of the clan typically maintained peace and order. The large Chinese population has shared about 500 surnames, many of which were uncommon. This did not mean, of course, that everyone with the same surname was involved in clan relations with one another; but the vague feeling of kinship was strong enough to support a rule that people of the same name should not marry. In addition, having the same surname did make introductions or voluntary associations easier between strangers, especially in areas distant from their birthplace. In general, those with the same surname were supposed to be helpful to one another.

The formally organized, *operative* descent group was, however, localized, confined to one area in a town, or to a single village. Since such a clan might well have been settled in the area for ten to twenty generations, other subclans descended from the same supposed ancestor might well dominate other nearby localities, villages, or parts of towns. These subbranches would not meet together as a unitary whole, but would know that they were descended from the same ancestor, and would probably even recognize which group was the senior or main branch, as well as the order of seniority of the subbranches in the clan. Each village clan maintained, or felt an obligation to maintain, a clan temple in which the ancestral tablets were kept, refurbished, and displayed. If sufficiently prosperous, the clan might have common land, which was used to pay for the upkeep of the temple or for other clan activities. This land would be rented to clan members, under various sets of rules, though usually it was the more powerful families within the clan who succeeded in controlling the land.

A village could be numerically dominated by one clan. All the wives had to be nonmembers of the clan, and therefore would come from nearby villages. In addition, an outsider might—because of the familistic loyalties of the Chinese—have some difficulty in political or economic competition with members of the organization. However, larger villages or towns would have more than one clan, and these vied with one another for honor. If a clan became prosperous, it might hire a scholar to "research" its history in order to prove its illustrious origins. At a death or marriage, clan members would contribute to the ceremony in order to display their wealth or past achievements. Since the Chinese government carried out so few tasks at the village level, a wide range of activities was the responsibility of clans, from building a temple to ridding an area of bandits. In addition, some clans established schools, since the most prestige would accrue to the clan who produced scholars, especially those who rose to high position in the imperial bureaucracy. The clan also served at times as a parole body for a man who had disobeyed the law but who had reformed. Its importance was recognized in the rule that a man should not be an imperial governor in his own province, because he could not dispense justice to all impartially. Nepotism was both expected and approved in Chinese society, and this rule at least reduced the temptation.

The head of a local clan was, ideally, the oldest member, but in fact education, power, and wealth counted for more in the actual clan decisions. A clan might have a council of elders, but perhaps most did not. In any event, seniority was respected, primarily in a symbolic fashion if an older man did not have other qualities that commanded assent. The clan did not often interfere in the domestic affairs of the family. Its importance lay outside the household, unless the male head could not maintain his authority. Precisely because the clan could concentrate both economical and political power, it was a significant resource to be exploited. Since individual poor families could not, except in unusual situations, call on governmental agencies for help, they were not able to escape or to resist clan influence. Where the clan owned agricultural land, it was supposed to be rotated among families according to clan rules, but the stronger families were more likely to use this land when they wished. If taxes were to be collected, the rich could pay less than they should.

In the cities, the poor families could more easily escape clan influence and obtain its benefits from other agencies. In turn, rich urban families did not wish to recognize their vague obligation to help their kin. After the 1911 Revolution, which destroyed the Manchu dynasty, the Republic created new political authorities in the villages, elected by the people.

These did not fully replace the clans, but they were sometimes a force to be reckoned with. By the 1930s, the clan seems to have become weaker in even those areas where it had once been strong.

As already mentioned, in Imperial China, and to some extent under the later Republic, the rule of the central government extended only partially to affairs at the village level. By contrast, the power of the clan was local. It was for this reason that the Communists aimed at destroying the clan, since they intended to control as much of Chinese life as possible. The clan was viewed as the locus of old superstitions and "feudal practices." It was a possible source of countervailing political authority. The Communists also saw it as the tool of the rich, and as an instrument of a corrupt regime. Therefore, they moved to eradicate the clan. Economic life was to be directed by the state, not the clan. Populations were moved about a good deal, in order to sever clan ties. Where ancestral graves, halls, and groves, existed, they were taken over. Where clan agricultural land existed, it was expropriated. Over the decade between 1949 and 1959, the Chinese supplanted the clan by their own corporate but nonkinship agency, the commune system.

The "core" of the Chinese clan was close to the ideal, symmetrical network of "mourning relatives" or mourning grades—the most important people for the purposes of mourning. These were (1) a man's direct male ascendants through his great-great-grandfather; (2) a man's lineal descendants through his great-great-grandson, and (3) the collateral relatives four degrees from the man at his own generation, three from his father and son, two from his grandfather and grandson, and one from his great-grandfather and great-grandson. In and of itself, this was not a corporate group, since obviously its limits would differ for different individuals. A full chart would also include all the obligations for mothers, who did not really become part of their husband's clan until the women died. Obviously, only a rare man would have great-great-grandsons, and if he did all his ancestors would be dead. The chart would thus tell us more about where respect was to be paid in the direct family line than who was administering the local clan. It would pay less attention to the juniors, but under the old system these would in turn eventually become adult, to be reckoned with in the day-to-day affairs of the village clan. It emphasized the main line of adult males.

THE JAPANESE DOZOKU

The Japanese, like most people in other nations, did not typically live in extended households. In late Tokugawa times (the nineteenth century until 1868), about half of Japanese households were nuclear in fact, and even about a half-century ago some three-fifths of all Japanese lived in nuclear families. But as mentioned earlier, the Japanese family was a *stem* family. One person inherited the headship of the family and thus represented the continuation of the family line, which could form part of a kin grouping called the *dozoku*. This head, usually the oldest male, took some responsibility for the younger siblings. It was expected that younger brothers would not remain in the household, and indeed Japanese folklore asserted that younger brothers were more likely to be daring and original than the oldest brother, since the young ones were pushed out to live on their own. As among the nineteenth-century upper-class English, whose families were also of the stem type, many younger brothers entered the expanding world of business after the Meiji Restoration of 1868. The oldest son was a kind of trustee for the line, however, and was responsible for maintaining its prestige.

If economic conditions were ideal, a younger brother might found a branch or junior family line. Both the senior and the junior families, it must be emphasized, represented a link in the unbroken chain of the family, and did not form a clan composed of many collateral kin. In rural areas, however, and among upper-class urban strata, a senior line might well link with one or more junior branches to form a *dozoku,* which in many ways acted as a corporate kin grouping. These links had deep roots in the Japanese family tradition. A "household" was not simply where a family lived, or even an aggregate of the living members. It was the repository of all the history of that family line, paying reverence to its dead members and maintaining, within the limits of its space and budget, mementos of the past. A wife was usually not inscribed in the family register until she had borne a child, preferably a son. A junior household was not simply a group of kin, but a bearer of the family honor, and shared that responsibility with the senior branch.

In any given *dozoku* there was only one *honke,* or senior branch. If economic and social opportunities had been favorable in the past, and the family had taken advantage of them, there might be one or more junior branches of varying historical depth. These people, with their wives, formed the nucleus of blood kin within the center of the *dozoku.* In some regions no other people were part of the kinship unit, but in many areas other nonkin families were also included in this grouping. For the most part, this larger organization was found in forestry and fishing villages. Such families did not inherit their positions without question, but had to validate them by working for the core higher-ranked families in the *dozoku.* Their status was not quite that of serfs, but this was not a free market either. Only certain families would be given the opportunity to work for the higher-ranking core members of the clan. These non-blood-kin families did not inherit land or authority, and their subordinate duties and rights were defined by tradition. The links among these families were reaffirmed on ritual occasions, such as the buddhist All Souls' Day.[3]

Japanese society was feudal, and the feudal relationship of patron-protégé, lord and master, extended into family relations as well. These "ritual kin" gave their labor and loyalty to the core families in the *dozoku,*

3. Chie Nakane, *Kinship and Economic Organization in Rural Japan* (New York: Humanities Press, 1967), Chap. 3; and Seichi Kitano, "*Dozuku* and Kindred in a Japanese Rural Society," in *Families in East and West: Socialization Process and Kinship Ties,* eds. Reuben Hill and René König (Paris: Mouton, 1970), pp. 248–269.

and in turn received some economic and physical security. The system had the approval of the imperial government, since the less advantaged social strata were thus held in place by a network of obligations and duties, and could be no threat to national order. This hierarchical system was also the model of a widespread social pattern in Japan by which many individuals recognized others as patrons, as a major source of present, past, and future benefits, to whom the protégés paid deference, loyalty, and service in turn. This *oyabun-kobun* relationship was found in cities as well as rural areas, and in all occupational areas, but was more personalized and individual than the relations among members of the *dozoku.*

As in China, the Japanese clan was of less importance in the cities, for without a landed base the family could not easily hold together both members and subordinates. The services obtained from subordinates could as easily be bought. However, an individual patron or *oyabun* might be needed by even an urban family of some standing because of new goals it wished to realize. The family might wish to enroll a son in the imperial university, or obtain a job for him in a bank (essentially new urban aspirations), and for this goal might need the support of a highly placed person. This more individual patron-protégé relationship continues in Japan in the traditional arts, in the form of the master-apprentice link, and in academic life.

By the Meiji period (1868–1912), the senior and junior branches of the *dozoku* had ceased to cooperate in vital matters, and acted independently of one another.[4] In rural areas this type of clan had lost its land base by the end of World War II. Before that time, the power of a few families over the land had very likely been increasing: In 1892, 40 percent of Japanese farmers were tenants, and by 1945 the figure had risen to 60 percent. The land reforms under the Allied occupation reduced tenancy to the point where between 80 to 90 percent were either owners, or owners in addition to being tenants. Thus neither the individual nor his family depended primarily on the *dozoku* for land, and of course the expansion of industry opened alternative opportunities for young men. Within the modern world, until very recently, the *dozoku* also remained of importance among the powerful Japanese families, called *zaibatsu,* who directed great commercial and industrial corporations.

THE KINDRED

This type of kin grouping was typically not organized, but its members did consider themselves to be a group. Since the *kindred* was likely to include blood kin in all directions, and was a residential unit as well (thus including many who married into the group, called *affinals*), its boundaries were much less clear than those of a lineage or clan. In part, who was in it was decided by local opinion: Whether one was to be called "one of the Peytons" would not be decided only by closeness in blood or marriage, but

---

4. Kunio Yanagida, *Japanese Manners and Customs in the Meiji Era,* trans. C. S. Terry (Tokyo: Obunsha, 1957), p. 104.

by whether "the Peytons" considered the individual one of them. Its boundaries differed for every one of its members. For example, an individual's mother's brother might be in it, but if he in turn counted as co-members everyone within, say, five degrees of *his* kinship position, he would have included some people who were further removed from that individual.

Kindreds were found in rural United States in the nineteenth century, but have not been genuine corporate bodies in the West since the beginning of the Middle Ages. Murdock found them in 30 percent of his sample, as against some 65 percent with lineages, but he argues that they are probably even more frequent than this figure suggests.[5] This form of descent grouping was found among the early Indo-European and Semitic tribes, and persisted until recently among some Polynesians and a few other tribes in various parts of the world. Notice that it is *not* exogamous, but endogamous. It contains many people, of different family lines, so that it is likely to contain a potential spouse. (In general, the smaller the kinship group, the more likely it is to be exogamous.) Of course an individual could also marry a very close "relative" in a unilineage system but not in his *own lineage*. Thus, in a matrilineage, a man might marry a first cousin, his mother's brother's daughter, but she would be in *her* mother's lineage. In a kindred he could also marry any cousin (father's brother's daughter), but neither would be members of an exogamous lineage. The central core of the kindred was usually the dominant families who bore the name of the kindred.

Since those who are closest to the main line of descent are viewed as the carriers of the traditions of the kindred, much attention was paid to genealogies. These had to be charted with great care because so many families had to be included, whereas in a lineage only the single line had to be reckoned. The kindred boundaries were not as clear as those of a lineage, and thus in a conflict or even in a matter of property ownership it could not function so effectively. Because everyone was in a different position in the total unit, and its boundaries extended indefinitely in all directions, people in it might be in conflict with one another, but call on a different set of relatives for support. Thus internal conflict was possible. In an external conflict, mustering everyone was not easy, since those distant from the core kin would not have felt the same definite sense of membership, and might instead feel just as close to another kindred. It is as though the McCoys of ballad fame were fighting with the Hatfields, but at many points they would be linked by kinship ties that made it difficult to mount a joint battle of the two groups as wholes. A person's duties in a unilineage were clear, however, because his other membership was clear.

So in general kindreds cannot be clearly defined segments of a society, and cannot easily act as a collectivity, either in owning land or administering political justice. On the other hand, they could achieve local control over their constituent families within a delimited area, and some analysts believe that at times their core of dominant families became the aristocratic stratum in more complex, stratified societies.

---

5.   George P. Murdock, *Social Structure* (New York: Macmillan, 1949), p. 57.

Although kin networks do not become corporate kin groups, acting together as a collective in industrialized nations, they merit comment in this chapter. First, as noted earlier, every recent inquiry into such networks reveals that they are alive and active in the technologically most developed nations. They show no signs of disappearing. When questioned closely, most individuals report some kind of active kinship links (visits, letters, gossip), and indeed the average number of people they think of as "kin" seems to range between 50 and 150 persons. Most also report some kinds of sharing activities (gifts, visits, services, help) with various members of their kin.

These patterns are not just remnants of older rural customs. They are maintained because a set of relatives is simply more effective for some kinds of help than even a competent bureaucracy. For example, kin can find out about one's needs faster, and can help more quickly. They understand one's particular or idiosyncratic wishes, and are more likely to take them into account in their decisions. Most family obligations do not require great expertise. Or they may be tasks for which there are no experts, or they may not fit exactly the categories of problems for which the bureaucracy has been designed.

On the other hand, people in a modern society engage in far more kinds of social relations with other people, groups, and organizations than in other societies, and some of these outside relations may be far more important for their lives than the interactions individuals have with an extensive kin network. Consequently, people can avoid some kinfolk altogether; engage in the most fleeting and rare interaction with others; or treat still others as very close friends. That is, in the modern setting, perhaps far more than in the distant past, people have a wider choice as to whether they will engage in intimate relations with any given kinsperson (uncles, cousins, nieces) or ignore that person altogether.

But though people do have that choice, and also exercise it, most people maintain relations with many kin. What determines the frequency of that interaction? In general, two major variables intersect to determine the amount of interaction that does take place. The first is *closeness* of kin. By and large, people are in more active contact with kin who are socially defined as closer.[6] This means, in *increasing* degree of distance: (1) the couple's siblings and joint descendant kin, their children and their children's spouses, together with their children's children; (2) the immediate family of one's spouse (both parents and siblings); and (3) the more distant kin, such as aunts, uncles, nieces, grandparents, and so on. That is, the farther out from the person's immediate family these kin are, as socially defined here, the less frequently will the individual have any social interaction with them.

6.   Here I am primarily following the analyses of George S. Rosenberg and Donald F. Anspach, *Working Class Kinship* (Lexington, Mass.: Heath, 1973).

The second variable is made up of all the factors that affect a kinsperson's *availability:* geographical proximity, the relative cost of transportation and communication, and of course whether an actual person of that kin type even exists. In one recent American sample of urban working-class respondents, 10 percent had no kin in or near their city, while two-thirds had "close kin"—descendant kin, or members of their parent's family. However, the *gradation* of interaction remains the same whether different categories of kin are more or less available. For example, if their children's families do not live close by, people do not compensate by frequently seeing their genealogically more distant kin who do live near. Aunts, uncles, grandparents, nephews, and nieces are seen less frequently than parents or children, even if they live closer.

Many family analysts have asserted that the Western pattern of kin interaction is *matricentric,* that married couples interact with the wife's family far more than with the husband's family. The explanation given is that women have closer ties with their mothers, and they also view the affairs of their kindred as more important. Two comments may put that claim in some perspective. First, the difference is very likely not great. The model pattern is for both husband and wife to see their *own* close kin, and when there are some differences, the wife's kin are seen more often. On the other hand, most spouses see their own kin *jointly,* and visit the two sets of relatives *equally.* If wives do not see their husband's kin, it is because their husbands are not seeing them either. Similarly, husbands see their wives' kin because they visit them with their wives. The pattern of joint visits also applies to their children. That is, for the most part, parents go together to see their children, or they do not see them at all. *Both* husband and wife play a key role in their visits to the other's kin. If the marriage breaks up, the links with in-laws become weak.

It seems clear that kin networks are active in even Western industrialized societies, though they do not form corporate groups. The social patterns observed between members are defined by positions within the conjugal family, but the sentiments and customs are not simply forms of family patterns. The kin network exists in its own right. However, we cannot yet answer with certainty an important question about these social patterns. Do people interact with more or fewer kin than in times past, or than in nonindustrial societies? Are the modern kin loyalties and social controls only thin copies of traditional feelings and behavior? Because of easier transportation and communication, perhaps contemporary families have more frequent contact with more members of their kin network than in the past. But it seems likely that interaction is of a) shorter duration, b) narrower in scope, and c) weaker in intensity. As to the second question, it seems at least plausible that kin do not play so central or so strong a part in modern life if only because the contemporary world offers far more alternatives, social relations, activities, forms of recreation or solace, and help.

One further question merits some attention. Research of two decades ago suggested that the *social networks* (made up of kin and friends) in which husbands and wives lived affected their personal relations considerably. Specifically, it seemed that when their network was "closed"—that is, its members formed a group and interacted with one another independently of the couple—husband and wife were more traditional in their allocation of domestic tasks, lived more of their day with friends or kin of the same sex, and in conflict enjoyed some social support from that same-sex group. By contrast, where the network was "open"—the couple's friends did not form a network or group independently of the couple—these patterns were not found. Subsequent research has suggested, however, that the closed network is found mainly in lower-class neighborhoods. Second, the differences are primarily based on whether or not the husband and wife separately interact as individuals in same-sex groups (kin and friends), rather than interacting as a couple. The differences depend little on whether those groups are tight networks. Third, among the better-educated couples, open networks are more common. Thus, the network pattern itself does not have the influence on husband-wife relations preliminary research once suggested. Perhaps the various types of social networks the couple takes part in do affect their relations, but at present this question has not been resolved.[7]

USES OF CORPORATE KIN GROUPINGS: PAST AND PRESENT

The corporate descent group could protect the individual family politically, since it could muster a greater number of men. It could act as a collective banker as well as tax collector, demanding of each family some contribution for a necessary collective enterprise, which might range from a marriage to the clearing of new land for growing crops. Often the chief rituals were organized and executed by the descent-group leaders. All these activities transcend both the interest and the power of the individual family. The family might wish the rituals to be performed, but could not pay for all their cost. If a young man was to be married, his own family was interested; but his kin were only mildly interested, and would contribute little to the expenses. However, a lineage could focus both interest and contribution on a necessary task whose completion ultimately helped to maintain it as a collectivity.

A further consequence of the relationships just noted can be seen. By virtue of the descent-group links, the family was drawn more firmly into the larger society. If quarrels were serious, they had to be submitted to the adjudication of clan or lineage elders. The individual family could not easily deviate far from community norms, because it had to continue to fulfill its collective kinship obligations, and was under the scrutiny of lineage or kindred members. A father who could not control a wayward son or wife could get help from members. Thus the forces that tend to turn

7. For a more extensive summary of the effect of networks, see Gary Lee, "Effects of Social Networks on the Family," in Wesley R. Burr et al., *Contemporary Theories about the Family,* vol. 1 (New York: Free Press, 1979), pp. 27–56.

a family in on itself, concerned only with its own problems, were partly countervailed by the demands of the larger kinship structure.

It is then understandable that when a society moves toward industrialization, the clan, lineage, kindred, or other corporate descent grouping weakens and decays. All these activities can be performed by impersonal, nonkinship agencies, whether governmental or private. A lineage is not needed to protect an individual family, if an adequate police system exists. Close kin remain a major source of small loans even in a modern economy, but banks become the main source (except among the very rich) of investment capital. In the early stages of industrial transition, a family that commands an effective kinship structure can often forge ahead of families trying to rise on their own. Nevertheless, such structures begin to disappear under industrialization. Even in societies where they existed for centuries before the modern era, for all these reasons they were much weaker in cities than in outlying rural areas.

One additional fact should be reported here. Although lineage systems remained strong in many great civilizations, it must not be assumed that all was harmony within them, or that they contributed services to all families equally. They were, after all, social organizations with resources, and members disputed among themselves as to who would make decisions and for whose benefit. Rich and powerful kin leaders directed poorer and weaker kin, ordered them to build roads or repair temples, and adjudicated disputes in their own favor. If lineage wealth could be used, they used it. Thus, if one can say that lineage created some services which in modern societies are furnished by the market or the state, one can also reverse that description in part: When alternatives became available, very likely most of the poor were not displeased to be freed of the burdens imposed on them by their more exalted kin within their lineage.

CHAPTER 8 WORKING WIVES: STEPS TOWARD EQUALITY IN THE SOCIETY AND THE HOME

Although it is common to think of "working women" as a relatively new phenomenon in history, the reality and its consequences are much more complex than the notion suggests. In fact, as a moment's thought will reveal, women have always worked, and not just as wives and daughters carrying out domestic chores in their homes.

Long before factories were introduced, peasant women worked in the labor market. In Southeast Asia, China, and Japan, for example, they often engaged in various forms of agricultural work—gathering tea, planting rice, winding silk from cocoons. When textile mills were established in such countries over the past century, women formed much of the labor force, and this was true as well of the early phases of nineteenth-century mills in England and the United States. Whenever men have had businesses such as innkeeping or brewing, wives have often furnished some of the skills that made those enterprises profitable. In Western societies, and doubtless Eastern ones as well, for many centuries a large segment of the poor women in each generation spent some years as domestic laborers or servants. Both women and children made up much of the labor force in the past because they could be paid very low wages, but their contribution to the total income of the family made it possible for all to survive.

For these reasons, even though the percentage of the labor force (only those who work for wages are counted officially) that is female does increase under industrialization over long periods of time, the changes in the great regions of the world over a single generation may be very modest. Since World War II, greater changes have occurred in the *kinds* of jobs women have entered, and how they feel about jobs, than in the total percentage that is female. More women have moved to industry as it has offered new opportunities. In the United States, a higher percentage have become bus drivers, bartenders, physicians, lawyers, and mayors. Great changes have occurred in communist countries after the revolution, which always seeks to utilize a higher percentage of female labor while industrializing. But although large changes have occurred in some specific countries, Table 8.1 reveals that in a number of great areas of the world, the changes over the past generation in the percentage of labor force that is female have not been very radical. What has been radical is the change in the position of the working woman. For though women have always worked, their position in an advanced industrial economy is different from their position in other systems in two fundamental ways, both of which have profound consequences for the family.

THE WOMAN WORKER IN INDUSTRIAL SOCIETY

In an industrial society, for the first time women have had the right, slowly conceded by men, to enter the labor market on their own, to obtain jobs or promotions without the help or permission of male kin, and even to spend their wages at their own discretion. They do not get this last right, among many groups, until a later stage in industrialization, whatever their rights under the law. This may be phrased in a stronger way: Industrialization is the first socioeconomic system (socialist or nonsocialist) in which the employer comes to have relatively little interest in whether his female employees fulfill their kin obligations; the primary stake is in how well those workers do the job. In plain terms, employers in a fully developed industrial system will not pay higher wages simply because their employees are dutiful daughters, obedient wives, or nurturant mothers.

Table 8.1   Percent of Women in the Total Nonagricultural Labor Force 1900–1978,[a] Western Nations

	ABOUT 1900	ABOUT 1930	ABOUT 1950	ABOUT 1978[b]
Germany[c]	(1907) 27	(1933) 30	(1950) 33	37
Belgium	(1900) 32	(1930) 27	(1947) 25	39
Denmark	(1906) 36	(1930) 35	(1950) 37	44
Finland	(1900) 27	(1930) 38	(1950) 41	46
France	(1906) 37	(1931) 34	(1954) 35	38
Great Britain	(1901) 32	(1931) 31	(1951) 32	39
Italy	(1901) 32	(1931) 30	(1951) 28	32
Holland	(1899) 27	(1930) 26	(1947) 25	27 (1971)
Sweden	(1900) 28	(1930) 35	(1950) 31	45
Switzerland	(1905) 36	(1930) 37	(1950) 34	
United States	(1900) 23	(1930) 26	(1950) 30	42

[a] 1900–1950 data from Jean Dirac, "Quelques vues sur le travail feminin non agricole en divers pays," *Population*, January–March 1958, p. 72.
[b] 1978 data from *Yearbook: Labor Statistics*, International Labor Organization, 1979, Table 2A.
[c] East and West combined for the pre-World War II period.

The second fundamental change is that it is only with industrialization that women's jobs separate them from their children. In the earliest stages of industrialization, as in agricultural and domestic labor, women have been able to carry out their tasks with the help of their children, or at least with their children close by. Most societies had little concern about this new development as long as these workers were poor laborers, and most women workers in the earliest factories were unmarried anyway. It is only in this century, when an increasing part of the female labor force is middle class or at least white collar, and mothers as well, that moralists and analysts have begun to worry about the fate of their children as well as the family generally under these new conditions.

A host of speculations about these consequences have been raised in every country in the world.[1] If the woman has a good job, will she bother to marry? If the wife works, is marital unhappiness or divorce more likely? Are her children more likely to be neglected, to become juvenile delinquents, or to have personality problems? Energy and time that are spent in career advancement will surely not be invested in the traditional duties of wife and mother. If the wife obtains an adequate salary, she will not be as dependent on her husband as she once was, and it can be supposed his authority might be less. Common sense would seem to be on the side of the traditionalists in every country who have predicted that these great changes in the position of women within the labor force might lead eventually and necessarily to the breakdown of the family. It is because of this widespread public concern that we devote a chapter to this topic. Such views are partly correct, but the reality is somewhat complex. Let us review the evidence to date.

The Research Base

Research on the impact of women's employment has been much more voluminous in the United States than in other countries. The strength of the findings is thus limited (a) because of normative differences among countries (for example, men in Islamic countries resist women's employment more successfully than men in Communist countries; (b) because of differences in substitute care facilities for children; (c) because the kinds of jobs women can get will differ from one country to another; and (d) because people's attitudes toward women's employment are likely to continue changing (for example, findings from the 1950s or 1960s in the United States are not correct now). Thus we must be wary of supposing that all the relationships noted here will apply to all countries.

On the other hand, many social patterns are created by very general social forces whose broad impact should be similar in different countries.

---

1. The reader should note that almost all of them contain a hidden assumption: That the traditional duties of caring for home and children are unquestionably *hers;* only rarely do men consider whether the father/husband should not simply take over some of them, to prevent them from being "neglected."

For example, such patterns as these ought to be visible in almost any country:

1.   As a higher percentage of women become better educated, more employers see some economic profit in hiring them, and the relative economic payoff to the family in permitting them to work will increase.

2.   As fertility declines, more women decide to take jobs; as more women take jobs, fertility declines.

3.   As the ideology that supports wives' dependence weakens, more women enter the labor market.

4.   As more women take jobs, the age of women at marriage is likely to increase (if it was low), and this may affect husband-wife adjustment.

5.   At lower levels of family income, or under inflation, more women feel the need to work in order to provide a margin for security.

6.   Husbands' and childrens' resistance to mothers working decreases as their percentage in the labor force increases.

7.   If husbands are better educated, they adjust more easily to the wishes of their wives (also better educated) to use their talents in a job.

Thus, in spite of the limitations of contemporary research findings, it is likely that many of them will describe with some accuracy what is happening in many other parts of the world.

Major New Socioeconomic Patterns

As in other family patterns, the socioeconomic forces that affect family relations when the mother works outside the home are often complex because of the continuing *normative* pressures on women. Specifically, in early socialization as in later social interaction, the role of *mother* (and *housewife*) is more central than any other role the woman plays. She is expected to continue her homemaking and maternal tasks even if she does work full-time. On becoming a worker she will not be permitted to be as independent as would, say, a nearly adult son in the family. In addition, although studies generally find that working mothers do not spend as many hours at home tasks as women who stay at home, husbands do *not* assume the domestic tasks that are not carried out. The evidence from studies in other Western nations, communist and capitalist, yields the same conclusion: Even when both husband and wife work, domestic tasks are not shared equally. Home and children are still expected to be her responsibility. It cannot be supposed, however, that as more women enter the labor force this imbalance will continue to be as great as it is now.

In the United States in 1979, women made up 42 percent of the civilian workforce; in 1950, it was 30 percent. This participation changes with age, but it has been moving toward a pattern much like that of men, which means that women's part in the labor force has been increasing at all ages beyond 20 years. About 80 percent of never-married women are working, and 75 percent of divorced, separated, and widowed women have jobs.

Fifty-eight percent of women with husbands present and with children under 18 also work. The figures are somewhat higher for black women, but this difference has been declining. Fifty-eight percent of all women with children aged 3 to 5 are in the labor force, and the rate for mothers has been rising faster than for other segments of the labor force. And all these rates will be higher in the coming decade.[2]

Just what effect has women's employment had on various aspects of contemporary family life? Family analysts have noted two possible effects of women working: One, because women can earn a living independently, and in a market economy can obtain housing and the array of services and commodities that people need for living alone, they might decide that they need not marry at all. Second, the woman's income may, on the other hand, serve as a kind of "dowry," which would ensure some economic stability for the couple and thus encourage marriage.

The first of these effects was observed in the first decades of this century, when most working women had relatively unskilled jobs and usually dropped out of the labor market about the time of their first child, but at least some women entered professional occupations and devoted their entire lives to a career. This latter group of women often did not marry, or married late. At that time, women viewed their alternatives as devoting themselves to a career or to a family, and some chose the first. However, now that almost all women work at some time in their lives, and a relatively high percentage of women continue to work for much of their marital careers, at least off and on, it becomes obvious that those were false alternatives: one can do both.

By contrast, the "dowry" effect seems stronger for most women in the present generation. Nevertheless, both effects (the postponement of marriage and the dowry effect) may still be noted, since the age at which young women marry rises when they have good employment opportunities. They do not have to rush into marriage at the first opportunity, and since they continue to earn money, they continue to be worth more on the marriage market. That is, precisely because women's earnings enable them to marry they can postpone marriage, but need not forgo a marital career altogether. For the immediate future what this means is that the age at which women marry will very likely be somewhat higher than in the past, but that almost everyone will eventually marry (about 95 percent). Since, moreover, more women are obtaining professional training of some kind, and thus extending the years of their own education, we can expect some additional support for the trend toward a somewhat later age at marriage.

A third set of effects has to do with divorce. In the past, as at the present, women at the upper levels of income and occupational rank are

2.   Kristin A. Moore and Sandra L. Hofferth have summarized the descriptive data on these points in "Effects of Women's Employment on Marriage: Formation, Stability and Roles," *Marriage & Family Review*, 2 (1979), 1, 27–36, which also contains a good bibliography of the important statistical sources. See also George Maesinck and Mary Jo Bane, *The Nation's Families: 1960–1990* (Cambridge, Mass.: Joint Center for Urban Studies of MIT and Harvard University, 1980).

more prone to divorce. Almost certainly this is an "independence effect"; women who experience an unsatisfactory marriage do not have to tolerate it, because they have the alternative of living independently. Moreover, the size of their income makes them continue to be somewhat more attractive partners, and thus they are more likely to remarry. There is a generally *inverse* relationship between class position and divorce; that is, there is a higher divorce rate toward the lower social strata. But this general pattern does not apply to women with postcollege education and higher occupational rank: their divorce rate is higher. We would suppose, in addition, that when the husband's income is unstable or low but the wife's is relatively high, the higher divorce rate would be accentuated. Let us look now more closely at what these trends mean within the individual family.

THE WORKING WIFE AND MOTHER

Division of Labor within the Home

Because the past two decades have witnessed a new effort on the part of women in the United States (and other parts of the world) to achieve greater equality within the marketplace as within the home, it is important to consider the extent to which the division of labor within the home has changed because of women's employment outside it. Most studies, in this and in other countries, suggest that very little change has occurred, although we believe that important changes are now taking place. Let us consider this problem.

Even without any ideological pressure toward a more equal division of household responsibilities, one might suppose that husbands and wives would move toward a greater sharing of domestic duties when the wife is engaged in a full-time occupation, just as her husband is. That is, since both are spending more than 40 hours a week at work or in traveling to and from work, it would seem likely that not only fairness, but the simple recognition of limited time and energy, would shift the burden considerably. But at present, very few bits of data suggest that this commonsense expectation is correct. Let us first consider the woman's time budget over the past decades. The introduction of household labor-saving devices in the United States did not reduce the number of hours housewives devoted to domestic tasks, although of course such inventions as free-flowing water within the home, gas and electricity for heating, and washing machines did decrease the actual physical labor of cleaning and cooking. Many studies of housewives' time budgets were made over this period of more than half a century, and during the past two decades time budgets have been made in other countries as well. Until very recently, the general finding of almost all these studies was the same: machines increased the productivity of the household as an economic unit, but they did not decrease the number of hours women worked. Various studies, based on different samples, have reported a range from 35 to 60 hours per week. These figures, of course, apply mainly to housewives not engaged in outside jobs. The hours will be longer or shorter, depending on the number of young children, region, class, and so on. The *direct* care of children adds somewhat to the total figure beyond the range already noted (to about 40 to 70 hours weekly).

Such studies report that men contribute very little to the total amount of domestic work accomplished, in socialist as well as nonsocialist countries. In some studies, two-thirds of the husbands are reported to do no housework at all. Among those who do some, the contribution ranges from about 6 to 11 hours per week, depending on which tasks the researcher decides to include (merely sitting in the company of children, or only direct supervision of children).

Since the total number of hours worked by housewives without a paid job is so large, it is difficult for many to work an additional 40 or 45 hours per week at a full-time occupation plus transportation to and from work. Men do not, however, take over the tasks this reduced number of hours may leave uncompleted. This means, therefore, that the husband works fewer hours per week than does the wife. In one study, the work week of wives (job plus housework) averaged about 8 hours more than that of husbands. Up to the mid 1970s in the United States, husbands increased their participation in domestic tasks by only a small amount, from one hour to a few minutes per week in different studies. Indeed, the broad finding of many studies is simply that whether or not a wife works has very little effect on the husband's contribution to domestic tasks. The most important change is, instead, that wives reduce the number of hours they devote to various tasks, as well as to gardening, sleeping, or television viewing. One recent estimate drawn from a sample in New York State is that full-time worker-wives reduce their domestic work to about 26 hours weekly. In cross-national studies as well, husbands are reported to contribute very little to domestic labor. Russian women continue to take on most of the household tasks, in a country that extols the ideal of egalitarianism.

Wives make do in various ways. Perhaps the most pressing problem is that of child care. About 13 percent of children in the 7- to 13-year-old age category are sometimes left to care for themselves. A majority of employed mothers pay for child care, even if not on a daily basis. Most wives also manage from time to time to obtain help from relatives. In China, grandparents, older sisters, and sometimes other kin and neighbors furnish this service. Women have not only coped; they have begun to change their attitudes as well. In the period 1962 to 1977, American women began to change their attitudes in the direction of greater approval of more equal sex role behavior, and thus a more equal sharing of housework. In studies carried out in the early 1970s, a majority of women reported that they did not feel their husband should contribute more to housework, possibly because they felt their husbands already worked enough. (Black women were more in favor of this contribution). In the 1960s, although many women held relatively egalitarian attitudes, they constituted a minority. By 1977, attitudes *against* a traditional division of the labor, with respect to housework, major decisions, and which kinds of jobs or tasks men and women should have, formed a majority of the total. In addition, as an apparent harbinger of the future, younger women, women with more education,

wives with better-educated husbands, black women, and those who had
held jobs for many years were more likely than others to move toward
egalitarian sex role attitudes.[3]

It can be predicted that such changes will also occur in other industrialized nations, as a higher percentage of women obtain better jobs and are
increasingly affected by the worldwide discussion about "woman's place."
From past history it can be taken for granted that men will resist these
pressures, but observations suggest that among better-educated, younger
couples, men are already moving to accept a greater share of domestic
tasks. In contemporary rural China, in spite of some moves toward
egalitarianism, women earn work points for their labor, but these points
are totaled as earnings for the family, and males are the heads of such
families. They do not receive wages independently, and what they contribute to the family over time does not become part of their property if they
are divorced. Moreover, they are hardly represented at all among the important political positions in the communes, except when they are in charge
of some kind of "woman's concern," such as birth control, indoctrination of
women, and the like. It is to be emphasized that their *structural* position is
not an independent one, and therefore we should not expect any substantial changes as yet in the allocation of domestic tasks, which remain pre-
dominantly the responsibility of women.[4] Changes are substantial, however, in urban China.

Marital Adjustment

Since women enter the labor force for a wide variety of reasons and
work at very different jobs, while their husbands vary substantially in their
attitudes toward this move, we can suppose that the impact of women's employment on marital satisfaction would be fairly complex. In most societies
until possibly the past few decades, most men in comfortable financial situations would have forbidden their daughters or wives to go outside the home
to work. Even in contemporary society, many men feel that it is their duty
to make enough money so that their wives "don't have to work," and they
feel some failure if financial need forces them to accept that new situation.
In addition, men have supposed that they would lose control over their
wives and daughters if they took jobs outside the home, both because they
could not continue to monitor their sexual behavior, and because an independent income would make them less willing to accept male domination.
On the other hand, now as in the past, husbands or fathers have derived
economic benefit from the additional income. And wives have not always

3. Arland Thornton and Deborah Freedman, "Changes in the Sex Role Attitudes of
Women, 1962–1977: Evidence from a Panel Study," *American Sociological Review,* 44
(October 1970), 832–842.

4. For other data on these relationships, see William L. Parish and Martin K. Whyte,
Village and Family in Contemporary China (Chicago: University of Chicago Press, 1978),
chaps. 10–12.

been eager to take outside jobs, because it was evident that they were expected to continue discharging their regular household duties, whatever
the demands of the outside work.

We should expect, in any event, that studies made in different parts of
the world, at different times, would reflect a very different set of outcomes
for husbands and wives. Obviously, if most of the women in a given nation
are already in the labor market, most men will feel less troubled if their own
wife or daughter goes out to work. In the Soviet Union, men expect their
wives to work as a matter of course. As a higher proportion of the labor
force is made up of women, more women will be found in higher-level
occupations, thus returning a larger income to the household that loses her
services for part of the day. As more challenging work opportunities are
opened up over time, more women actually want to work and will be
unhappy if they are not given that chance. Many children object to their
mother's working because they feel deprived of her attention; while they
may also be proud of her accomplishments. Thus, in reviewing the evidence, we have to be aware that changes in labor-force composition and the
attitudes of men, women, and children will affect whether or not people
feel greater satisfaction when the mother enters an occupation on a full-
time basis.

In spite of these cautions, some relationships seem fairly likely, as we
noted earlier. One is simply that wives with more education, who therefore
obtain more challenging and higher-paid jobs, are more likely to go to work
out of choice, and also to report more marital satisfaction. If their husbands
approve of that employment, they are also likely to report greater satisfaction with their marriages. On the other hand, most women (like most men)
can enter only relatively uninteresting jobs at modest pay, and they continue to shoulder most of the burden of housework. Their husbands, in
turn, feel deprived of some of the services they normally would expect.
Moreover, most studies show that when wives work, they obtain a stronger
voice in family decisions. This effect is greater toward the middle and lower
social strata, because the difference in income between husbands and wives
is *smaller* there than in upper-middle or upper-class positions. The difference between the incomes of black husbands and wives is likely to be still
smaller, and wives' share in family decisions somewhat greater.

Thus, some studies report that husbands of working wives experience
less satisfaction with their marriages and a generally lower mental and
physical well-being than husbands whose wives stay at home. Women who
work part-time only, as well as their husbands, are more likely to report
their marriages as good—perhaps because in this case the husband loses
fewer of his wife's services, but still gains from the added income. It should
be kept in mind that the findings of these studies are likely to become
dated, simply because both attitudes and behavior change over time, and
also because the samples themselves may be made up of very different
kinds of people. Men whose wives do not go out to work may be married to
women who themselves hold traditional attitudes, in harmony with the
traditional attitudes of their husbands. Some of the lesser marital satisfaction of men whose wives go out to work may come from the fact that these

women are already less willing to remain under the control of their husbands, and want to have an independent base for their lives.

It is difficult to disentangle the effect of all of these separate factors, because almost no studies follow a group of marriages over time in order to ascertain what happens to each marriage when the wife goes out to work. Instead, reports come from a cross section of marriages at a given time. In many cases the husband and wife lived together in conflict to begin with, before the wife decided to enter the labor market.

Children of Working Mothers

When most mothers in the labor market were lower class or black, relatively little social concern was expressed as to whether this might have a bad effect on their children. However, as women have come to form a larger proportion of the labor force, and have entered middle- and higher-level occupations, they have threatened men somewhat more and have also made stronger claims to equality in the workplace as in the domestic sphere. Consequently, more voices have been raised to predict that the children of the future will be harmed by these changes. Of all mothers (with or without a husband present) with at least one child at home under the age of 18, almost 60 percent are in the labor force. What can we say now about the effect of mothers' employment on the development of their children?

Perhaps the most important finding is that it has *not* been possible to demonstrate that children who grow up in households with working mothers develop psychological problems or are more prone to various kinds of deviance than children whose mothers stay at home to supervise them. The small differences that do appear seem to be simply a reflection of class differences: More working mothers with or without a husband are to be found toward the lower middle or lower social strata, where somewhat more juvenile delinquency and poor school performance are likely to be reported.

A second important finding negates another widespread fear: Many studies have been made of the effect of child-care agencies and organizations in various countries, and these show that children who spend part of their day in the care of substitute mothers in such organizations do not show evidence of psychological harm or social delinquency. In rural regions, of course, these substitute agencies are likely to be simply relatives of the working mother, while in various European countries (France, Russia) the agencies are likely to be supervised by the government and staffed by professionals.

In conformity with our earlier discussion, children whose mothers work part-time are less likely to feel deprived. Part-time workers have more hours at their disposal, and it is possible they represent a different sample—that is, mothers who simply wish to devote more time to their children. Children of mothers who like their work are also less likely to feel deprived. This pattern is made up of several elements. Women who like their work are more likely to be engaged in somewhat higher-level jobs that pay more and are somewhat more fun. They bring more material comforts to the home, and try to make up to their children for their lesser gifts of time. On the other hand, the women who do not like to work are more likely to be lower class and to have less pleasant jobs. Such mothers may therefore feel put upon and are more likely to insist that their sons shoulder some of the burden of household chores. Such mothers feel less need to compensate for their absence, and their daughters are more likely to feel somewhat neglected. Children of mothers who hold higher-level jobs may not suffer much from neglect for another reason. Although such jobs may be more demanding, they are also likely to bring more satisfaction to the mothers who engage in them. As a consequence, such mothers report more marital satisfaction, and thus psychologically are better able to give more affection and attention to their children. The added income also enables the family to hire more household help or child care services.

Of most importance for the behavior of future generations is the effect of sex role attitudes on the children. In general, when mothers work their children are more likely to approve of mothers working and of a more egalitarian division of domestic tasks. Girls are less likely to accept traditional feminine roles, and are more likely to take jobs themselves. Lower-class boys with working mothers are less likely to evaluate their fathers as highly as lower-class boys whose mothers stay at home. Middle-class boys of working mothers are more likely to view their fathers as warm and nurturant. Both boys and girls with working mothers are more likely than others to view women as competent.[5]

On the other hand, we cannot suppose at all that present reports are adequate. First, almost all begin with the widespread assumption that it is the *mother's* responsibility to take care of the children, and it is *her* working that creates problems (if any) in the psychological and social development of the next generation. That general assumption is shared by most men and women in this and other countries. And, as we have noted repeatedly, both the behavior and the attitudes of men, women, and children are changing with respect to a wide range of definitions about appropriate sex roles within the home and the marketplace. As people's attitudes and understandings change over time, the sociopsychological effects of mothers working will also change.

In addition, of course, we lack an appropriate historical *time base* for our comparison. We simply do not know what percentage of traditional mothers in past generations would actually have contributed to their children's well-being by entering a full-time occupation. Many mothers, at all class levels, were not nurturant or attentive, sensitive or responsible, in former times as well as at present. Doubtless many child-care agencies as well as other relatives give better mothering to some modern children than they would get from their real mothers. In short, even aside from the complexity of contemporary data, and the difficulty of weighing the impact of maternal employment over the first two decades in the life of a child, we

---

5.   E. M. Rallings and F. Ivan Nye, "Wife-Mother, Employment, Family and Society," in Wesley R. Burr et al., *Contemporary Theories about the Family,* vol. 1 (New York: Free Press, 1979), pp. 215ff.

have little knowledge about the psychosocial development of children under traditional household arrangements in the historical past, when most women stayed at home. We know, at least, that it is only in very recent times that childrearing was felt to be a full-time occupation for adult women. The most cautious but robust conclusion is this: If the mother's employment has a harmful effect on the psychosocial development of the child, contemporary studies have not discovered it.

A MOVEMENT TOWARD EQUALITY?

Recent changes in the structural position of women in the market-place should not be overstated, but they must not all be viewed as trivial, either. The Saudi Arabians have tried to keep their educated women from entering many jobs they could perform, because it is feared they would be corrupted. Both the Soviets and the Chinese have put most adult women in wage-earning positions and have proclaimed equality (easier than achiev-ing it), but women in both countries are burdened with nearly all the traditional domestic duties along with their tasks outside the home. Should we focus on the radical changes in these two countries, or on their failure to reach equality?

The question of women's liberation is theoretically important, and it should be treated here as part of our continuing analysis of how societal forces affect relations within the family, and vice versa. If women continue to improve their position in the marketplace, will they also move somewhat more toward equality with their husbands in the home? Or will men man-age to subvert the political thrust of the women's movement?

Here we focus mainly on the United States, but we remind the reader that women in every major country are now attempting to assert their claims to equality, and not only in the area of work. Their "rebellion" is part of a worldwide demand for equality, pressed not just by women, but by ethnic and racial groups, castes, colonies, and subnational groups such as the Scots and the Basques. Oppressed groups all over the world are no longer willing to admit they deserve their lowly position. They increasingly argue that they have been victims, and each year a larger percentage of them clamor for equality. The first stage of liberation is often the recogni-tion that one's misery or deprivation is not *personal;* it is caused by social institutions, in this case familial institutions.

In this country, blacks, the more educated women, and younger women are more likely to feel this than others, and of course rural Chinese women are less likely to do so, but the movement can be observed worldwide. More and more women are experiencing this revelation. If the movement continues, it will have important consequences for the family. But even in Sweden and the United States, where the most organized efforts in this direction have been made by schools, governmental agencies (once women begin to care, their votes are a threat), and private organiza-tions, we suppose that the last reader of this book will not live to observe complete sexual equality firsthand.

Will the movement toward equality continue? Running the risk that all prophets of the future must run, we assert that males will stubbornly resist but reluctantly adjust. They will do so because women will continue to want more equality than they now enjoy, and they will be unhappy if they do not get it. Men, on average, will prefer that their women be happy. The adjustment will continue because neither women nor men will find an adequate substitute for the other sex, and neither will be able to find an alternative social system. When dominant classes or groups cannot rig the system as much in their favor as they once did, they will work within it just the same. To revise an old adage, if this is the only roulette wheel in town, men will continue to play even if it is honest and fair.

We shall go on to formulate the basic cause for these changes in an abstract but powerful socioeconomic relationship. For now, we wish to state at least a few of the subtleties that are to be found in the resistance of men to accepting an egalitarian relationship with their wives, even as they come to recognize that women's potential and their achievement are greater than has been recognized. Of course, men have enjoyed an exploitive position throughout history, just as all dominant groups have, and such groups do not easily give up their unearned profit in money, power, and prestige. However, if relations between men and women were simply those of oppressed and oppressor, then the greater power of men would have moved all societies toward male-vanity cultures, and women would have been kept behind blank walls, forced to work at productive tasks only with their sisters, while men lazed away their hours in parasitic pleasures. Instead, it is easy to observe that men work all over the world, and the position of women varies a great deal by class, by society, and over time. Indeed, we assert that there are strong socioeconomic contradictions within any attempt by males to create a fully exploitive set of material advantages for all males. There are also inherent *emotional* contradictions in any effort to achieve full domination in that intimate sphere.

As to the first contradiction, women—just like men in the same situation—who are utterly powerless, slavish, and ignorant are most easily exploitable, and there are always some male pressures to place them in that position. Unfortunately, such women do not yield very much surplus product; they do not even produce much. Women who are freer and also more in command of productive skills, as in hunting and gathering societies and increasingly in modern industrial ones, produce far more, but they are also more resistant to exploitation or domination.

As to the emotional ties, men would like to be lords of their castle and to be loved absolutely—if successful, it is the cheapest exploitive system—but in real life this is less likely to happen unless one loves in return. In that case, what happens is what has happened in real life over history: Men do care about the joys and sorrows of their women—and in spite of some modern historians, we believe that this was almost as true of the thirteenth century in Europe as it is in the twentieth century. Mutual caring reduces the degree to which men are willing to exploit their own wives, mothers, and sisters. More interesting, however, their caring also takes the form of wanting to prevent *other* men from exploiting these same women, when the women go into the outside world. Thus, over several centuries, English

laws defining the position of wives and daughters expressed those contradictions: At times, some of these laws expressed the wish of husbands
and fathers to dominate; other laws expressed their need to create protec-
tions for these women against the evil intentions of other men.

Some part of the resistance of men against any move toward equality
in jobs or the home comes, of course, from the obvious sociological fact that
the observations made by both men and women are limited and somewhat
biased by what they are most interested in, and by their lack of opportunity
to observe behind the scenes of each other's lives. As Jesse Bernard has
commented, there are always at least two marriages: *his* marriage and *her*
marriage. Because their structural positions are different, wives watch husbands much more closely than husbands watch wives; that is, what men do
affects women far more than what women do will affect their men. Nevertheless, since men do not typically understand the problems women face
when they work, they do not at once feel that this change has earned equal
rights for women.

Husbands, and men generally, know that they themselves did not
create the system that gives them their advantages, and thus they reject any
charge that they are following a plan to dominate women. They have
throughout history taken for granted the system that gives them their
position, and (like other dominants or subordinates) they are not aware of
how much the social structure pervasively yields small, cumulative, and
eventually large advantages in most competitions. Generally, men believe
that their greater accomplishments are actually due to their inborn
superiority. Moreover, when men are asked, they express far more awareness of the burdens and responsibilities they bear than of their own earned
advantages. As we noted much earlier, husbands have not in the past seen
much wisdom in giving their wives or daughters more opportunity for
growth, since they already had their familial roles laid out for them and
they were not deemed capable of much growth, and especially not in the
areas of men's special skills.

Neither men nor women easily organize as a group. After all, the two
sexes do not live in set-apart communities, neighborhoods, or families.
Both husbands and wives are separated from their own sex by having a
stake in the family organization that gives each a set of different roles.
Women especially come to have a vested interest in the social unit that at
the same time imposes inequalities on them. And one response of men to
the liberation movement is surprise, as well as deep resentment. Men are
also hurt, for they feel betrayed, and this response can be observed in men
of many countries. They do not wish to believe that the previously contented
or pleasant façade their women presented to them was false. They feel they
were giving protection against anyone who wanted to exploit or hurt their
wives or daughters, and they respond with anger to the discovery that they
were deceived, or to the charge that they have selfishly used the dominant
position they feel they have rightly earned.

At perhaps a deeper level, very likely most men (especially outside the
privileged stratum of professionals and managers) see their work in a
modern industrial state as not yielding much intrinsic satisfaction, as not

being fun in itself. On the other hand, they pride themselves on their hard work and personal sacrifice as breadwinners—they have made, in effect, a gift of this to their wives and children. Now, they are being told that this was not a gift, and they have not earned special deference for it. The charge is now made that women work longer hours, sleep less, and play less, and they have earned far more than their husbands actually gave them.

As to whether there are any changes in either the domestic sphere or the marketplace, the data reveal just what would be expected in any social movement that entails so many facets of people's lives. In Communist as in non-Communist countries, as we have already noted, men contribute very little to domestic tasks, and they contribute hardly more when their wives work than when they do not work. This is true of every country for which we have time-budget data. It is only in the last few years in the United States that some few survey data have begun to show a possible trend toward greater sharing.

With reference to jobholding, several basic facts should be noted. Communist countries have made far greater strides toward job equality than were made in perhaps any comparable time in Western nations, and it is possible that there is somewhat more job equality in the Soviet Union at the present time than in the United States—although to demonstrate that assertion would require a relatively elaborate analysis. On the other hand, in both Communist and non-Communist countries, the basic pattern remains the same. At every upward step in the job hierarchy, a smaller and smaller percentage of women is to be found. For example, a majority of ordinary physicians in Soviet Russia are women, but a very tiny percentage of women are professors in major medical institutes. Since the 1950s, American women have made no visible progress at all in closing the earnings gap with men. There are more women in the marketplace, but about the same percentage are now to be found in sex-segregated types of jobs: teaching school, librarian, typist, and so on. On the other hand, it is also true that in more and more job classifications, when men and women are to be found in exactly the same job, the earnings gap does begin to close. Moreover, far more women are in nontraditional jobs (bus drivers, bartenders, garbage collectors). In addition, there is less occupational segregation in most of the professions than formerly.

As to public opinion, the changes in the United States are much more substantial. In spite of the frequent reference to "backlash"—supposedly the change of opinions that comes when people see that proposals they had supported before will actually lead to social behavior that they disapprove—in fact there is no visible backlash. Public opinion, as expressed in numerous questions that have been asked over the past several decades, has steadily moved toward greater approval of equal rights for women in all areas. We do not suppose that public opinion is the prime mover here, or that action automatically follows attitudes. It would be difficult, however, to assert the contrary—that values, norms, and ideology all have no effect on behavior. For example, a nation that proclaims equality and liberty in innumerable abstract formulations is embarrassed at being confronted with strong evidence of crude discrimination and unfairness. The ideology would have less effect if women in the United States were not in fact almost as well educated as men generally, except for postgraduate training; and if women had not demonstrated again and again their capacity to do first-rate jobs in a wide range of tasks; and if they were not increasingly needed in the labor force to maintain productivity. Nevertheless, ideological factors give expression to these changes, justify them, and organize sentiments in favor of them.

In the domestic sphere as in the larger society, groups and segments of the population are engaged in day-to-day negotiation and renegotiation of advantages. This occurs among husbands and wives, fathers and children, or bosses and the people who work for them. The fact that so many relationships must be negotiated, rather than being decided by tradition, creates some tension between husbands and wives, but this process is not likely to end soon. The negotiations are partly personal, but their outcome on a mass basis is mainly determined by the advantages each segment may hold in the structure of law, economic demand, or political power. They are determined in part by the achievements and failures of subgroups, as they are faced with new opportunities or new disasters. All these socioeconomic conditions in advanced industrial nations are different from those of any prior civilization, and they give less support to men's claim of superiority than in perhaps any other historical era. When these new conditions weaken that support, men can rely only on previous tradition, or their personal attempts to socialize their children, to shore up their faltering advantages. That rhetoric is not likely to be successful against the new objective conditions as well as the political claims of aggrieved women. Men are quite correct when they feel they are losing some of their privileges, worry that women will vote against them because of their failure to implement a law supporting equality, or worry that some women may perform a job better than they can.

In the modern world, there are fewer tasks that require much strength because of the increased use of various mechanical gadgets and devices. Some still require strength, but most men today cannot do them either. Women can now do more of the household repair tasks that men once felt only they could do, but still more are not done by husbands anyway, but by repair specialists. There are few if any important combat activities that only men can do, though in this area men still want to protect women from actual battlefield conditions, even if all of us are threatened with destruction by the nuclear bomb. With each passing year, in this and other countries where serious research is done, psychological and sociological research reduces the areas in which men excel over women, and it also discloses there is far more overlap in talents. Thus, even when males (in some tasks) still appear to have an advantage, it is but a slight one. It is also becoming more widely understood that the top posts in government and business are not best filled by the stereotypical, *macho* male, but by persons, male or female, who are sensitive to others' needs, adept at obtaining cooperation, and skilled in social relations. Under these conditions, new laws in almost every country are proposed or passed that express both the concern of men about the new women's activities (and thus try to hold women in their place) and also support their demands for equal treatment. The new laws have their direct effect on the conditions described here, but the laws themselves arise from a sensitivity to the new forces that have been unleashed in the modern world.

In theoretical terms, the underlying shift may be phrased as movement toward the *decreasing marginal utility of males.* That is, fewer people continue to believe that what the male does is indispensable, nonsubstitutable, or adds such a special value to any endeavor that it justifies his extra "price" or reward—on the job or in the home. In wars of the past, males enjoyed a very high value, because it was felt not only that they could do the job better than women, but that they might well make the difference between being conquered and remaining free. In some societies, their marginal utility came partly from their contribution of animal protein through hunting. Even when most men did not engage in such activities, they felt that their activities as revolutionary heroes, plowmen, hunters, warriors, and daring capitalist entrepreneurs was a contribution beyond anything women could do, and doubtless most women thought that as well. In any event, it seems likely that through most of history, and in spite of much grumbling, both men and women have thought that the contribution of men deserved some extra privileges of rank, authority, and creature services. Now, that marginal utility is increasingly under suspicion. It is not that, as individuals, males will be deemed less worthy in the future, or that their contributions will be less needed. It is rather that there will be an increasing number of people in the world who will be reluctant to grant *extra* rewards to men *solely* because they are members of the male sex-class. This is part of a still broader trend of this generation worldwide, which increasingly denies that being white, or an upper-caste or upper-class person, produces a marginally superior result and thus justifies extra privilege.

We wish to emphasize that these changes will not occur tomorrow, in any country. In some contries just after a revolution, important changes seem to occur (for example, Algeria), and then women's rights are taken away or the effort toward equality is dropped. In the Soviet Union and China there were radical changes at first, and it is fair to say that there has been no substantial backward movement, but political leaders have mainly decided that attention to productivity should take precedence over concerns about women's equality. As they discover that they will achieve higher productivity if domestic duties are also allocated more fairly, they may inaugurate new policies. In any event, we can never take for granted a simple, steady movement of change.

On the other hand, it seems unlikely that the massive forces we have described can be totally negated by the personal efforts of men to retain their privileges within the domestic sphere. As noted, we believe there is already evidence that changes are taking place in the more advanced societies, and we are arguing that the shifts in socioeconomic opportunities and advantages make it simply profitable to some segments of the society to grant more equality to women. As that movement continues, we argue that however husbands may deplore this ongoing movement, they cannot stop it by their individual efforts or the cleverness of their personal negotiations.

If such a movement toward equality continues, at whatever slow or fast pace in various countries, and beginning from different advanced or retarded points on the curve, how will that affect relations within the family? We have reviewed some of the modern research data about the present. Let us now look at some future changes that seem more likely than others.

First, as this chapter has repeatedly argued, change in the domestic sphere will continue only to the extent that women obtain jobs and promotions without respect to how well they carry out the traditional obligations of mother, wife, sister, or daughter; and that women move toward closing the earnings and power gap that puts them below men in the job system. It seems likely that fertility will continue to drop under such a system. Men have had the luxury of being sentimental about children, because they had only a modest share of the burden. Any change in the direction of equality will mean that their share will be greater than before, and they will be much more likely to count the costs than in the past.

Equality will necessarily move toward sharing far more domestic duties. There are many complexities in this change. We suppose that the first result of greater sharing will simply be that the hours devoted to domestic tasks will be shortened considerably. If men are pressed toward a more equal division by public opinion and by their inability to control their wives, they will doubtless decide that many tasks need not be done, or can be done much more poorly than at present. We do not suppose that this will necessarily lead to communal kitchens, but it might well lead to other arrangements that are no longer based on the assumption of free labor contributions from the wife. In addition, since many women are in fact quite handy at doing tasks that were formerly thought to be masculine, very likely the sharing will become complementary; men will not simply do half of all the labor expended on the various types of household tasks, but husbands and wives will sensibly decide to do what they do best, or most easily, and work out some arrangement for the remainder that seems fair to them.

Sex role socialization is already changing toward equality in at least the educated social strata of the United States, but we suppose that the movement will continue in the direction of making fewer distinctions between boys and girls in the kinds of traits their parents praise or punish, types of playthings or toys given to them, vacation activities, and career orientations. Some commentators have remarked that in the past decade men have finally been given "permission to cry"; they are no longer exhorted to keep a stiff upper lip, to bear grief without showing it, or to feel love without expressing it. Precisely because traditional sex role allocations will weaken still more, men and women will have to be much more open in stating their attitudes, preferences, and specific willingness to perform various types of tasks.

Whether or not marriage contracts become popular, it seems likely that more husbands and wives will, both before and after marriage, engage in explicit negotiation about how tasks are to be divided, who will support whom during the process of getting an education, who will determine residence, how property will be divided, and who will decide about having children. Since more and more women will want to live under somewhat more egalitarian arrangements, while men will continue to be reluctant to give up some of their privileges, it seems likely that the age at marriage for women will continue to move up somewhat. It also seems likely that the growing pattern of living together before marriage will become in part a testing ground for ascertaining whether each individual can live up to some adequate standard of fairness and justice.

If there is greater equality between husbands and wives, the divorce rate is unlikely to drop; we suppose that it will continue to rise. This will occur because far more women will be able to live independently than in the past. In addition, although giving both parties an equal voice in making decisions and independent actions may eventually create a strong solidarity if the unit endures, it also creates substantial conflict. We do not believe that egalitarian relations within the family will necessarily yield more happiness, although to be sure those who suffer or those who feel oppressed under the present system would be happier under different arrangements. We simply do not know which marital arrangement might yield the greatest happiness for its participants, and thus have no way of predicting whether greater equality within the society and the home will make people happier with their lot.

CHAPTER 9 MARITAL DISSOLUTION

Households and families, like all other living things, require continued inputs of energy and resources if they are not to dissolve; and ultimately all will dissolve. In the United States about a million marriages are formally broken through divorce each year. Others rock along shakily from one year to the next, in various states of disrepair. Even those that do hold together firmly are eventually unmade by death.

From this point of view, all family units are headed for eventual dissolution, earlier or later, and we may think of the breakdown of families as a normal, expected fate. That view is not adequate, since in the lifetime of each individual we can also observe many forces that help to maintain the stability of any given family unit. Thus, neither view is complete. In this chapter, we face the fact that any given family unit will finally cease to exist, but we also continue to explore some of the factors that help to create whatever stability is observable in family role systems.

THE ROOTS OF TROUBLE: INTERNAL OR EXTERNAL?

The causes for what happens at the level of the individual family unit can be observed within it, but we must also consider the larger social structure if we are to understand the dynamics of marital dissolution. Husbands and wives, parents and children, have fought each other in all societies. But the social definitions and the prohibitions or supports from the larger society were likely to determine just what action flowed from that conflict. Each divorce is an individual experience, but when there are many divorcees, this has consequences in turn for the larger society. Thus, all those who are now married know that there are many potential spouses among the large number of people who have divorced. As the number of people who have ever been divorced increases, so that it becomes a more common experience, it is also less likely to be disapproved by the society at large. Let us consider further these mutual effects.

We can take for granted that when a society undergoes considerable disorganization, as during a civil war, revolution, famine, or epidemic, some aspects of the family may change, and very often these changes will be viewed as "disorganization." Nearly always, large-scale disorganization in the entire social system is likely to lead to a high rate of marital dissolution of all kinds among the family units of that society. As a consequence, some commentators who look back in history can suppose that the fall of some great civilization such as Rome was "caused" by a breakdown of the family system, though surely one can argue equally strongly that the Roman family was breaking down because the entire social structure was breaking down. As analysts we must be alert to the interaction between the smaller unit of the family, numbered in tens of millions in large countries, and changes in the larger social structure. It should also be kept in mind that individual family units may dissolve at a rapid rate, even when the larger social system as well as the family system itself continue relatively unchanged over long periods of time. That is, a high rate of dissolution by death or divorce may simply be a normal part of the "traditional" family pattern. In Tokugawa Japan, before industrialization, a high rate of divorce was normal at the very early phases of marriage; it was not an index of the breakdown of the family system.

Legal systems may also be viewed as a main element of social structure, and they may have a great effect on marital dissolution. Large-scale societies typically have codified bodies of family law, while some analysts would argue that in tribal societies the folk customs that guide the patterns of marriage and the family can simply be viewed as "the law." In any event, when new nations arise they are likely to create an explicit, new body of family law. Since World War II, revolutionary societies have typically written into law a new set of provisions that were somewhat counter to folk customs or even ordinary public opinion at that time. Inevitably there are conflicts, then, between the individual family unit and the new legal structure—though the new legal structure is not always victorious. At any given time, we can expect to observe that what happens in the larger society affects marital dissolutions, while these in turn may have consequences for the society as a whole.

TYPES OF MARITAL DISSOLUTION

Family analysts have proposed many classifications for the types of marital dissolution, but have come to no general agreement about which is theoretically more fruitful. If we use a simple definition of marital dissolution—when one or more members fail to perform adequately their role obligations, as these are viewed by other members—then the following main types of family breakup will cover most cases:

1. *Illegitimacy* (the uncompleted family unit). It may be objected that this family unit cannot cease to exist, since it never came into existence in the first place. We would nevertheless include it here, simply because one or both of the parents are absent, and conspicuously fail in their role obligations. It is the father who usually fails most completely; and in most cases the parents of both the young mother and the young father fail to some extent in their parental obligations to control the courtship behavior of the two young parents. It should be kept in mind, nevertheless, that the stigma of illegitimacy has decreased over the past generation in this and other countries, and a small but significant minority of women now decide to have a child independently, and thus do not feel that the father is failing at all in his role obligations when he is absent.

2. *Annulment, separation, divorce and desertion.* The voluntary departure of one or both spouses.

3. *Changes in role definitions (resulting from the differential impact of cultural changes).* Members of the family disagree sharply with one another about their role obligations, and by that standard one or more persons fail to live up to those obligations. Cases in this category include conflicts that arise from new definitions of women's roles, but more common problems arise from parent-youth conflict.

4. *Involuntary failure in role obligations because of external events.* The temporary or permanent involuntary absence of one or more members of the family because of death or imprisonment, or catastrophe such as flood, war, or depression.

5. *The empty shell family.* Members of the family do live together, but conspicuously fail in their obligations to give emotional support to one another; they live together and have minimal communication and contact with one another.

6. *Unwilled major role failures.* Internal catastrophes such as mental, emotional, or physical pathologies, such as psychosis of the child or spouse or chronic or incurable physical conditions.

Both the underlying definition and the types that evolve from it suggest the key fact: that a family unit is a social system made up of continuing inputs of goods and services; and if these people fail in important role obligations to one another, the family unit may simply cease to exist. Note that the larger society may be more concerned with some of these types than with others. For example, in industrial societies the cost of welfare is likely to be greater if the illegitimacy rate is high, while government agencies are not at all concerned with the "empty shell" family. Both kin and neighbors feel obliged to help family members through their first days of difficulty if the husband dies, but they do not feel the same duty if there is a divorce. Separation is a common event, but no official action is likely to be taken because of it unless a wife asks for government help in order to force her husband to pay for the financial support of his family.

In this one chapter we cannot analyze all these types of family dissolution. In an earlier chapter, we discussed some of the important social patterns of illegitimacy; here we focus on divorce and death as types of marital breakup. We give somewhat more attention to divorce because (a) so many of the other types of family dissolution are likely to end in divorce sooner or later, because (b) in most countries it is the focus of much moral and personal concern, and because (c) changes in divorce rates are usually accompanied by changes in other elements of the society's family system.

The Social Effect of Voluntary Departures

The four modes of voluntary departures from the family—separation, divorce, annulment, and desertion—are given different legal definitions in different countries, but they show much similarity of behavior. In all of them, at least one adult leaves the family unit, and those who remain behind must somehow cope with this loss. Separation may or may not lead to a divorce, but almost all divorces are preceded by a separation, which in most countries does not require specific legal action. For most people, divorce is the most public statement that one or both spouses have decided to end the marriage permanently.

Divorce is likely to be a personal misfortune for one or both spouses, but it may also be viewed as a social invention, one type of escape valve for the inevitable tensions of marriage itself. It is permitted in nearly all nations of the world (Spain and Ireland are still exceptions) and has been common in most tribal societies. Indeed, some calculations show that the rate of divorce in most primitive societies has been higher than in the United States, while some nations in the past have had higher rates than this country (Japan, 1887–1919; Algeria, 1887–1940; Egypt, 1935–1954). Common sense, if not law or theology, has generally recognized that the personal anguish as well as the social consequences of continual fighting may be worse than a divorce. On the other hand, divorce has not been viewed as one of the happier ceremonies, and it is not celebrated with festivities or joy, as other changes in status are likely to be. It expresses hostility between husband and wife, and breaks the bonds that once united two family lines. It creates adjustment problems for adults and children. Consequently, even in societies with a relatively high divorce rate, there is at best a grudging approval of divorce as necessary though regrettable. Societies express that reluctant acceptance by creating various social mechanisms for keeping the divorce rate lower than it otherwise would be. Let us consider some of these social patterns.

Mechanisms for Lowering Conflict

Tensions are inevitable in marriage, because it requires at least two adults to live together in some intimacy in spite of their many differences. That intimacy brings rewards, but it also brings costs, and no marriage system has ever promised happiness for those who take part in it. On the other hand, the marital system is maintained by voluntary participation, and we can observe that all systems contain various social patterns for reducing hostility, or reducing its effects.

Perhaps most widespread among the traditional societies of world history was lowering the individual's aspirations about the delights to be found in marriage. For example, getting married in both prerevolutionary China and in Tokugawa Japan was viewed as a duty; children were not taught to expect either romance or happiness from it. They were told instead that if they were wise and carried out all their obligations, they might achieve contentment or peace over time. Most traditional societies also attempted to control marital conflict by laying much less stress on the husband-wife relationship and more on the interaction with other kin. We noted earlier that in the joint Hindu family the fathers were ideally not to show excessive affection for their own sons over their brothers' sons, and young husbands and wives were not supposed to spend much time together. Elders directed the affairs of the family, and arranged all marriages. They also intervened in quarrels between husband and wife. Spouses were pressed to contribute to the good of the larger set of kin, rather than turn inward to their own little family unit for individual satisfaction. Under these circumstances, husband and wife are much less likely to develop intense, continuing hostility.

In addition, perhaps all societies attempt to avoid some marital tension by affirming that some actions are more important than others; for example, making a living is more important than dressing neatly. As a consequence, as long as the two spouses can live up to the minimum levels of performance in important areas, other members will not support them in their quarrels about trivial matters. Assigning a higher value to some types of role performances may decrease or increase the divorce rate by defining what is a *bearable* level of disagreement between husband and wife, as well as the socially approved solutions for marital problems. We are likely to think of marriages a hundred years ago as being relatively harmonious. It may be wiser to think of them as family units in which it was taken for granted that even substantial difficulties were not viewed as adequate grounds for breaking up. Perhaps in most Western societies it has been assumed until fairly recently that spouses who did not love one another and who fought in private should nevertheless be civil in public and maintain the marriage simply for the sake of their children and their respectable standing in the community.

In many Catholic societies, divorce was not permitted until recently, only legal separation. This did not prevent spouses from deciding upon an informal separation, but it did express the general social disapproval of divorce. Nearly all informal solutions gave more options to the husband than to the wife. Before Italy permitted divorce, hundreds of thousands of husbands established separate residences with other women, but the community strongly disapproved of wives doing the same thing. In a polygynous society a man might decide to ignore one of his wives, but she could not take an additional husband. In both China and Japan a man might bring a concubine into his house, but a woman could not choose a parallel solution.

Divorce differs from informal solutions primarily in that it permits both partners to remarry. It expresses dissension between spouses, and creates additional problems for the two kin lines. Prior marriage agreements are broken, problems of custody and child support arise, and unhappiness is an experience common to many or most of the participants. Nevertheless, we cannot correctly speak of divorce as a more extreme solution than all other alternatives. One might argue that it is more extreme to bear the misery of an unhappy marriage, or to bring in a concubine to reduce the misery of a husband, while leaving the wife to be unhappy alone.

CHANGES AND TRENDS IN DIVORCE RATES OVER TIME

In each of the four years 1975 to 1978, there were over one million divorces in the United States. In every decade since the Civil War, the rate of divorce has increased, and at present it is very likely the highest rate in the world. Other countries with current high rates are Cuba, Puerto Rico, Soviet Russia, and Hungary, although as we noted earlier some nations have had higher rates than the United States in the past. Table 9.1 presents divorce rates for various countries for comparison.

The Case of Japan

From the 1890s until the 1970s, the divorce rate in Japan fell. From having one of the highest rates in the world, it came to have one of the lower rates among industrialized countries (the rate is now rising again). Traditional Japan prior to the Meiji Restoration in 1868 was a stable society, but with a high divorce rate. However, divorces were not typically based on conflicts between husbands and wives; they were caused by the elders rejecting the young bride for one reason or another. Most of these were, of course, rural

Table 9.1   Divorce Rates for Selected Countries

COUNTRY	AVERAGE DIVORCE RATE
United States	22.0 (1978)
Tunisia	5.6 (1966)
Canada	6.2 (1971)
Cuba	21.8 (1973)
Costa Rica	1.3 (1973)
Mexico	3.4 (1970)
Puerto Rico	20.4 (1970)
Israel	3.9 (1972)
Japan	4.2 (1975)
Czechoslovakia	7.2 (1970)
Denmark	8.8 (1970)
France	3.2 (1968)

Source: Most of these figures come from the *U.N. Demographic Year Book 1976*, pp. 482–489. The divorce rate is calculated as the average number of divorces over a three-year period, centered on a census year, per 1000 married couples.

marriages among relatively poor people. Marriages were arranged by the elders of the two families through a marriage broker. If the groom was an eldest son, the bride came to join the household of his father, since the eldest son would inherit the property after his father's death and would become the representative of the family line. The young bride was under an obligation to pay respect to her elder in-laws, to defer to their wishes, and to obey them. If she failed to obtain their approval, she would be sent back to her parents. If she obtained that approval, and bore sons for the family line, her position was secure.

The divorce rate was lower in the upper social strata, as it is for other countries of which we have any knowledge, in part because marriage among the nobility was often a family alliance, so that divorce would be more likely to cause conflict between the two families. The young bride also had no way of resisting her powerful in-laws. Finally, a higher-ranking groom could, if necessary, adjust to marital problems by introducing a concubine into the household.

The divorce rate in present-day Japan is the result of several factors, some of them in opposition to one another. First is the traditional set of factors that generated high rates of divorce in the premodern as well as the modern period. As these traditional forces declined in intensity (especially the harsh rule of the mother-in-law over the bride, and the decisive voice of the groom's parents as to whether the bride would be permitted to remain), the divorce rate fell. That is, as theoretically predicted, under industrialization the divorce rate did *not* rise at first, but fell. Under the old system it was already high, while the forces that made it high would ultimately be weakened by the social relations of industrialization (lesser control by elders, independence of both young men and women who obtained jobs, and so on).

It is not anomalous, of course, that some traditional countries once had high divorce rates, or that with industrialization they would fall. They will not continue to drop indefinitely, however. All the modern forces we have described before, which generate both marital tension and the opportunity to decrease it through divorce, are common in highly industrialized countries (seeking "happiness," demanding love and not traditional behaviors from one's spouse, available alternative spouses, and so on). Thus, over the past two decades, social forces in Japan have pressed toward *both* high and low divorce rates. Until recently, divorce rates have dropped as the traditional forces were weakened. Now, they appear to be rising again, and as marital stability comes increasingly to be based on the personal adjustment of husbands and wives to each other, the divorce rate will rise or remain moderately high, even though it may be lower than under the traditional system.

The Effect of Economic Trends and Fluctuations

Almost all countries are now experiencing a general upward trend in divorce rates, and this trend is likely to continue for some time in the future. Since rates reflect the massive forces of both social change and the ups and downs of large-scale events, we can expect that they would vary somewhat over time, aside from the contemporary upward rise.

Both divorce and marriage rates follow the business cycle, increasing during periods of prosperity and decreasing during periods of depression. Before divorce was a real possibility in Western countries, rates of marriage were influenced by good times and hard times in a similar fashion. Obviously, the correlation of divorce with prosperity does not mean that families are less happy during prosperity, or more contented during a depression. Instead, the cost of the divorce itself and the still greater cost of establishing new households prevent people from breaking up households during hard times. For example, during the Great Depression of the 1930s, the U.S. divorce rate dropped by about one-fifth. With the return of better times, divorce rates rose once more to new highs.

The effect of war on divorce rates depends partly on how long the war endures, and how massive its general effects are on the society. Usually, immediately after any major war the rate will rise sharply, because there are more marriages at that time (and thus more couples at risk), and because some returning soldiers and their spouses find that their reunion causes more unhappiness than they had anticipated. Any large-scale dislocation of social life, such as war or revolution, is likely to increase the divorce rate. It should also be noted that such periods generally bring new laws, which in modern history are likely to move in the direction of liberalization of divorce.

The Effect of Long-Term Social Trends

If we think of divorce as a kind of decision that is quasi-rational, we can consider some of the long-term social changes that would cause its frequency to rise. One basis of all decisions is the norms and values people hold with respect to any course of action. Without question, these have moved from a strong disapproval to at least tolerance: thus divorce costs less in social esteem. Even when communities or nations feel divorce should be avoided, they accept the fact of divorce and understand that not everyone who divorces should be censured. This change in attitude can be read from newspaper editorials, speeches, books, and of course programs presented on radio and television.

In the United States, this attitude can be seen as well in the spread of no-fault divorce, which first began in California in 1969. A slight majority of all states offer at least the option of a no-fault divorce, and it can be expected that more states in the future will adopt a pure no-fault pattern. Under such a law, the husband and wife may not make moral or ethical accusations against one another, and neither can prevent the other from obtaining a divorce. Problems of support and custody are worked out by the court, under the general norm of equality, but just who "caused" the divorce cannot be an issue. Such a law does not express approval of divorce, but it does tell us that the disapproval of divorce has decreased substantially.

When people make decisions, they also weigh the *alternatives* that are available to them. When one course of action offers alternatives that are unacceptable, that course of action may well be given up, even though it seems desirable in other ways. At the present time, almost any married person can feel that he or she has some alternative if the present marriage is very unhappy. This was not so in the past. When almost no one got divorced, there were few potential spouses left in the marriage pool. Since most of the population was engaged in farming, almost everyone needed a spouse simply to help carry out the necessary tasks. Wives could not support themselves without a husband, for there were few opportunities for employment except in domestic service. By contrast, in the high-divorce Arab countries, when a man divorced his wife he had to complete all the payments to her household he had contracted for, and she in turn was available for new marriage negotiations, with an additional (though smaller) bride price.

Our decisions are also affected by social pressures. These pressures may move in many directions, depending on the attitudes of kin and the local community. In the main, advice or pressure is likely to be somewhat cautious; almost everyone will point out the problems and difficulties of divorce. On the other hand, people increasingly understand that a marriage may not work out even if both spouses do their best, and few elders or kin will now threaten a spouse with ostracism if he or she does not give up the idea of divorce.

At a much deeper level, one change in values has affected choices in most of the modern world. This is the belief that people have a right to make decisions on the basis of what they believe will bring them happiness, or satisfy their self-defined needs. This is given the negative label of "hedonism" in some discussions, and the positive label of "self-fulfillment" in others. The general belief, widespread in all traditional societies, that individuals should carry out their duties even at the cost of their own happiness, has weakened a great deal. Almost certainly this change is more widely accepted in the United States than elsewhere, but it is growing in almost all countries.

Will the general trend toward higher divorce rates continue indefinitely, until there are as many divorces each year as marriages? Many family analysts believe that the trend is slowing down, but that view supposes that we now know exactly which factors have caused the great increase, and that those factors will no longer have the same effect in the future. If more young people live together before marriage, and thus marry later or after a long period of adjustment, perhaps the impact of hasty marriage will be reduced. On the other hand, modern society will continue to present many alternatives to both spouses, as well as alternative marital arrangements. Spouses will be even less dependent on each other in the future, since both husband and wife are likely to be earning an income. Even if, as many claim, we are now witnessing a politically conservative trend, there is no evidence that people are becoming more conservative in the areas of intimacy and sexuality. Therefore it seems more cautious to suppose that the divorce rate will continue to rise somewhat in the near future, even if the rate of *increase* slows down.

DIVORCE, DESERTION AND SOCIAL POSITION

Just as peoples' marital decisions will be affected by their experiences in different historical epochs, or over the fluctuations of the business cycle, so are they affected by their different positions in the social structure at any given time. We can expect that class ranking, religious affiliation, race, or rural-urban background might also give rise to different rates of divorce, separation, or desertion. People in different social positions are likely to be socialized differently, feel more or less committed to remaining married, and even have different expectations of the marital relationship.

The Effect of Class

Common sense has long suggested that economic factors may create marital difficulties, while many family analysts have asserted that fighting about economic matters may hide more basic conflicts, such as who should do what within the household, personality differences, or differences in attitudes. Almost certainly both positions contain some truth. Neither view, however, predicts whether the divorce rate will be higher among the lower classes. After all, the well-to-do also experience financial problems, and deeper types of conflict might well be found at any class position. In any event, a study by the author disclosed, a generation ago, that divorce was more usual among the lower social strata, contrary to both common opinion and the assumptions of family analysts at that time. Very likely the more common belief, that people in the upper social strata divorce more, was based on the much greater publicity given to such divorces. The author's study, the first full-scale theoretical analysis of this pattern, disclosed that the basic correlation was *inverse:* The divorce rate drops toward the upper socioeconomic levels, whether the index used is occupation, income, or education. It was also ascertained that the divorce rate among blacks is higher than that among whites and has been for decades.[1]

Phrased in historical and cross-national terms, where divorce is extremely difficult and thus requires considerable resources it is a privilege that mainly the upper social strata enjoy. As each country moves toward a more or less "free market" in divorce, the basically greater marital instability among the lower social strata is revealed. In Arab countries or in Japan, where divorce was relatively easy to begin with, instability shows itself as divorce, rather than separation or desertion. To be sure, this fact runs contrary to the popular picture of lower-class family life as stable, warm,

---

1.   These relationships are more complex than can be summarized here. The relationship is inverse for males of either race, but is positive for women of either race, mainly because women toward the upper socioeconomic levels are more prone to divorce. The first analysis of this pattern was reported in 1949, and later studies have confirmed it. There were earlier sets of data that reveal this relationship, but it was glossed over or ignored as theoretically unimportant. The inverse relationship varies somewhat depending on which class index (education, income, occupation) we use.

and inviting, tightly knit against the outside world, which has been a widely used literary stereotype. Table 9.2 shows an example of this inverse class correlation for males in the United States.

Without question, only the well-to-do were able to divorce in the distant past, for only they could afford it. For example, in many jurisdictions, a special act of legislature was necessary to get a divorce. On the other hand, if we consider only marital *instability*, lumping together the cases of divorce, desertion, and separation, it is clear that the pattern holds *cross-culturally* and very likely *historically* as well: The total rate of marital instability is greater toward the lower social strata, in this and in all other countries for which we can obtain adequate data.

What causes such a correlation? Although philosophers have tried to convince people for centuries that the poor need not be unhappy, since a wise and serene mind is the key to contentment, ordinary people have apparently felt otherwise. People with higher-level jobs enjoy greater work satisfaction, and though there is financial strain at almost any level of income, there is nevertheless more financial strain at lower levels than at higher. At high and low socioeconomic levels, women may hold jobs, but toward the lower economic levels men are more likely to feel they are failures because their jobs do not bring in enough money to support their household alone. If people do in fact express some of their economic discontent through their marital relations, we should expect more tension in the lower social strata, and indeed there is more tension there.

Other class-distributed factors may also increase or lower divorce rates. Social networks in the upper social strata are larger and more closely knit, so that the social consequences of divorce are likely to be greater. Women are also much less likely to want a divorce at higher levels, because the discrepancy between their possible or real income and their husband's income is much greater than toward the lower social strata, and thus their loss will be greater. In addition, a much greater percentage of men toward

Table 9.2   Male Proneness to Marital Instability by Urban Occupation in the United States, 1970

OCCUPATION	INDEX TO PRONENESS TO MARITAL INSTABILITY[a]
Professional, technical	72
Managers and administrators	90
Clerical, sales	97
Craftsmen	103
Operators	112
Laborers	124
Service workers	135

[a] Separated plus divorced plus married more than once as % of total in each of those categories for each occupational group; divided by number "ever married" as % of total ever married for each occupational group, times 100.

Source: U.S. Bureau of the Census, *1970 Census of the Population, Subject Report PC (2) 4C, Marital Status* (Washington, D.C.: Government Printing Office, 1972), p. 142, Table 5.

the higher social strata will pay alimony and child support, and though they are likely to exaggerate this reality (since most men manage early or eventually to get out of these obligations just the same), it is their perception of these difficulties that affects their decisions. More income at higher levels is already allotted to long-term expenditures and complex ownership of property, so that the difficulties of breaking up a marriage are somewhat greater. Note that by this line of reasoning men toward the higher social strata enjoy more power and freedom to leave their wives and seek another but they face higher costs; women *whose independent* money or power is greater also have that freedom and are more likely to see that they could make it on their own if their marriage is not a contented one. However, apparently their costs are not as great. In fact, their divorce rates are higher. This applies to both black and white wives.

It should be emphasized that this is a *class,* not a *cross-national* pattern. That is, divorce rates are not necessarily higher in poor countries than in rich ones. The comparison to be made is only among classes *within* one country, and the difference will be observable whether the nation is rich or poor.

As might be expected, rates of desertion and separation also show class differences. Lower-class husbands can more easily move and avoid being traced, while they are less likely to leave behind any substantial amount of property. Although the actual number of desertions has not dropped, a higher percentage of lower-class instability is now expressed in legal divorce than in the past. This occurs in part because divorce is legally simpler, and costs less. In addition, husbands are more easily traceable than in the past. Finally, states have begun programs for tracking down husbands who are derelict in meeting their obligations to support their children. Thus, cost-free desertion is not as easy as it once was. Note that we speak of desertion by *husbands.* The last ten years has undoubtedly seen an increase in the number of wives who desert, perhaps because more wives have come to decide that taking care of home and children is not necessarily their supreme obligation; it is in part the duty of their husbands as well.

Desertion rates, then, are higher among the poor, higher among blacks than among whites, and more common among Catholics (perhaps because more Catholics still feel that divorce is to be avoided if possible). It should also be added that many "desertions" are really separations of some kind, in that the whereabouts of the husband are known. In many instances it is not clear whether the act is to be viewed as a separation or as a desertion, and many husbands who have deserted do return eventually to their families.

As in other areas of family behavior, a large part of the black-white differences in divorce rates are likely to be caused by class differences. That is, the marital patterns of lower-class whites and blacks are similar in many ways (both have higher rates of premarital pregnancy and illegitimacy, of desertion, separation, and divorce, of mother-headed households). But since a higher percentage of blacks than of whites live at the poverty level or have low-income jobs, the *averages* for blacks as a group are more similar to lower-class patterns than are the averages of whites as a group.

With reference to the rates for blacks, two regularities are worth noting. One is that blacks have a more difficult experience during a depression (again, like the lower classes generally), and also show a wider fluctuation than whites in divorce rates over the economic cycle. Second, some evidence also suggests that as the black population becomes more assimilated into U.S. society, its divorce patterns will become more like those of whites. We should also expect that differentials in marital instability by religious affiliation should decline over time, since the *doctrinal* differences relating to divorce become fewer. Differences still remain, but they must be cautiously interpreted, since findings are based on relatively small samples.

The Effects of Religious Background

The effects of religious background on divorce rates are both complex and obscure. They are obscure for several reasons. First, with reference to the United States, the U.S. Census does not ask questions about religion, and most private research is based on relatively small surveys that have no historical depth. Second, although religious affiliation seems to have some effect on divorce rates, it is not clear just how much religious *beliefs* contribute to these differences, because the doctrines of most U.S. religious systems are set to some extent against divorce anyway. Third, religious *affiliation* data are typically obtained from surveys, but regularity of church attendance or religious commitment are probably of much greater importance. Fourth, some of the differences may arise from class differences associated with religion. For example, Jewish couples have lower divorce rates than Protestant couples, but a higher percentage of Jewish than of Protestant couples have a college education and upper-class jobs (which are both *negatively* correlated with divorce).

The lack of good descriptive data keeps us from dealing adequately with the apparent complexity of these relationships on a cross-national basis. For example, in many Western countries almost everyone is Catholic, but we cannot suppose that divorce rates are the same in all segments of the society; Protestants in such countries form a subgroup that is different in many social characteristics, not religion alone. Islam is the dominant religion in a wide arc that extends from northwestern Africa to Indonesia, but divorce patterns seem to vary a good bit in this great region, while we have no adequate analysis of those differences. In India there are dozens of fairly large religious sects with many doctrinal differences, but it is not clear that these differences are reflected in corresponding differences in marital dissolution. Most important, research on these topics has been of great concern primarily to Western social scientists, in part because divorce was a moral and social problem in the West, while in most non-Western countries other issues (the joint family, the Chinese clan) were given more attention.

With all these cautions in mind, several social patterns are worth noting. First, at least in the modern Western world, where people seem less ready than in the historical past to kill others for their religious beliefs, the differences in marital dissolution rates are likely to be caused more by the social pressures and opportunities of the larger society than by differences in religious doctrines. In the United States, for example, Catholic attitudes about many family behaviors (contraceptives, divorce) are very close to the attitudes of the rest of the population. Second, even when religious differences are evident (Catholics divorce less than Jews, and Jews less than Protestants), class differences will still be observable (people at higher social ranks divorce less). Blacks are mostly Protestant and have a higher divorce rate, but this is much more likely caused by their class position than by their religious affiliations. Third, although religious commitment may affect divorce rates, there is no evidence that people who are more devout have more harmonious marriages. They are simply less likely to break up the marriage because of their conflicts.

Perhaps the most important general finding is that marriages between couples of different religious backgrounds are more likely to end in divorce, and people of the same religious background are less likely to divorce, whether they are Catholic, Protestant, or Jewish. It does not seem likely that this difference is caused by disagreements about religious doctrines, although doubtless these do have their effect. The more important relationship is to be found in the strong finding that people who claim no church affiliation are perhaps the most inclined to divorce of all subgroups. That is, those whose beliefs are weak or nonexistent, who feel little allegiance to traditional values, and who are less likely to be rooted in a local neighborhood with its religious community, are less likely to be committed to marital stability. People who marry outside their faith are also likely to be less committed to the religious beliefs of their parents, and are thus more similar to the subgroups who admit that they are not affiliated with any church.

The Effects of Differences in Social Background

Let us now look at the effects of still more specific background traits of couples on the rates of marital dissolution. It should be emphasized that these are simply associations between a given social characteristic and the likelihood of divorce, with no specification of just how this relationship occurs. In addition, these associations are likely to be weak. That is, the effect of each trait may be consistent, but it is relatively small. The findings of various research studies are summarized in Table 9.3. Most of these traits have a fairly obvious connection with the rates of marital dissolution. For example, rural populations usually have stronger attitudes against divorce than do residents of urban areas. Similarly, when husband and wife come from very different social backgrounds, they are less likely to adjust easily to one another in a marriage.

The disapproval of kin and friends may seem to be unimportant in modern urban life, since commentators frequently argue that all modern urban dwellers live a rootless and disorganized existence. However, this approval or disapproval is of considerable importance. First, it is basically a *prediction*. These people do know the engaged couple, and how they feel about the marriage expresses in part their judgment of future adjustment

Table 9.3   Background Characteristics Associated with Greater or Lesser
Proneness to Divorce

GREATER PRONENESS	LESSER PRONENESS
Urban background	Rural background
Marriage at very young ages (15–19 years)	Marriage at average ages (males, 23; females, 22) or older ages
Shorter acquaintance before marriage	Acquaintance of two or more years prior to marriage
Short engagement, or none	Engagement of six months or more
Parents with unhappy marriages	Happily married parents
Couples who do not attend churches, or are of different faiths	Couples who attend church regularly, are Catholic, or adhere to the same church
Lower social rank	Higher social rank
Kin and friends' disapproval of the marriage	Kin and friends' approval of the marriage
General dissimilarity in background	Similarity (homogamy) of background
Disagreement of husband and wife on role obligations	Agreement of husband and wife on role obligations.

or conflict. Second, their approval may actually help to bind the couple together and to help them to adjust to one another. Length of acquaintance or engagement has two clear connections with rates of marital dissolution: First of all, a longer period of time gives the couple more opportunity to know one another well, and those who stay together over a longer period of time are more likely to be those who have in fact become better adjusted. These relations also reflect in part a class factor, since longer engagements are more common toward the upper social ranks. Common sense would also suggest that age at marriage has a *curvilinear* effect on marital dissolution, and the exact ages that would be viewed as "older" or "younger" vary from culture to culture. Unions at very young or very old ages are likely to be deviant for many reasons (for example, teenage marriages in the West are likely to be preceded by pregnancy, and hastened by family pressures) and are less likely to survive than unions at more conventional ages.

From the beginning of divorce research, analysts have tried to pin down the "causes" of divorce, but with little success. Inquiries have reported what legal grounds the divorcing couple uses, what complaints they make about each other outside that legal action, and many of the factors associated with higher or lower rates of marital dissolution. It seems unlikely that we shall locate any simple set of causes.

More liberal divorce laws "cause" higher divorce rates, but they are passed because more people want to get a divorce. Changes in legal grounds also have a causal effect, but they in turn are caused by changes in people's attitudes. In general, people have alleged whatever legal grounds they needed to allege in order to obtain the divorce that one or both parties wanted. They have usually chosen the legal accusations that were strong enough to guarantee the divorce, but mild enough to persuade the other party to accept that charge. Three great time phases may be noted in the changes in the divorce suits filed in the United States since the Civil War. From that time until about the time of World War II, the legal grounds did not change fundamentally, but the interpretation of those grounds did change. During that long period one spouse was presumed to be "guilty," but over time less serious complaints were gradually permitted as a basis for divorce. In the period before World War II and continuing after it, "cruelty" was increasingly used, but it came to mean almost any kind of behavior that the complaining spouse did not like. The third phase is the period after World War II and continuing to the present, in which more and more states have added a "no-fault" provision, or permitted no charges at all to be made against either spouse. That system is increasingly used in European countries as well, for example, in Denmark and Sweden. This change will make it more difficult to make time comparisons, since the court record will not contain specific charges against one or both spouses. The net conclusion to be drawn from this long time period is that legal grounds have not afforded us much basis for understanding the underlying causes of divorce.

Because the causal relations are so complex, it is likely that spouses themselves do not really know why their marital conflict was so intense, although they, of course, can express what they believe are the main causes. The more objective analyst is likely to suspect that these are typically one-sided allegations, and may or may not describe the underlying problems. For example, they may make specific charges about each other's behavior, but not perceive that much of the tension was due to economic problems of various kinds. In any event, if we tabulate all the various complaints that husbands and wives make about one another, these are likely to coincide with the main areas of social life together.

The more deeply we probe the complaints of husbands and wives, the less likely it is that we feel much certainty about the successive phases of conflict, or their underlying causes. A few marriages doubtless end because of some single large cause, such as the husband's violence or the wife's neurosis, but very likely most modern divorces are the result of many diverse difficulties. These create a continuing cumulative process of conflict, during which both spouses gradually come to reject both the relationship and each other. In that process, both persons begin to change. At the end, neither is likely to see in the other the pleasant, attractive person he or she originally married, for that person does not exist anymore—at least not for his or her marital partner.

DIVORCE AND BEREAVEMENT

As we noted earlier, in modern, high-divorce, industrial societies, the average individual spends more years within a marriage than in societies of the past, because people live longer. In the past, people experienced on average fewer years within marriage, simply because they died sooner. On the other hand, because most people who divorce marry again (and most do live out their lives within a marriage), most people will end their last marriage with death. Sociologists have pointed out the similarities in the processes of adjustment that are required by divorce or bereavement. In both, a set of role relations has been disrupted, and adjustments are required throughout the family network. Because each marriage relationship is unique in many ways, it is not possible to find an adequate replacement for the missing partner. The easy sexual satisfaction that is sometimes alleged to be characteristic of modern society is likely to be experienced as a poor substitute for the sexual intimacy of marriage. Economic problems are likely to be pressing. The problems of finding emotional solace, friendship, and love are difficult in modern urban societies. In both divorce and bereavement, the spouse remaining with the children is likely to feel that controlling and supervising them is much harder than before the breakup, while the children are likely to feel abandoned, and often guilty as well.

In contrast to these many emotional similarities, perhaps all societies are better adjusted to dealing with death than with divorce. That is, death is surrounded by rituals, ceremonies, and obligations, in part because death has always been viewed as an unwilled intrusion, an unwanted tragedy, while divorce continues to be viewed as a state that one or both parties intended. It is possible that as more societies come to view divorce as basically "no-fault" in its character, more institutional patterns and supports will grow up around this change in status. Let us consider the structural differences in these two social patterns.

In apparently all societies, the death of a spouse creates an obligation for kinfolk and friends to help the bereaved person, to offer solace, to make small or large gestures of support. If possible, they should attend the funeral, and they may offer financial help. The bereaved person is permitted, even encouraged, to accept this support, and to express grief. Note that in divorce, even when one spouse is very unhappy about the divorce, only a very close friend may feel any obligation to offer emotional solace.

The rituals and ceremonies of death have a further aspect, the duty of the bereaved person to carry out some formal tasks that are within his or her capacity. In Western countries, these activities may be organized by funeral directors, but they do call for physical movement from the home to the place where the body is to be disposed of, greeting and talking with relatives and friends, and in general much participation in social activities. Each person dies alone, but survivors are pressed to cling together for a while. In addition, the funeral service itself expresses the finality of death, unlike the many complex stages of divorce, from separation and filing suit to the final action by the court. And unlike divorce, bereavement does not generally create hostility toward the former spouse. Sometimes the bereaved person feels guilt, but in any event is likely to idealize the past relationship and the person. Indeed, there is a general norm that kin and friends are supposed to praise the dead person, whereas the talk about the absent divorced spouse is likely to be critical. People who divorce are likely to feel a sense of failure. After death, the bereaved person may feel some regret that he or she did not "do enough" for the dead person, but it is less likely that the general feeling tone is one of having contributed in a major way to the death.

In general, in divorce there is no agreed-upon set of rights and obligations that kin, friends, or even the spouse are supposed to meet. There are many similarities in the social patterns of people who divorce, but these are not the result of specific divorce customs. Rather, they grow out of common social experiences. For example, the economic needs of the broken family require the wife to get a job or to seek help from a welfare agency. The loneliness of the divorced person moves him or her to begin dating again, or the day-to-day difficulties of working out life adjustments may cause some unhappiness.

The customs of death include a period of mourning, in which the individual is supposed to avoid intimate relations with the opposite sex. In Western nations, widows were praised for revering their dead husbands to the point of never marrying again. This ideal was strong in China, and of course in India the older ideal (which a small minority continued to follow even in the nineteenth century) was for the woman to throw herself on the funeral pyre to join her dead husband. In the United States, twice as many widowers as widows remarry during the first five years after the death of their spouses, but both are more likely to marry than in the past. It should also be added that in Western history, widows with property were very likely to marry, in spite of the sentimental ideal of "remaining true to her husband."

Unhappiness in divorce is a common experience, while the major form of postdivorce adjustment is remarriage. In Western countries no moral norm states that people should remarry after divorce or bereavement, but innumerable social pressures lead toward that solution. Adults in our society live in couples, entertain in couples, and talk with one another about their families. The percentage of people who live alone at any given time continues to increase, but almost everyone who does live alone is moving toward a marriage, with or without intending to do so, for all the reasons that make married life somewhat easier than single life. Taking care of children, if there are any, is wearying and difficult without a spouse. Children themselves are likely to suggest to their parent that he or she should remarry. In spite of occasional embarrassments, friends are likely to introduce the formerly married to eligible partners. Even sexual relations, which are described in newspapers as easy and tolerant, are in fact somewhat awkward or difficult outside of marriage, and in any event are much less likely to be satisfying.

As a consequence, most people begin to take part in courtship and dating before they have fully adjusted to the loss of their former spouse, whether by divorce or death. The ability to do so is partly an index of how far they have moved toward adjustment. In turn, it leads to a fuller adjustment, since the bereaved or divorced person begins to see himself or herself in a new light, as an attractive partner, or simply as a person rather than as the former spouse of so and so. In general, acquaintances at work as well as friends are simply uninterested in trying to keep alive old memories or to cherish past relationships. People lose their interest in helping any individual to maintain his or her grief, whether it arose from death or divorce. So almost everyone who loses a spouse by death or divorce will eventually remarry, if this event occurs roughly between the ages of 20 and 40 (after that age, people find it more difficult to find new partners).

CHILDREN AND FAMILY BREAKUP

What happens to the children when the family unit loses the mother or father? For decades, husbands and wives who were miserable in marriage were urged to stay together "for the sake of the children," and doubtless many marriages remained intact because of this belief. In the United States, at least, that belief has weakened considerably over the past generation. At the same time, research on the consequences of divorce for the personality development and happiness of children has continued, with ambiguous results.

The most obvious finding is that children who are reared in a happy home are themselves more likely to grow up happy and psychologically healthy. Since present data suggests that some 40 percent of all marriages that begin during this decade will end in divorce, that choice is not one most people will be able to make. That is, almost all spouses would prefer to have a happy home, for themselves as well as their children, but accomplishing that end cannot be achieved by simply willing it. Psychological analysis would suggest that children from an "empty shell" family are less likely to grow up happy or psychologically healthy, precisely because members of the family fail in their emotional obligations to one another, and child development specialists have argued that warmth, nurturance, and love are necessary for adequate socialization. It seems equally likely that divorces where both spouses engage in great hostility, seek to involve their children in the dispute, and tell their children how evil the other spouse is, are more likely to have a bad effect on the personal development of the children.

However, if we wish to understand the effects of marital dissolution on children, we should compare not merely the two extremes of "happy" families at one end and hostile families at the other; we should also ascertain the effects of death, divorce, separation, and desertion on children. Moreover, since it seems clear that it is the *quality* of the relations between parents and children that is most important, we need some data on how parents and children interact with one another before and after those dissolutions, since the mere fact of dissolution itself may not be the key variable.

We do not even know exactly how many children are involved each year in these various forms of dissolution, although we do have fair estimates. Of the 65 million children under 18 in the United States in 1976, 80 percent were living with two parents, and two-thirds were living with parents who had been married only once. Eleven million children under the age of 18 were living with one parent. Four million were living with a parent (mother or father) who was divorced, while 3.4 million were living with a parent who was separated from the other spouse, and 1.5 million were living with a widowed or widowered parent. The remainder lived under various arrangements, and of course most of these were living with a never-married mother. In 1976, 40 percent of black children under the age of 18 were living with their mother in a household without a father present. Note that these figures apply to a particular time. It is estimated that of all the children born in 1977, as many as 45 percent are likely to live for a period of at least several months in their lives as members of a one-parent family.[2]

These data give an estimate of the numbers of children who are involved in certain types of marital dissolutions, though of course they do not cover all such problems. For example, we have no data on how many families are torn apart by the presence of a severely mentally retarded child or a psychotic parent. A consideration of the range of possible role failures suggests, by their complexity and potential severity, that many superficially intact homes may have an unhealthful impact on children; by contrast, we know that many children who are reared in well-run child-care centers in this and other countries, or by a loving, concerned parent (without an additional spouse) may grow up to become a well-adjusted adult. Moreover, longitudinal data from recent studies have begun to suggest that our knowledge about what produces *healthy* children is less secure than is widely believed. Consequently, studies that argue for giving sole and absolute custody to one parent (without any substantial socialization experiences with the other parent) or studies that report on the unhappiness and hostility of children who undergo a divorce experience should not lead us to assume that we already know exactly which type of child-care arrangement after a divorce or death will be the most satisfactory for all children. That research has yet to be done.

With reference to simple behavioral problems, studies have shown for decades that juvenile delinquency is associated with "broken homes," most of them of course broken by divorce. That finding remains unshaken, but now we know it is largely based on the fact that juvenile delinquency is associated with class position (with higher rates toward the lower social strata). Thus, the relationship shows in part that both divorce and juvenile delinquency are more likely to be the experience of children of less advantaged homes. The association may, then, be partly spurious. At least one research report has suggested that for blacks, the effect of divorce, or living in a one-parent family, is relatively minor at the lower social strata. More bluntly put, the black child born to a mother toward the lower social levels faces so many problems that the difference between having or not having a divorce experience is of relatively small consequence.

However, studies do suggest that even when class position is held constant, delinquency rates are somewhat higher for broken than for un-

---

2.   These and related figures are to be found in Paul C. Glick and Arthur J. Norton, "Marrying, Divorcing, and Living Together in the U.S. Today," *Population Bulletin, 32* (October 1977), 27ff.

broken homes, and higher for children for homes broken by separation or divorce than for homes broken by death. The latter difference would be expected, because of the help and social support the bereaved person receives, and the lesser likelihood that children who have lost a parent by death have gone through a period of dissension, hostility, or problems about loyalty to one or the other parent. Studies have also revealed that children who have grown up in homes where parents avoid divorce but continue fighting have more emotional problems than those who experience a divorce.

All such studies are limited, but they are in agreement with what we understand about the processes of socialization. First, almost any kind of domestic trauma is likely to have at least some effect on the children who experience it. Second, it is the quality of the relationship between parents and children that is of most consequence. Thus, hostility and anger, and coldness and withdrawal are likely to have more destructive effects on children than the simple absence of one of the parents. A substantial segment of black children are reared in mother-headed households, but with some elder kin to give additional nurturance and help. It seems likely that this experience is a more healthful one than remaining in a household that is superficially intact, but torn by internal feuds.

Each year in the United States, over one million minor children are involved in divorce and annulment cases. Very likely most of their parents wished to live harmoniously with one another, but instead decided to break apart. If everyone could simply *decide* to be happily married, almost no divorces would occur. For most people, the real choice is whether to continue to live together in disharmony, or to divorce. Most of those who face that decision will be concerned about the effects on their children but in the modern world only a small minority will decide to remain miserable and married. In choosing divorce, they must also choose the complex and often unhappy consequences they and their children will then experience. The data on postdivorce adjustment for adults suggests that though most do have some unhappy experiences during divorce, they eventually enter a relatively more contented marriage afterward. This also means that most children who experience a divorce are likely to acquire a step-parent later on and to live in an intact home. All these experiences do require adjustments, and some are very painful. It is not yet certain, however, that these experiences have a lasting, destructive effect on most children.

CHAPTER 10 UNDERSTANDING FAMILY CHANGE: THEORY AND METHOD

Since human beings are pleased to believe they are the only animals that think about their own history, and because their own past seems endlessly fascinating to them, very likely they have discussed the topic of family change for thousands of generations. "How did things get to be the way they are today?" may well be the oldest question in social science. We do not make much progress in solving it, perhaps because the problem itself is very difficult, and we may have phrased it unfruitfully. Whatever the causes, social change is the least secure area of traditional social theory, although every aspiring theorist has probably tried to analyze it. Consequently, we shall set modest goals in this chapter. Rather than aiming at a comprehensive theory of family change, we wish only to clarify some methodological and empirical issues in this area, and to analyze some actual processes of changes in family systems of the past and present.

TYPES OF QUESTIONS ABOUT FAMILY CHANGE

Almost all the main social science questions about family change are of two broad types: (1) How or why did various family patterns (the rise in divorce rates, neolocal residence) alter over long or short historical periods? and (2) is there some regularity or determinate sequence in these changes? For example, are we able to say that matrilineages appeared before patrilineages or patriarchal polygyny before monogamy?

The first of these aims at explaining why particular changes occurred. For example, in our discussion of divorce we analyzed a number of the factors that seem to have led to a continual increase in divorce rates in the

United States over the past hundred years. Typically, this is done by applying common sense or social science regularities to some element in family patterns. As an illustration, we can assume that legitimacy rates are kept relatively low by an extensive set of social control processes, and if they rise over a historical period we can at least look for some of the factors that may have caused those social controls to weaken.

The second type of question is an evolutionary question, and very likely it is beyond our ability at this time.[1] All such comtemporary formulations are highly speculative. Such theories seek to locate patterned or *determinate* sequences of family change. A mere chronology of events, or even a long-term tabulation of continuing change, is not such a theory. An evolutionary theory must state that the history of family changes is not a mere fluctuation of patterns, or a series of ups and downs in some family behavior, but a set of developmental steps, comparable to the steps through which the various species and subspecies of plants and animals have arisen over thousands or millions of years and transformed themselves into other species or subspecies, in response to environmental pressures.

Many such sequences in animal evolution have been unearthed from fossil beds, and many regularities in these sequences have been noted. It seems almost certain that the amoeba had to appear before the flatworm, and the lion could not have appeared when the first ostracoderms appeared in the seas. In the realm of technology, determinate sequences appear even more robust. The automobile cannot appear before the wagon. The fore-and-aft sail is developed only after a long line of evolution in sailing technology. Microcomputers cannot occur until a great many prior discoveries in electrical circuits have been made.

By contrast, it is not at all clear that the "modern" conjugal family of industrial society is a new invention, or that it can come only after several prior steps in family evolution. Indeed, if we suppose that evolution proceeds from the simple to the complex, we might reason the opposite. Moreover, we know from research about contemporary family systems that the simple conjugal family is associated with a relatively *low* development of technology. Unfortunately for either speculation, the conjugal family is more likely to be found among tribal societies with a relatively low development of the economy, and *also* among societies that are industrialized. When we move to such before-after queries as whether low divorce rates come before high ones or polyandry must come before polygyny, even common sense will not help us much. Some rather complex hypotheses about linked sequences in kinship structure have been developed, but they are very difficult to test.[2]

1. Two good examples of this approach are P. L. Van den Berghe, *Human Family Systems: An Evolutionary View* (New York: Elsevier, 1979); and Gerhard Lenski and Jean Lenski, *Human Societies—An Introduction to Macrosociology,* 3rd ed. (New York: McGraw-Hill, 1978).

2. See, for example, George P. Murdock, *Social Structure* (New York: Macmillan, 1949), p. 251.

The task of a developed theory of family change, then, is not just to discover that certain social patterns did happen before others, but that the historical sequence is determinate, caused by social forces we can understand and predict. We do not believe that such a goal should be taken seriously in contemporary sociology. This renunciation is not caused by excessive modesty: other sciences have also shown a similar self-restraint. Cosmology, the study of the origins and developmental stages of stars and planets, has been the focus of far-reaching theoretical development over the past quarter-century, but it remains the least rigorous field of astrophysics. Chemistry seems not to take such an aspiration seriously, for it assumes that the patterns of chemical combinations under specified conditions are the same now as they were in the past. Biologists have meticulously charted the life cycle of many plants and animals, but the result is many descriptions without rigorous theory. Perhaps the best that sociology can do is to chart numerous longer-term changes where these can be found, and to explain them as well as possible with existing generalizations about social processes.

PROBLEMS OF METHOD AND PROOF

Obviously, before we can develop any adequate theory about necessary sequences in the development of family systems, we must first find out what they were. In pursuing that question, we can quickly eliminate one traditional question as being impossible to answer: what the human family was like when it first began. The origins of the family are totally lost to us. Even if we could penetrate the obscurities of known history, we would then have data on only the last few instants of human experience, for it reaches back to at least a million years ago and possibly four million. *Homo sapiens* certainly appeared as early as fifty thousand years ago, and possibly a hundred thousand years ago. We have no data at all on family patterns of that time, and because no traces remain we shall never know what they were. As we noted earlier, the family patterns of our four great anthropoid ape cousins do not help us at all, because they are very different from one another and because they branched off from the main human evolutionary line so long ago.

Even if we wish to analyze only the historical record, we face formidable technical problems in simply tracing the changes that have occurred. Most family events do not usually leave traces in the form of laws, documents, or treaties, much less systematic continuous records. Some formal events (births, deaths, marriages, lawsuits about inheritance) may be recorded, though of course there are fewer and fewer as we move back a few centuries into history. These, in any event, yield only a few insights into family patterns. These problems have been well analyzed by Peter Laslett and Lawrence Stone, who have perhaps contributed most to our understanding of family changes over the past few centuries in England and Europe.[3] Stone's

3. Peter Laslett and Richard Wall (eds.), *Household and Family in Past Time,* (Cambridge: University Press, 1972), esp. chap. 1; and Lawrence Stone, *The Family, Sex and Marriage in England 1500–1800* (New York: Harper and Row, 1977), chap. 1–2.

analysis of the aristocracy was especially rich, because peers left more records.[4] The comments of literary or philosophical figures about their times are at best the guesses of wise but untrained amateurs, for they did not carry out empirical investigations in order to test what they believed they observed. In addition, records and comments focus mainly on the top social strata, leaving nearly in obscurity the family behavior of most of the population. The records are written, then, by people who are literate, not by the lower strata, women, children, or slaves. Most changes in family laws were decided by the upper social strata, because of problems they faced in their own family situations; they tell us very little about the families of other social strata.

Equally important, as we noted much earlier, a single individual is not likely to be an excellent observer of an entire society, or the whole family system, because he or she has not had much opportunity to observe those other families firsthand. It is even more difficult for individuals to be accurate about time trends that extend beyond one person's lifetime. This difficulty creates perhaps the commonest error in attempting to chart family changes. It is an error that is self-contradictory: The commentator asserts that in his lifetime family patterns are changing rapidly, but that in some relatively recent past (usually his grandfather's time) family patterns were much more stable, for they followed the ancient and rightful ways of old. Since people are likely to have made such remarks in almost every generation, clearly they cannot all be correct. Another myth is that preliterate societies lived out their family patterns "unchanged for thousands of years until white men came." No such assertion has ever been proved. That claim may instead be seen as a mode of social control by which the old persuade the young that the traditional ways were best. We simply do not know how much change occurred in most of the societies without a written history, but we believe that a more fruitful assumption is to suppose that social and family change is universal; those changes may occur rapidly or slowly, but they take place continuously.

Thus, methodological barriers make it impossible to analyze the first beginnings of family systems in the human species, or their early changes over hundreds of thousands of years. Those technical problems make it difficult even to chart the exact history of family changes since the invention of writing. It is difficult to measure change if we do not have a secure base point. For that reason, the most important work in family change has been done in the past generation, when serious historians have attempted to mine the available archival material in order to specify whatever family changes those materials permit us to infer. Often, some of the most important relationships and factors are not recorded at all, but we are beginning to have at least a fair knowledge about some of the changes that have occurred in Western family systems—but only over the past several centuries. Although this knowledge will become more secure over time, very likely we shall still be unable to find out about some important social patterns. For

---

4. See Stone, *The Crisis of the Aristocracy, 1558–1641* (Oxford: Oxford University Press, 1965).

example , we may not find out whether family life was much more harmonious in England two centuries ago, and people more contented with it.

FACTORS IN FAMILY CHANGE

The methodological difficulties of formulating an adequate theory of social change have not, of course, prevented social analysts from developing theories just the same. The most popular "theories of social or family change" are not theories at all, but are unifactorial hypotheses—that is, they assert that family or social change has been shaped or caused primarily by one great factor such as race, climate, or economics. A common notion among social scientists, for example, is that technological or industrial change is *the* great factor in family change. That hypothesis derives its strength from a commonsense plausibility. Clearly, family life *is* different in industrial England from life in Stone Age Australia, just as it is different from life in England when most of the population was engaged in agriculture.

This and similar unifactorial explanations seem additionally persuasive because the global causal factor eventually is asserted to encompass almost everything. Since it *is* everything, of course it must cause everything. "Industrialization," like "urbanization," can be expanded to include almost everything, because it embraces not merely machines, but also the science and engineering that produced them. It includes the secular attitudes of the modern era, and thus antitraditionalism in many areas. Accompanying industrialization is the social pattern of placing people in jobs on the basis of competence. It is a society with high geographical mobility, and an open class system. In short, it encompasses all the social traits that set off this particular epoch in Western history. Thus it can be said that industrialization in this vague but enveloping sense does "cause" the modern social and family patterns, but only because it is identical with them. Such a hypothesis is true, but trivial.

To transform such a truism into a worthwhile exploratory probe, we much first attempt to locate which factors or elements of industrialism first enter a society, and the precise points of impact of those elements on various sectors of family life. Still more specifically, we suppose it is necessary to ascertain just how any of those elements might change the levers of power, prestige, or wealth, so that different members of the family, or different relationships within the family or the larger kin group are put under strain, or allowed to escape it. Or, just which alterations in the economy or technological system give greater or lesser opportunities to different members of the family. We shall discuss this problem in more detail in subsequent sections.

A more dramatic theory of family change, *evolutionism,* was dominant throughout the nineteenth century, and was widely accepted until as late as World War I. It began before Darwin's *Origin of the Species* (1859). That work revised fundamentally our thinking about the evolution of plants and animals, and it was quickly seized upon by social scientists who hoped to reconstruct the evolution of human societies and family systems. This was the only comprehensive theory of family change. It was mainly discarded in the 1920s, but no satisfactory substitute for it was found. In the last two decades, it has been resurrected in new forms, but with hardly any more secure foundation than it had before.

That theory was a reconstruction of the unknown past built on guesses about other animals, some tales and observations about tribal societies, and deductions from supposed "social survivals." These survivals were thought to be a kind of social fossil, and thus afforded social scientists the possibility of reconstructing the past from them, just as paleozoologists were reconstructing bygone animals from a few bones. Here is one example of one such supposed survival: In many societies the groom and his party once engaged in a mock battle in which they tore the bride away from her kin and carried her off to join the groom. From this custom it was deduced that in the distant past brides were obtained by capture. Ignored in this analysis was the fact that if a group actually succeeded in kidnapping a young woman, or several of them, they did not have to bother with marriage at all, for they could use such women in any way they chose. They did not have to give them the legitimacy of wifehood. Since the victim tribe could hardly be supposed to remain indifferent to this state of affairs, one would have supposed that such a custom must have been confined, if it existed at all, among a very small number of societies, those successful in war.

In a similar fashion, social scientists engaged in formulating the unknown developmental steps of the human family by reference to their technology or economy. They supposed that they could study Australian aborigines or Polynesians and thus learn about Stone Age family customs of fifty thousand years ago. To be sure, both the Australians and the Polynesians had as long a history as the nineteenth-century British, but if each stage in the development of stone or bronze tools was correlated with a specific family stage, then we could infer from those stages just what were the family patterns of many thousands of years ago. The core of this speculative edifice was the notion, then, that with each step in technology human beings also "advanced" in religious and familial behavior. It seemed reasonable to suppose that at some indefinite time in the past, human beings must have wandered about in a kind of horde, just as animals do, engaging in a sexually promiscuous life. At some later point, it became evident that the mother's line was known, while the part that men played in procreation was less clear, and of course the fatherhood of a specific child might be doubtful in any case. After the state of matriliny (in many versions this was viewed as matriarchy) came the stage of polygynous patriarchy, the patriarch with numerous wives and progeny. Much later, of course, came the highest spiritual pinnacle of all, Victorian monogamy.

This speculative reconstruction was not destroyed by contrary evidence, since we do not have any real data about family systems in the Stone Age period. Rather, under the new standards of evidence in the early twentieth century, this set of stages was viewed as having no real empirical support. No trace of an actual system of promiscuity has ever been found, nor of any matriarchal system. There are some low correlations between types of economy in a family system—for example, horticultural systems are correlated modestly with matrilineal systems, and herding societies are somewhat more patriarchal than others. However, robust correlations between economy or technology and family system are uncommon except in a crude form. We noted, for example, that there is a curvilinear relationship between the extension of the family system and the type of economy, in that the conjugal family appears to be common both at the lowest levels of technology and the highest level.

Although the thought of Marx and his collaborator and friend, Engels, did not ignore this reconstruction, Marx himself was not a social evolutionist. In his view of history, each epoch was distinct in its characteristics and in its social regularities. On the other hand, the position of women has been important in Marxist theory, largely through the work of Engels (who based his evolutionary ideas on the research of the American anthropologist Morgan), and it is essentially asserted that female subordination occurred when the phenomenon of private property appeared in human societies. The more important private property became, the more exploited and subordinated women were, and they will be liberated only when private property is abolished. Marx himself focused his empirical inquiry on the changes in the British family under the impact of the factory in the middle of the nineteenth century. In his view, the crucial change was the introduction of the machine. It can do the work of the human hand, and thus can be multiplied, speeded up, and driven by an inanimate source of power. Since it substitutes for the skilled hand, it can be operated by women and children. Thereby, a vast new supply of labor is available, which reduces the price of labor. Wages can be reduced to the level where all *must* work in order to survive. Since the capital costs of the machine continue whether it operates or stands idle, it is most efficient to run it long hours. The factory owner must hire the cheapest labor and work the laborers as hard as possible if he is not to be squeezed out of business by competitors.

Marx believed his ideas were buttressed by the reports from numerous empirical inquiries conducted by the investigating commissions of his day. Women and children were put to work, mother and child were separated, and children were neglected. Mortality rates of infants and children rose. Fathers sold their children's labor, and sometimes in effect their children, on harsh terms.[5] Later historical analysis does not fully confirm Marx's observations. The actual processes of development from the late eighteenth through the first half of the nineteenth century seem to have been somewhat more complex. Economic historians have argued that real wages did not in fact fall. Children were exploited (as they always had been), although in earlier phases of the factory system men could supervise their own children within the factory and thus retain some of their parental authority. The economic misery and the neglect of children and family during this period cannot be denied, but it is not at all clear that this was a

---

5.   A good example of his data and reasoning may be found in *Capital* (New York: Modern Library, 1936), chap. 15.

new development among the lower classes. In any event, the British family system did not continue to disintegrate.

Marx had not aimed at a generalized theory of family change. He was rather trying to focus on the developments he expected to take place as the capitalist mode of production generated its own contradictions, separated all social strata into workers and exploiters, and moved toward an inevitable revolutionary period whose outcome eventually would be socialism. Unfortunately, the modern socialist countries have not, of course, ushered in the harmonious, egalitarian family system that was envisioned by Marxists of either the nineteenth or the twentieth centuries.

Many thinkers who are politically not Marxist have utilized one or another facet of his thought. Many analysts, as noted earlier, have supposed that some elements of industrialism or technology have had a major impact on social or family structures. In his early work, the sociologist William F. Ogburn asserted that the prime mover of social change is technology ("material culture") and that the nonmaterial (family, religion) elements adjust to it after a time ("culture lag"). His actual research and his later theoretical position were more eclectic. He saw a wide range of new elements as sources of family change, from ideologies to airplanes. Like many family analysts of the past generation, he saw the modern family as "losing its functions" because industrial production took place in factories, education in schools, religious training in churches, and so on. Although this view of family change is widely shared, it is rather vague in meaning and for the most part is simply an incorrect statement of what has been taking place.

Ogburn's "theory" is a general approach rather than a set of linked hypotheses, and simply directs us to look for the origins of family change in specific technological innovations. Along with many others, for example, he saw the automobile as freeing individuals from family controls, because they could drive to places where they were free of observation by family members. He took for granted that engineering innovations would mainly be accepted on the grounds of rationality, and they would eventually have some impact on social patterns. As against this looseness, however, he was careful to prove false a number of assumptions about changes in the family, for he was basically an empirical researcher. For example, he pointed out that the average size of the U.S. household did decrease from 1850 to 1950 (5.5 to 3.5 persons), but obviously the swarming multifamily household of nostalgic speeches was not common even a century ago. Similarly, he summarized research data to show that the labor-saving devices of the American home had not reduced the number of hours the housewife worked each week.

INDUSTRIALIZATION AND THE CONJUGAL FAMILY

The author's research, along with that of many others in the period after World War II, has documented one gross empirical regularity whose processes are not yet clearly understood: In all parts of the world and for the first time in world history, all social systems are moving fast or slowly toward some form of the conjugal family system and also toward industrialization. In agreement with the intuition of social analysts for over a century is the finding that with industrialization the traditional family systems—usually extended or joint family systems, with or without lineages or clans—are breaking down. On the other hand, since each system begins from a somewhat different base point, the *direction* in any given family pattern may be different. The divorce rate dropped for over half a century in Japan (it is rising now) and for a shorter period in some Arab countries, while it has been rising in the Western countries. The age at marriage has simply fluctuated without much change in most Western countries, but it has been rising in most of the countries of the world where the traditional age had been set relatively low.

Before continuing with this analysis, let us keep clearly in mind what is being asserted. Even though this large-scale regularity can be observed in the data over the past century, we must narrow its content by pointing out the following limitations:

1.   Some family patterns appear long before industrialization (for example, most families in most great societies have been relatively small).

2.   Family changes occur in any society, not alone those undergoing industrialization.

3.   Many family patterns resist industrialization, for a generation or two or indefinitely (for example, kin networks continue to be of importance).

4.   Even under industrialization, other factors (ideology, laws) can change family behavior.

5.   Most family patterns do not change rapidly (the dowry does not disappear in a generation); and most family changes associated with industrialization begin among some parts of the population before industrialization has developed very much.[6]

Let us now consider the factors in industrialization that might have some impact on family patterns. Earlier, the structural characteristics of the conjugal family system were outlined, most of them derivable from its lesser extension of kinship relations. These traits fit rather well the demands of industrialization, although as we shall suggest subsequently, this does not mean that industrialization is a strong support of the family system itself. Under the industrial system, the individual is supposed to be hired because of his or her competence, and in promotion the same standards are to be applied to all who hold the job. That is, the standards for performance are ideally achievement-based, and universalistic. The person's relationship to the job is functionally specific—role obligations are ideally confined to getting the task done. Put another way, the extended

---

6.   For a more extended historical analysis of these problems, along with trends, see William J. Goode, *World Revolution and Family Patterns* (New York: Free Press, 1963). Many of the figures in this monograph have been brought up to date in an Italian translation to be published by Nicola Zanichelli, S.p.A., in 1981.

family system, with standards of ascription, particularism, and diffuseness, is ideally not permitted to interfere with the efficient functioning of a modern enterprise. As I and many others have noted, this interference occurs to some extent just the same, but it is not so great as in most previous types of economy. As a set of prescriptions for efficiency, these notions began with commercial capitalism, and at least two centuries before industrialization began to have much of an impact, but they are most fully implemented under industrialization.

Because of its emphasis on performance, such a system requires that the person be permitted to rise or fall in social rank, and to move about wherever the job market is best. A lesser emphasis on land ownership also increases the ease of mobility. The conjugal family system is neolocal (each couple sets up its own household), and its kinship network is not strong, thus putting fewer barriers than other family systems in the way of class or geographical mobility. The relationship may also be put another way. Since increasingly an industrializing society (China, the Arab countries) creates formal agencies to handle the major tasks of any kinship grouping larger than the nuclear family, such units as lineages, clans, or even large extended families lose some of their tasks as well as their resources. Thus, they cannot command the allegiance they once had, as they do not enjoy the social controls that were once in their hands. They cannot ensure that the individual who subordinates himself or herself to the elders will do better over the longer run than those who embark upon an independent career. Thus individuals and families are more likely to go their own ways, ignoring such extended kinship ties.

Although family elders always attempt to control the major new economic or political opportunities, they cannot do so as easily under an industrial system, and thus family authority slips from them over time. The young groom can obtain his bride price on his own, and need not concern himself as much about the good will of his elders. In a modern Chinese commune, he is sure to obtain employment, whether or not he is obedient to his elders. A couple need not obey anyone outside their family unit, since it is their performance on the job that is mainly relevant for their advancement. As new types of tasks proliferate, young people need not even rely on family elders for job instruction, since schools, the factory, or the plantation or mine will teach them the new skills. They do not need to continue working on the land, if it is still in the possession of the elders, since the new jobs and political opportunities are likely to be in the city or factory. Thus, industrialization is likely to undermine the traditional systems of family control and exchange. Each member is in a different structural position; the terms of the role bargaining between generations have been altered.

Upper-strata families, of course, are more likely to keep many controls in their hands as a society undergoes increasing market development and industrialization. When Western societies underwent industrialization, the new opportunities remained in the hands of middle- or upper-class families who owned these new enterprises. At least their bargaining power was not reduced so much as that of lower-class families. By contrast, the formerly upper-strata native families in newly conquered regions were apt to lose *more* than families toward the lower social strata. In the New World, for example, after the initial period of conquest, the indigenous tribal leaders were removed. The Spanish and Portuguese local rulers took all the important positions and opportunities. Native rulers lost control over their families, and their political authority collapsed. More often, at least in the early development of plantations in Africa, many European empire builders tried to rule *through* the tribal leaders, so that fewer chances for economic or political advancement were available to young natives independently of their elders. On the other hand, over time, as a larger percentage of the tribe or society is drawn into the new economic enterprises, and people are hired and promoted on their own merits, the large kinship groupings weaken and leaders lose their ability to elicit obedience to traditional family customs.

The conjugal emphasis on emotionality within the family also serves somewhat the needs of industrialism. At lower job levels, the worker experiences little intrinsic job satisfaction; at higher levels, he or she obtains more job satisfaction, but is also subject to great demands. At any level, the enterprise has no responsibility for the emotional balance of the individual, for that remains the responsibility of the family. At least, there is nowhere else to go for it. In the following chapter we continue this analysis by noting the major trends over time that accompany industrialization.

CHAPTER 11
HOW DOES INDUSTRIALIZATION AFFECT THE FAMILY?

By emphasizing how the modern conjugal family system fits the needs of industrialization (without fully considering whether the latter meets the needs of the family), we only partially explained how industrialization has its impact on traditional systems. We did note the key point: As new jobs and opportunities develop (first under commercial capitalism and later under industrialization), family elders lose some control over the younger generation because they no longer command as fully all the available resources. Let us explore this set of complex processes in a bit more detail.

PROCESSES THAT WEAKEN FAMILY CONTROL

We suggest that three main processes arise with industrialization and weaken the traditional system of family control. First, an increasing number of people earn their living from *jobs,* positions that pay wages for a particular task. They do not depend on eventually obtaining a share of the land, or a right to rent land, both of which are usually in the hands of family elders. Second, the needs of efficiency in the industry and the economy require that jobs and promotions be given out mainly for competence and by people who basically *have little stake in the familial position of the worker.* Therefore, those who hire, fire, or promote will feel little concern about whether the rewards they give will support any existing set of familial roles. For example, if the worker does not fulfill his or her family obligations, the employer is not very interested. In that case, individuals who wish to avoid or defy family controls will not lose much by following their own inclinations. It should be noted, however, that this is less likely to be true at the upper levels of corporate life, for high corporate executives are expected to lead relatively stable family lives. Third, work positions in the market economy offer the possibility of gaining a living as an *individual,* not as a member of a family. If individuals can earn more in the economy by their own efforts than by pooling their labor with members of their family or their kin network, they can become independent of their kin or elders.

In all three processes, the result it that the traditional flow of rewards and punishments given to the younger or older family member on the basis of his or her conformity to family wishes is interrupted or altered. It is not that these industrial processes directly and universally work against the family; but all family systems are under some strain, and always some individuals would break away from traditional rules if they could do so easily. Industrial patterns give much less support than did the traditional system to the maintenance of older family loyalties and contributions. In many social changes, some traditional supports are undermined, but new supports emerge. At the present time, it seems likely that industrialization has not developed many alternative patterns of support for traditional family obligations.

Such changes do not occur swiftly. Males became more liberated from family controls at an earlier stage in industrialization than did females, and at a different rate in different parts of the economy. For example, a teenage factory worker in the late nineteenth century did not have to obey his father nearly so much as a teenage daughter, or so much as a son of a farmer-owner, or of an industrial owner. That was because the young factory worker did not have to stay on the farm in the hope of inheriting it; instead, he could live off his wages. On the other hand, the authority of elders was not undermined to the same degree by the fact that young women took jobs in nineteenth-century Japanese and Italian spinning mills. They worked under various arrangements, but it was taken for granted that they would not have full command over their own wages. In Japan it was expected that some part of their money would be set aside for their eventual marriage. They did not continue to work after marriage, and so did not develop an independent career. They were not promoted on their own. In short, at every point the system of law and authority was focused on obtaining a heavy work contribution from young women for a period of years, but both the mill managers and the family elders continued to be concerned about these workers' conformity to family tradition. By contrast, modern U.S. factory managers simply do not care, in general, whether their expert computer analyst obeys her husband or is respectful toward her father.

These processes may be viewed in another way by asking why family elders have attempted, in so many societies, to maintain lineages and clans, strong and extensive kin networks, or large extended households when they could do so. First, all such units can be productive enterprises, in the narrow sense of creating goods and services for sale, and in the broader sense of yielding a wide array of rewards for the elders who control the units. Elders gain prestige, comfort, deference from the young, and the pleasure that comes from making decisions for others. If many are pooling their resources, and there is a sufficient amount of land or a large enough enterprise to support everyone, some measure of social security is achieved. Some economies of scale occur, and in general individuals will feel that their best chance of long-term profit will be found in staying with the large family unit, contributing to it, and hoping that eventually they will become privileged elders in turn.

A final, major process through which industrialization has an effect upon kinship patterns is to be observed in its creation of a wide array of impersonal services that can be obtained in the open market. *Corporate* kinship groups such as lineages and clans always engage in different kinds of capital accumulation, lending, the development of some collective properties such as a temple, protection of the group, and so on. Earlier, we analyzed some of these patterns as they appeared in Japan, China, and India. The modern type of political economy develops easier banking facilities, public schools, political protection, and many public services. This enables *individuals* to live more adequately apart from the controls of the kin network. Equally important, it undermines the controls of such large-scale kin units over individual families. The services and help they once provided can now be obtained elsewhere.

DOES INDUSTRIALISM "FIT" THE CONJUGAL FAMILY?

Although several of the characteristics of the conjugal family are useful for an industrial economy, does the latter support the conjugal family? We cannot assume that the interaction between these two great institutions is naturally harmonious, or conducive to the total welfare of the society or its members. In the course of history, sometimes one institution gains at the expense of others, and may even gain at the expense of much of the population. Large-scale institutions are the unplanned result of individual desires and initiatives. All are systems of forces, each with its own needs, and in various ways any one may fail to serve the needs of the others.

In order to achieve the goal of placing everyone in his or her job solely on the basis of merit, we would have to destroy the family system entirely, for it is an inevitable result of any family system that members attempt to give special advantages to their young whenever they can. Industrial enterprises, focused on profits (whether in the Soviet Union or the United States) have little interest in the idiosyncracies and needs of aged parents, the emotional problems of adults, or the insecurities of children. On the other hand, if the family system failed completely to deal with such matters, very likely there would not be enough adequately functioning people even to staff the industrial system. That is, family and industrial factors have some independent weight, but do interact with one another. Neither fully determines the other, and as we shall note later, family forces continue to resist industrializing pressures. Thus, we cannot suppose that industrialism supports even the conjugal family, though it may be ultimately dependent upon its effectiveness.

We may answer the question by pointing out some of the problems that are common in a conjugal system, or are partly generated by the demands of an industrial system, and then asking whether the modern political economy helps to solve them or to prevent them. We believe that in general the answer is negative. Since we do not wish to explore this question in depth, we will simply list some of these junctures at which an advanced technical society does not appear to offer much support.

1.   The family unit is fragile because of separation and divorce, but the larger system offers little help in the crises for adults or their children.

2.   The industrial system fires, lays off, and demands geographical mobility by reference to the *individual,* ignoring the familial strains these actions may cause.

3.   For most of its history, the industrial system has operated through the fiction that only the individual worked at the job. The major contributions of the wife to the worker's productivity were ignored. Moreover, the technical system offered women more economic goods, but has not relieved them of their household tasks. Labor-saving devices merely raised the standards of cleanliness and general performance, permitting more work to be turned out, but they did not reduce the hours of work.

4.   With the recent increase in the use of women in the labor force their total work burden has increased, but only a few corporations have attempted to develop programs for helping them in child care, or for inducing men to share these tasks.

5.   The modern system, with its neolocal, independent household and its accompanying values in favor of separate lives for each couple, leave older parents and kin in an ambiguous position. It has been estimated that the 1980 U.S. Census would find that about 12 percent of the total population is 65 years of age or over, or about 27 million people. Because it focuses on the importance of the individual as a jobholder, this type of society has not yet developed any position of respect or even economic security for such people.

Doubtless the reader will think of other problems common to the contemporary family which the industrial system passes over or ignores as being irrelevant to the tasks of the enterprise. Most of them are tackled, if at all, only when they are thought to create *political* problems, such as the "welfare burden," high illegitimacy rates, school failures in the ghetto, or the complaints of upper middle class men that they have to pay too much alimony.

MAJOR WORLD TRENDS IN FAMILY PATTERNS

Before going on to consider some of the points at which family systems may resist the ideological, economic, and political pressures of industrialization, let us summarize the major world trends that seem to be observable in most of the world's societies at present. These general trends do not suggest that in some relatively early future all family systems will be exactly alike. Even if we confine ourselves to the purely technical structure of the factory, it is evident now that the organizational processes of the factory are likely to be different in China, Japan, Russia, and the United States for many decades to come. The time perspective should be even longer if we make prophecies about the family.

What are some of the major changes now going on in family patterns the world over? They appear to be the following:

A Decline in Matriliny.   In matrilineal kinship structures, property and power descended through the mother's line, with a number of important structural consequences that have been generally analyzed in the anthropological literature, and were presented in an earlier chapter. In the contemporary world, matrilineages begin to dissolve for all the reasons that corporate kin groups dissolve. In addition, both social and economic decisions place the responsibility for the family on the father, rather than the sister's brother; new laws are imposed that give testamentary freedom to the father, so that he can pass on his property to his own children, rather than to his sister's children. In many matrilineal societies, some women had high symbolic rank, but these posts tend to disappear in the industrial world, as being of no politico-economic importance. Thus it is likely that people in matrilineal societies begin to move toward a patrilineal or bilineal pattern.

A Decline in Influence of Corporate Kin Groups.   The wide range of lineage systems in tribal societies could be expected to decline in power and importance, for all the reasons we have noted earlier. The Chinese clan was, of course, also undermined by the direct political attack of the Chinese communists.

A Decrease in the Prevalence of the Dowry or Bride Price.   This is not a prediction that the *amount* will decline, since where such systems are maintained at all, inflation alone would increase the sums of property demanded. Both dowry and bride price can, in modern settings, approach more closely the Western pattern of gift exchanges on both sides—a system that looks similar but is very different. But the prediction is nevertheless that there will be a decline in the prevalence of the dowry or bride price, especially as young people increasingly make their own decisions about marriage, and have jobs of their own that will permit them some freedom to set up their own households. Even where they continue, they do not continue to serve the needs of the kin line, but of the new family unit.[1]

An Increase in Age Homogamy.   The average difference in age between men and women narrows over time partly because of a rise in women's age at marriage, in countries where that age was once very low. This trend also occurs because older men cannot so easily buy young brides as in the past, and young people increasingly make their own decisions about

---

1.   Because in the Chinese commune the bride's family loses a worker, the bride price continues in China, against official policy, but its meaning has been radically changed.

marriage, while their preference is likely to be in favor of mates about their own age.

A Decrease in Kin Marriages.   A smaller percentage of marriages occur between people who are relatively close kin, such as cousins of various degrees. This means a decline in the wide range of preferential marriages in traditional societies, but it also includes a large number of kin marriages in Western countries, where elders made efforts to "keep the property within the family."

A Movement to Medium or High Divorce Rates.   Any conjugal system will have a relatively high divorce rate. On the other hand, as we noted, some traditional systems (Japan, certain Arab countries, and some tribal societies) generated a very high rate of divorce, and the change from the older system may actually reduce those divorce rates in some social settings, at least for a while.

More specifically: What the *trend* will be in any country depends on where it *started:* Japan had a very high divorce rate *before* industrialization and as its family system changed its divorce rate *fell*, as this theory predicted. It has also begun to rise again. Taiwan's divorce rate was also high, though only by Chinese standards, and as the forces maintaining it weakened the divorce rate fell. It is once more rising. Malaysia had one of the highest rates in the world, and again as its traditional family patterns changed, the rate has been falling. Mainland China's rate fell from the late 1950's until recently, but for mainly bureaucratic reasons (for the purpose of total mobilization it was made very difficult). The author predicted a temporary fall in Arab divorce rates, but though some analysts confirm this it is not clear that the data will ever permit us to know what the exact trends have been

In any event, the prediction would not be that divorce rates in traditionally high-divorce areas would fall indefinitely; but that eventually they would, after falling, rise to medium or high levels.

An Increase in the Number of Women Holding Jobs Independently.   In all societies throughout world history, women have worked. In many societies they also held jobs that paid wages. Until very recently in world history, very few women got those jobs, or were promoted in them, without the permission or the active help of their male kin. The modern movement is toward greater independence in this area.

An Increase in Women's Rights.   This descriptive statement will occasion some controversy, since many ardent feminists assert there has been no significant change under industrialization, while others have argued that women were given equality with men in some legendary period of the past. No such historical epoch exists, as far as our present knowledge goes. However, if we confine ourselves to the era preceding industrialization, and to the period of relatively moderate or advanced industrialization, the trend toward greater equality of women's status seems clear enough.

Less Control by Parents over Children's Courtship and Mate Choices.
Parents steadily lose the ability to decide whom their children will court or marry. We have already noted the many factors in the modern world that generate this loss of control.

More Sexual Freedom.   Here it may be necessary to remind Western readers that most tribal societies have been sexually more liberal than the great civilizations of the past, and than Western societies. It may also be necessary to remind some Western readers who have been beguiled by myths concerning the "natural, guilt-free approach to sex" found in Eastern countries that the historical data do not support such a description, though rich males could enjoy relatively free sexual lives. In any event, wherever sexual freedom was highly restricted, industrialization brings greater freedom with it, because its idology asserts the right of individuals to choose, and its job system supports the individual who does not wish to follow traditional ways.

Unmarried Cohabitation in Western Countries.   It is one of the paradoxes of modern family change that as divorce becomes much easier, a larger number of people decide they do not wish to enter marrige at all. The paradox can be resolved, but the phenomenon itself deserves mention.

Not many analysts of unmarried cohabitation have sufficiently emphasized how radical a change this phenomenon is in world history. Living together outside a legal union has been common in Latin America for perhaps centuries, and more recently in urban sub-Saharan Africa, but in both cases this is a social pattern among the poor, in societies whose social and normative structures have been undermined or weakened. Very likely, in contemporary Latin America and the Caribbean the trend will be in the *opposite* direction: toward less unmarried cohabitation. In non-Western societies this phenomenon has not been common in the historical past, but where found the respectable classes did not engage in it. Occasional nobles in western society openly kept mistresses, but were expected to maintain the forms of proper marriage with their official wives, as was also true in non-Western societies. Only in our era has a large segment of respectable people moved toward openly living together outside a legal union, while engaging in ordinary social activities with their peers.

This is unlikely to be a passing aberration, and we shall not move in a pendulum fashion to Victorian sexual restraint. It is increasing (in 1980, about 1.5 million couples in the United States were living together unmarried) and especially in the countries that are the vanguard of the modern world (U.S., Denmark, Sweden).

It is not a full substitute for marriage. Both do offer the advantage of the "marital package"; but while marriage yields more benefits it also contains more potential costs.

More people will very likely engage in unmarried cohabitation, while a high percentage of those who do so will not be as committed to that union as they would be to a marriage. The stability of such unions is less than that of marriage. Most who cohabit will not eventually transform *that* particular union into a marriage, though most will, sooner or later move on to a legal marriage. Some, of course, will not be content with their cohabitation union, but will stay in it just the same because they do not locate a better opportunity.

Very likely for some decades into the future, cohabitation will become a widespread phase of the total marital cycle in Western nations, both before the first marriage and before the second marriage, just as dating has become. This pattern has become so widespread, and its consequences so ramified, that laws and courts are now setting about the task of working out what legal or other rights the individuals in such a union may acquire through living together. Finally, almost certainly both the recent delay of marriage and re-marriage, and the increase in the percentage of couples living in unmarried cohabitation, arise in part from the increasing reluctance of women to enter a relationship in which men are still unwilling to share burdens equally. Even women who have not openly joined the women's liberation movement have nevertheless become more conscious of the extent to which they are exploited in a legal marriage. While they have not as yet gained enough power to alter the terms of that legal contract much, they can express their wishes by their lesser eagerness to accept those formal terms, and to attempt to work out a more informal set of rules that will be less binding upon them.

Increasing Age at Marriage for Women.   Child marriages steadily decrease in societies where that was common.[2] This occurs partly because women obtain more education, and are worth more on the marriage market when they do; because adults cannot so easily control their male or their female children's choices; and because political pressures are set against very young marriages.

A Decline in the Birth Rate.   As people experience industrialization, they exhibit a generally downward secular trend in the birth rate, aside from the usual rises and falls that accompany prosperity or depression. For the most part, we do not see this as occurring because of any strictly *familial* impact of industrialization. We suppose the primary direction of causation is that public health measures, medical intervention, and an increase in affluence permits the survival of a much higher percentage of the baby population. When people are assured that they will have a fair number of children to survive them, the burden of additional children seems much clearer than in the past, when in many segments of traditional societies perhaps only a bare majority of infants ever became adult. In addition, more education for women and a higher percentage of women in the work force will reduce the birth rate.

The Passage of Family Laws Far Ahead of General Public Opinion. As new nations are formed, and successive revolutions write new constitutions and codes of laws, the new provisions express a set of wishes or aspirations (the equality of women, the protection of children, freedom of mate choice) that will be in advance of the day-to-day attitudes and wishes of ordinary people in a society.

Not all these trends are self-explanatory. Some are fairly secure as trends, but the direction of causation is not clear. Obviously, in almost every instance the *ideology* of modern freedom, individualism, the right to upward social mobility, and so on are part of the total set of forces that

---

2. For a substantial body of data confirming this change, see *Population Reports,* Series M, No. 4 (November 1979), esp. 115, 127.

generates such trends. Some of these trends are fairly robust if we consider nations as wholes, but we must keep in mind that there are many exceptions with specific subgroups, or subregions of any nation. Those exceptions should stimulate us to seek more closely the exact relationships between industrialization and family change.

SOME RESISTANCES TO INDUSTRIALIZING FORCES

If, as we have repeatedly insisted, ideological changes may (in modern times, typically through political action) alter some parts of the family before industrialization has made much of an impact, and some "modern" family patterns (a relatively small household in Western countries) may also begin long before industrialization, it seems reasonable to suppose that the social structure of the economy and of the family may be at least somewhat independent. Let us take the further step of exploring the relations between industrialization and the conjugal family by noting some points at which family forces appear to resist those of industrialization.

Birth Control

One such resistance has been analyzed at great length over the past generation—that is, the difficulty of reducing the birth rate in countries attempting to modernize, so that much of their increase in production is consumed by an ever-mounting population. That occurred in spite of a worldwide effort to reduce the birth rate in such countries. Those rates are dropping, but the decrease has been relatively slow. The reasons for the long period of resistance seem to be fairly clear. In all societies fertility has been accorded high priority, because the ranks of the living are depleted by death, and until recently a high mortality rate among infants was typical. Thus, in most societies, from the earliest period of socialization the child is told that he or she will eventually marry and produce children, and the full privileges of adulthood are typically not conceded until the individual has become a parent. Great effort is expended to inculcate fertility values in everyone, and even in industrial societies a high percentage of people will answer in surveys that they would prefer to have more children than they in fact intend to have. This emphasis is in sharp contrast to the relative lack of cultural emphasis on an individual's taking care of his own life and avoiding death. Apparently, human beings need very little special socialization to try to avoid death. However, the obligation of producing other persons, to whom we owe extensive and burdensome obligations, requires much social reinforcement.

In less industrialized, high-mortality societies, the main adjustive controls in the social structure—abortion or infanticide—come *after* conception. Thus, if the population is sharply reduced by war, epidemic, or famine, the constantly high fertility values lead individuals to produce replacements very quickly; and indeed all they need to do to adjust is to stop engaging in infanticide for a brief time. It would not be possible suddenly to bring in a set of high fertility values, since that type of socialization would take a generation to have any important effect. In a parallel way, however, it is difficult for a society quickly to take up a contraceptive pattern when mortality is suddenly reduced and the population begins to grow faster than the increase in productive capacities. In many countries since World War II, the death rate was reduced by 25 to 50 percent within the span of a few years, with little reduction in the birth rate. The interaction of those factors creates a special problem for the modern era, the world population explosion. It seems clear that no reasonable projections of possible increases in productivity can possibly take care of the projected population for future generations without a drastically decreased level of living.

To reduce mortality rates requires no more than a modest amount of cooperation from the population. A clean water supply can be introduced, or a more effective sewerage system, without a vote or any individual decision by those affected. Pesticides have nearly wiped out one of the great killers, malaria, without much help on the part of individuals. In any event, cooperation seems not to be difficult to obtain in ordinary medical problems, since people can be readily convinced that modern medicine and science can save their lives, and this is a goal desired by all. Contraception, by contrast, is an intimately personal and familial matter, not a mass decision. It requires an important shift in the attitudes, habits, and values of individuals with respect to family roles. Contraception is costly in poor countries, and requires much discipline. Moreover, until recently the main thrust of most great religious systems was set against the use of contraception—not only in India, China, or Islam, but also in Western countries. On the other hand, within the last decade this resistance has been reduced considerably, perhaps because mortality itself has decreased so much. No nation seems to have a *low* infant mortality for long without moving toward a somewhat lower birth rate. In addition, of course, there are increasingly strong political and governmental efforts to reduce birth rates, to give more education to women, and to open jobs to women.

The Retention of Kin Groups

Let us now consider some of these resisting processes at different levels of kinship complexity. First, at the highest level of complexity, industrialization has the most destructive effect on corporate kinship groups, as we have already noted. Such kin groups acted as a unit to develop facilities for loans, education, help in obtaining jobs, political protection, the repair of temples, and so on. The new economy undermines these socioeconomic foundations, and does so in a socialist country such as China, as it does in a capitalist country such as Japan. However, here and there in developing countries, some members of a kin group may perceive that not all these public facilities have been well developed, and kin members can sometimes best exploit the new market opportunities by continuing to pool their skills and resources. The great *dozoku* (called *zaibatsu*) of Japan did that until after World War II. Some lineage groups still do in Africa. Thus, the general undermining process may be visible, but many kin groups will continue to prosper as partial or truncated collectivities within one area of activity or another.

Let us consider a second family form at a somewhat lower level of organization than lineages and clans—that is, the large, multigenerational extended household. As we know, these were not typical even under traditional systems, for many reasons—the mortality of children and of the older generation, the lack of organizational skills necessary to hold larger household units together, inadequate land to support many people, and so on.

To be sure, if public health measures are suddenly adopted in technologically less developed countries, so that mortality rates drop quickly, for a time a modest increase in such household units might occur, or at least no great decrease. Nevertheless, over longer periods of time it is unlikely that any substantial increase in the talent for family organization will occur, and a higher percentage of people will earn their living from jobs, not from the exploitation of commonly held family land. Since people then depend far less on the communal group, that group controls them far less, and individual members will see fewer advantages to staying together. Thus we would expect such households to decline. On the other hand, at less developed levels of industrialization, jobs are often poorly paid and underemployment is common, so that individuals may well have to continue pooling their small incomes in order to survive. This happened in the early phases of English industrialization, as Marx amply documented. It is also reported in a very modest way for one small region of Muslim Libya. Doubtless, it continues to be common.

This type of pooling may occur even when some members actually object to it. It has been described in Africa as "family parasitism," for often a successful urban worker finds he is expected to honor his obligations to tribal relatives who come to live with him, though in fact they do not get jobs. He may have to support them in various ways, or send members to school, because of social pressures from members of his lineage or direct family line, even though the members who live with him do not actually contribute much, or anything, to the household. In one study in the Philippines, it was ascertained that there are more extended households in some of the urban regions than in surrounding rural regions. Closer examination discloses that these household members are often not direct descendants of a given family line. That is, they do not form a traditional extended household. Instead, the household has been increased by cousins, nephews, nieces, or more distant relatives who have come to live with an urban family, because there are more economic opportunities in the urban settlements and a chance for further education. In contemporary India as well as in Taiwan, extended households may still be observed, sometimes in the form of geographically separated family members who engage in both exchanges and pooling with one another. Some members of an extended family may farm, others hold jobs, and still others engage in entrepreneurial activities. Many may live under the same roof, or in the same compound, while others live at least part of the time elsewhere. We can suppose that this will not be a continued upward trend, but it is one example of the process we are describing—some type of family pooling when individual advancement or economic security is still limited in the industrial system, and the economy has not yet developed enough to utilize marginal members of the society.

Let us note a third type of kin resistance, the maintenance of kin networks as active sources of help. As the author noted over two decades ago, a key paradox in the apparently simple conflict between industrialization and family forces is that the most successful families and family networks in the industrial economy, the members of the upper class, very likely engage in more familistic behavior than almost any other stratum. Although the data on this point are not secure, it seems likely that at upper-class levels in industrialized societies, more political-economic opportunities are determined through family-linked social connections than at lower-class levels. This applies to lucrative contracts with corporations and governmental agencies, as well as to high-paying jobs of great prestige. This occurs in part because members of the upper class are in structural positions where substantial opportunities occur, and members of their kin network are the most easily available persons in command of enough resources to make exchanges workwhile. After all, if one is a member of an extended Rockefeller or Rothschild kin network, it is surely as profitable to seek help from kin as it would be to go outside it as an individual and seek help from strangers.

Thus, there is no mechanical relationship between industrialization and the undermining of specific kinship patterns. Rather, the destruction is less likely to occur when the socioeconomic environment does not offer better alternatives than various types of kinship pooling can offer. As further evidence of the vitality of kinship network processes, we repeat our earlier comment that in the most industrialized of Western societies, a wide array of research since the 1950s has disclosed that kinship networks are very much alive. Almost everyone seems to maintain continued relations with a substantial number of kin—in some research, from 50 to 150 persons.[3] The reasons can easily be found in our direct experience: For some activities the exchanges, help, advice, and even loans we get from kin may be easier to obtain, and less costly, than from the relatively awkward and inefficient bureaucracies of the state or the corporation. That is, under various socioeconomic circumstances, family structures possess advantages that modern bureaucracies and corporations cannot achieve.

EFFECT OF THE FAMILY ON INDUSTRIALIZATION

Let us now consider another relationship between family factors and social change, the possibility that the family system may have an independent,

3. For a brief summary of the data on the United States, see F. Ivan Nye and Felix N. Berardo, *The Family* (New York: Macmillan, 1973), pp. 407–434.

facilitating effect on the modern shift toward industrialization. No full-scale research into this hypothesis has been carried out, but a few suggestive facts may be noted here. Negatively, of course, many observers have pointed out that extended and joint family systems prevented free utilization of talent as well as the easy introduction of innovations. Positively, it should be kept in mind that the family systems of the West have been different from those of other major civilizations for over a thousand years.[4] Child or early adolescent marriage was not the ideal or the statistical usual. There was no ancestor worship, and *individuals*, not families, were responsible for crimes. There was no lineage or clan system, and the eldest male was not necessarily the leader of the family. Young couples were expected to live independently, for the most part.

These differences were accentuated when the individualistic, antitraditional ideology of ascetic Protestantism began to spread. The Puritans in the United States, for example, defined husband and wife as loving companions rather than simply part of a family network, and their children had more freedom of marital choice than was possible in the traditional European family systems. Divorce became possible, even though disapproved. It seems likely that by the time the new factory jobs opened in the late eighteenth century in England, the family system of at least part of the population was in some harmony with its new demands. Their extended kinship ties and obligations, and their links with family land, did not interfere with the new type of work obligations.

A more striking instance of the importance of family patterns in facilitating or hindering social change may be found in the contrast between the success of Japan and China in their attempts to industrialize during the late nineteenth and early twentieth centuries.[5] Both were opened to the West at about the same time, and both faced a somewhat similar set of problems: Threat of conquest, an agrarian economy, rapid population growth, extensive bureaucracies that had become corrupt and inefficient, an emphasis on families, strains between town and country, and the low prestige of merchants, who would have to assume important roles in any modernizing process. As against China's essential failure to cope with its problems, within about half a century after 1868 Japan had established heavy industries with almost no outside capital, altered its system of distribution, made both male and female literacy almost universal, and introduced a new set of social relationships characteristic of the Western market system.

Several differences between the Japanese and Chinese family systems

---

4. For a persuasive but much criticized analysis of this point, see Alan MacFarlane, *The Origins of English Individualism* (New York: Cambridge University Press, 1979).

5. Marion J. Levy, "Contrasting Factors in the Modernization of China and Japan," in *Economic Growth: Brazil, India, Japan,* eds. Simon S. Kuznets, Wilbert E. Moore, and Joseph J. Spengler (Durham, N.C.: Duke University Press, 1955). For another view giving more importance to international power relations, see Francine V. Moulder, *Japan, China, and the Modern World Economy* (New York: Cambridge U. Press, 1977).

contributed to their varying successes in coping with the problem of industrialization. One was the pattern of inheritance. Under the Chinese family system, all sons inherited equally, so that family capital could not usually be kept intact. In Japan (as in England) one son (usually the oldest) inherited all the property. Thus wealth could be accumulated, and one person could more easily make a decision to invest it. Perhaps the most important family differences lay in the relationship between family and state. In China personal loyalty was owed to the emperor, but not if it conflicted with family loyalty. A man owed his first duty to his father, and through him to clan elders. Being unfilial was the greatest of Chinese sins. Of course, the Japanese man owed loyalty to his father, but the system was feudalistic rather than familistic: An unbroken chain of fealty linked each individual, through his father and his father's leader or lord, through successively higher ranks to the great princes and the emperor. Orders from above were backed by family pressure. The radical alterations the Meiji leaders tried to implement called for much sacrifice—for example, former warriors might be put to work, or used as policemen—but the links of fealty between family and family, and family and state, remained strong.

The Chinese regarded nepotism as a duty. A man could not reject his family if he improved his station in life, and he was expected to carry upward with him as many members as he could. In Japan, social mobility was more difficult. Ideally, in contrast to China, people should remain in their places. However, *adoption* was an important mode of social ascent in Japan. A father might even disinherit a son in order to adopt a talented young man. The individual so chosen rose alone: He became part of the new family, and was no longer a member of his old family. Both in fact and predisposition, this pattern favored innovations under the Meiji leaders: (1) The Japanese were somewhat less handicapped by nepotism; (2) those who rose did not need to help the undeserving members of their family of birth; and (3) men could seek out talented young men for placement in positions of opportunity.

One long-term family process also lowered the capacity of the Chinese to meet the problems of the new era. Since both in fact and ideal the Chinese system permitted social mobility but accorded the merchant a lowly social rank, a common mobility path was to acquire wealth through commerce, but then to leave that occupation. The gentry were landowners and scholars. Those who acquired wealth sought to achieve prestige and power by becoming members of the gentry or training their sons to become members. The humanistic learning of the mandarins was essentially irrelevant to the problems of the modern era, there was no steady accumulation of a technical and financial tradition by the successful families. By contrast, the Japanese merchant was confined to a narrower type of mobility: financial success. He had little chance of moving out of commerce and into high social ranks. But as a consequence, Japanese merchants and banking families had developed a considerable technical knowledge and tradition and were much better prepared to cope with the complex financial problems that accompanied the rapid industrialization of Japan during the Meiji period.

It must be emphasized that these cases are extremely complex, and family variables cannot be said to be the prime creators of the dramatic contrast. Nevertheless, it seems clear that they did make a contribution to the striking differences in the industrial achievement of the two countires.

A FINAL COMMENT

In these final chapters we have tried to clarify some of the methodological and theoretical issues in the area of family change. Some of these problems are likely to prevent forever our knowing certain important facts about the distant history of the human family. On the other hand, historical work over the past two decades has produced a substantial body of strong data that were simply unavailable even a generation ago, because so few historians aimed at analyzing the history of the family with the same seriousness with which they approached, say, the French Revolution.

It is important to understand the methodological and theoretical problems we outlined earlier, in part because mainstream sociology has often been attacked (usually under the label "functionalism") for being unable to deal with the theory of social change. As we have pointed out, other, much more advanced, fields suffer from that same difficulty. Sociology's much more distinguished cousin, economics, becomes much less impressive when it embarks upon the problem of economic development—change over even relatively short periods of time. As we pointed out, a real theory of social change must not merely try to explain why certain things happened in the past, but must also specify a determinate sequence of stages, such as evolutionary theory attempted to do in the nineteenth century, and more recent work attempts to do again. Such a theory may be too grandiose an ambition for now and for the foreseeable future. No other body of thought within sociology can claim to have achieved such a theory, and the various Marxist versions have never earnestly faced the problems of reconciling that theoretical approach with an adequate theory of family behavior.

We do not wish to discourage speculations on such a broad scale, because in the modern period of research they have considerable utility. First, they aim at destroying prior theories, and thus must gather empirical data to support this goal. Such accumulations of information will help us to construct more adequate explanations. We must have the facts, because our experience has been narrowly confined to only a few types of families, and we have taught many "facts" that turned out to be myths. We have pointed out a goodly number of these throughout the book.

Such myths sometimes get in our way when we are attempting to reconstruct the past, or to understand the stages of changes in the history of a given family system. We cannot, for example, suppose that modern courtship behavior among young people is really "looser" than in the golden past, for as we learn of former courtship patterns in the eighteenth century in Sweden, France, or England, we find very similar behavior. The dramatic events in adolescent rebellion are likely to be painful for parents and children, but very few of these adolescents turn out to be rebellious a few years later. Most Americans did not once live in large, rambling houses that sheltered a numerous extended family, but rather lived as conjugal families in one-room dwellings, with perhaps a cooking lean-to attached. It is important that we not merely cast out such myths, but that we begin understanding how changes have occurred from one century to another over the few hundred years for which we may be able to obtain adequate information.

If we come to understand at least how the modern family arose over the past several hundred years, perhaps colleagues in other cultural regions will be able to do the same, and eventually we may be able to construct a global history of family patterns. Almost certainly, it will turn out that very different kinds of major social factors have had an impact on the family at different periods of time: In one period, perhaps great religious changes may have affected family patterns; in another, war, famine, and revolution; in still another, fundamental changes in property relations. But it cannot be supposed that from such a reconstruction we shall be able to make excellent predictions about the *future*. In any scientific field, exact predictions about the particular events of daily life are relatively unlikely. With all our science, we do not predict the weather very well; and everyone has had problems in predicting how a machine such as an automobile will operate on successive days during the winter. Our best prediction for a relatively slowly changing institution is that behavior patterns are very likely to be the same tomorrow as they are today. From one year to the next, the birth rate is not likely to change by much. We can also predict that in the future, even if there is a steady trend, the trend will not move in any single direction indefinitely: The mortality rate will not drop indefinitely; the age at which women marry will not rise indefinitely; the percentage of young people who live together without marrying will not rise indefinitely; and so on. These are all relatively safe predictions, but they do not form a theory of social change.

What we do obtain from a closer examination of global changes in family patterns, and from a close analysis of just how and where political ideologies or industrialization have an impact, is a much better understanding of relationships between various aspects of the society and family patterns. Even if we assume that industrialization affects the family, we must entertain the possibility that the family has a reciprocal effect on the industrial system as well. In any event, the goal of the analyst is not simply to find out which variables are more powerful, but to trace out all important relationships, whatever the direction of their effect. In this chapter we have noted some of the points at which family forces actively resist the undermining effect of industrialization. The importance of those facts is that through them we can better understand exactly through which processes the larger economic patterns may affect the family.

As we noted two decades ago, it is not so important to prove that societal variables shape family variables more than the reverse. We want to locate the prime causal relations, whatever the major variable turns out to be. The vast accumulation of more reliable data about the history of the family challenges the family analyst to test his or her theories about family process far more rigorously than in recent decades. A robust theory should be able to explain not merely some family behavior in twentieth-century urban United States, and not alone in other Western countries, but also in countries more distant culturally as well as historically. We shall never have data from five centuries ago that are as rich as the descriptions and observations we can obtain about contemporary life. However, we are increasingly able to describe certain aspects of those family patterns, and our theories about family behavior ought to be enriched thereby. As always, in any field, the challenge of the immediate future is both to ascertain the facts more accurately, and to develop adequate theories to account for them.

INDEX